MW00913319

Barefooted Soul

IMELDA ROBERTS

FIRST MAGNITUDE INTERNATIONAL
Imena Azul - Blue Dreams, USA

BAREFOOTED SOUL

Visit http://www.barefootedsoul.com for more information.

Request for information should be addressed to:
FIRST MAGNITUDE INTERNATIONAL
605 Hunting Ridge Drive
Frederick, MD 21703
info@barefootedsoul.com

Printed by Signature Book Printing, Inc.
www.sbpbooks.com

Library of Congress Control Number: 2006902133
Barefooted Soul / Imelda Roberts 2006
ISBN 13: 978-0-9777459-0-6
ISBN 10: 0-9777459-0-2

1. Nonfiction Adult 2. Memoir 3. Inspirational/Spiritual 4. Women's Issues
5. Music 6. Poetry 7. Asian American Studies - Filipino Americans

Edited by: Colleen Wilson, Johnny Pecayo and Socorro E. Tiongson
Cover and Interior Design by: Johan Erik Cerrada

This edition is printed in acid-free paper.
Printed in the United States - 2006

Barefooted Soul

Footprints For A Better World

May the Barefooted Soul's stories, heart songs, and reflections touch your heart and leave an indelible footprint into your own soul.

Let the Barefooted Soul inspire you to unleash your inner gifts, find your own perfect state of mind, and leave behind your own...

Footprints For A Better World!

Imelda Roberts

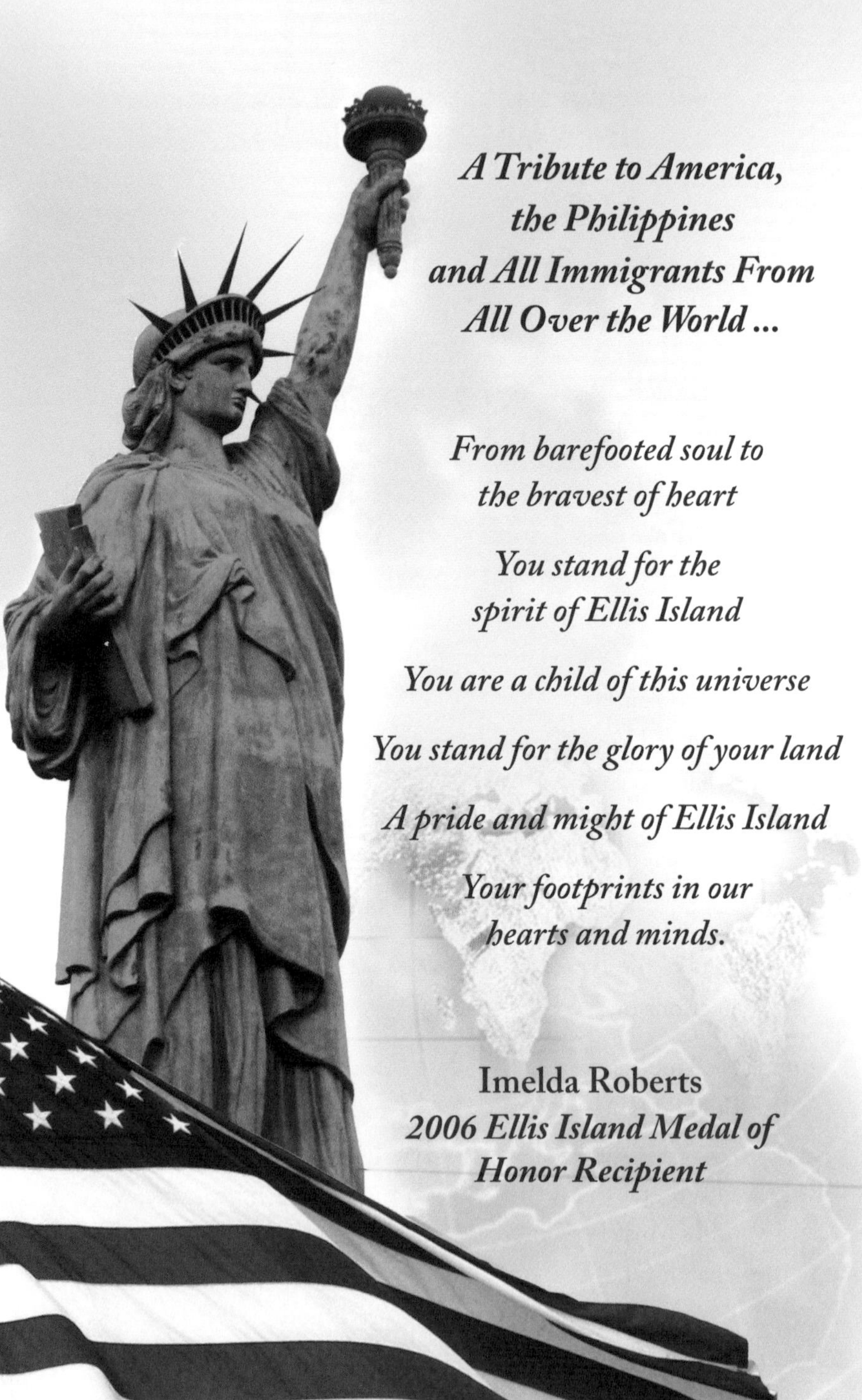

A Tribute to America,
the Philippines
and All Immigrants From
All Over the World ...

From barefooted soul to
the bravest of heart

You stand for the
spirit of Ellis Island

You are a child of this universe

You stand for the glory of your land

A pride and might of Ellis Island

Your footprints in our
hearts and minds.

Imelda Roberts
2006 Ellis Island Medal of
Honor Recipient

Barefooted Soul
Footprints For A Better World

Contents

Contents

With love to my children and future grandchildren!

We come to this world barefooted . . .
we leave this earth barefooted, but our

BAREFOOTED SOUL

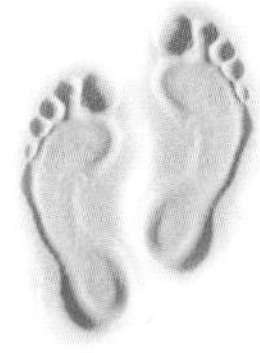

is a legacy we leave here on earth and
will stay forever within the hearts of those we love.

Dedication

First and foremost this book was written as a testament to the greatness of *God*, our *Creator*. It is also for all my angels who have touched my life in a profound way.

To my mother, ***Ana Roque***, for her love and the many sacrifices she has endured. To my sisters and brothers for the pure joy and laughter they have given me. They humbled my life with their appreciation of every moment and every blessing. I ask God to continue to bless them.

With it I honor two very important men in my life; though they left this earth too soon, their spirits and memory will forever live in my heart. To my father, ***Miguel Roque***, whose passing left a great void in me. I honor you for your kind heart and for teaching me to forgive everyone, especially those who hurt us throughout our lives. To ***David Roberts***, my hero and my children's hero. I thank you for being a great father to Alberto and Andrea. Your gift of unconditional love made each one of us a better person. We are indebted to you!

To all my friends, mentors and relatives for their support and their belief in me! For the 2.9 billion women in the world who inspire my inner being, and to more than a billion poor children whose lives are interconnected to mine. My love to my nieces, nephews and to my future grandchildren.

And most of all - to my children, ***Andrea Grace Tabian*** and ***Alberto Tabian***, whose gentle hearts and beautiful souls bring pride to my heart! To my forever love, best friend and my soulmate ***Jeff Snively***. Where would I be without you? FOREVER, you will always be in my heart. My love to him as well as to his dear children, ***Stacie Gilmore*** and ***Brian Snively***; and grandchild, ***Rory Margaret Gilmore.***

Thank you all for filling my life with love.

Imelda Roberts

Message and Praise for Barefooted Soul

Embassy of the Philippines, Washington, D.C.

Ambassador
Albert Del Rosario

Every individual has greatness in himself or herself that is waiting to be discovered, expressed, lived and shared with the world. Whatever kind of life one has, one should realize that every person has a path towards self-fulfillment and achievement. Imelda Roberts' book, ***Barefooted Soul***, is a sensitive narrative which proves that no matter how lowly one may at first be in life, one can climb up the ladder of success.

Imelda Roberts epitomizes this story of triumph. Her personal journey is a true to life fairytale, showing how one could rise to a position of high standing in government service in a country that is not even her native land.

I wish to warmly congratulate Imelda Roberts for coming up with this inspirational book, ***Barefooted Soul***! It will surely move those who will read it and impress on them that in life nothing is impossible.

Albert Del Rosario
Ambassador

"The book's contents are equivalent to a full-length movie with 40 episodes, and each episode is laden with an electrifying story that will thrill the reader to no end. Go through this book, and don't miss a page. Seldom do I find a book as powerful and interesting to read and to recommend to others. This book is for you and me. Read it, and it will help chart your own destiny. It will definitely touch your life!"

Johnny M. Pecayo, Chairman, Publisher and Editor-in-Chief
MANILA-U.S. TIMES - Venice Beach, California

"Imelda's story has written an indelible footprint in my own soul. It is a footprint that wants to venture to places where only the brave would dare go... a footprint that carries the mark of our friendship, that knows no bounds... knows no distance. I praise and thank God for gifting her an Easter experience...a new life indeed! The Barefooted Soul is a living testament of God's faithfulness and unfailing love. Read it and it will breathe life into your being and nourish your impoverished soul. A book for all seasons!"

Susan Romero-Vidal, Author, Agent for Life and The Gospel According to My Kitchen Sink - Makati, Philippines

"Imelda truly knows why God made her go through all those dark days ... if only to appreciate the bright and blue horizon ... as a part of His perfect plan. May the Barefooted Soul be a wake-up call for each single soul that is hurting or in deep slumber to finally claim its pain and unleash its own innate calling. May it also be a gong to alert leaders to address issues this book has brought forth - racial prejudice, abuse of any kind, migrant workers, divorces, corporate stress and poverty.

Socorro E. Tiongson - California
Former Vice President, San Miguel Corporation

"Imelda is absolutely an exemplary, courageous, brave barefooted soul. This book will for sure touch the hearts, souls and minds of everyone who reads it! She was crushed but had risen to the occasion. Her strong determination and empowered human spirit will truly be an inspiration to us all to live to our highest human potential."

Jhet Torcelino van Ruyven, White Rock, B.C. Canada, Author, The Tale Of Juliet; 2005 People of the Year Awardee - Asia People Magazine

"Imelda has added her story to the archive of memory-making of Filipinos in the diaspora. Each of us seem to be drawn to the recall and recovery of cultural and personal memories that are now begging to be rediscovered and retold as we find that there is now space and place to honor those stories. Imelda has done her part...now do yours."

Leny Mendoza Strobel - San Francisco, California
Author, A Book of Her Own: Words and Images to Honor the Babaylan

"I've worked with Imelda on several music projects. I'd already been impressed with her natural ability for writing inspired music and I was struck by the depth of her book, CD and website. It is truly beautiful, inspiring and uplifting. She has an important message for people that are struggling - a message of hope, a message that life can turn around no matter how bleak, if the person has faith and persistence. Her songs and words come from the heart, and are guided and inspired by the Holy Spirit. She has an important purpose in life that is unfolding more all the time. I'm sure people from all over will be inviting her to speak and share her art and life with others. She's building a mansion in heaven one beautiful and carefully crafted stone at a time"

Gerry Peters, - Nashville, TN
Music Producer & Engineer, Midi Magic Studio

"It has been my privilege to know Imelda Roberts and to learn of her story. The Barefooted Soul is an inspirational story of one soul's transformational journey to realize the promise of her inward spirit. It is the story of humanity's evolution in consciousness to embrace those who, while appearing to be different or apart, are the other parts of ourselves. She writes compelling stories which help us to know that we cannot be complete while making others invisible and denying their full humanity. I am uplifted by her message and her living example of courage, faith, undying hope, undiminished spirit, and compassion for others. Could it be that "the barefooted" among us are leading the planet to rediscover its collective soul?"

Jim Robinson, Executive Director
Center for Excellence in Public Leadership
The George Washington University - Washington, D.C.

"Often an author gets in the way of a good book. In this case Imelda Roberts steps aside and lets her soul do the writing and it wonderfully expresses itself with vulnerability, clarity and great courage. The book is not about Ms. Roberts, it is about all of us who've spent our lives in constant and insatiable accumulation. It is about a few of us when we finally grow up and discover a frightful emptiness in the midst of accumulations and accomplishments - when that happens, what then?"

Joe Avelino - Houston, Texas

"I have known Imelda Roberts for over 12 years. Since the first time we met at the Georgetown University, Organization Development Program, I have been struck by her incredible energy and joy for life. She brings a tremendous amount of enthusiasm and creativity to all she does. Her enthusiasm is born of her great faith, which has sustained her over a long eventful journey.

Imelda lives a life both inspired and inspiring to others. The word that best captures the sense of Imelda is courage. She is truly strong at heart. Her daily manifestation of the courage of her heart encourages all around her to be courageous, too and to step into their own greatness as well.

Imelda's story as told in her book, ***Barefooted Soul***, is as inspiring as any I have heard. To have known her makes the story even more compelling. Read it and you just may find yourself inspired to take on life 's challenges in a more courageous way."

Frank Ball, MCC
Organizational Consultant and Coach
Warrenton, VA

"Truly, working with Imelda has been a journey and a great experience for me. I enjoyed working on this project with her and Jeff Snively. As I went thru Imelda's inspiring book, I could not help but share some simple lines I wrote on how the ***Barefooted Soul*** helped me change my outlook and perspective in life. I am sure many others will be inspired by this book in the same way as I was.

Let all imperfections be seen perfect in our eyes,
As the Lord God has a perfect plan for these.
Let all sufferings forecast victory in our hearts,
For the Lord God has His righteous purpose with these.

Thank you very much Imelda and Jeff for allowing me to be in this journey."

Johan Erik Cerrada
Graphics Artist and Designer, Barefooted Soul

Meet the Author & Composer

Imelda Roberts
2006 Ellis Island Medal of Honor Recipient

You are about to read a powerful book that will change and profoundly touch you! *Barefooted Soul* introduces you in vivid fascinating details to the life of a remarkable lady whose faith, dreams and hopes will awaken your own spirit. Written by Imelda Roberts, *Barefooted Soul* is a true testament to one individual's passionate quest for a purposeful fulfilling life.

As a recipient of the prestigious *Ellis Island Medal of Honor* for 2006, Imelda joins the remarkable roster of distinguished Americans receiving this singular honor. She considers this award and being listed in the Congressional Record as an incredible honor and a pinnacle of her life as an immigrant in this country. Her enormous success and what she became capture the essence of her life's transformation for others to follow.

From an extremely poor family she overcame poverty and graduated as a scholar from the Pamantasan ng Lungsod ng Maynila (University of the City of Manila). From a maid to a life made in heaven, her inspiring journey from the Philippines to America reflects upon the tenacity of the human spirit. Though she was Head of Corporate Testing at the time she left in 1984 from San Miguel Corporation, the Philippines largest private company, she did not hesitate to start all over again in her new country. From a maid, a baby sitter, and a domestic help at the Embassy of Australia, today, Imelda Roberts has blossomed as an award-winning executive in the world's most powerful city, Washington, DC.

A recipient of numerous awards, she was featured in the media for several awards in human resources, information technology, and songwriting. Holding the highest position as Chair of the National Certified Public Manager® Consortium serving 28 states, the USDA Graduate Schools, and the Virgin Islands; and Director

of Human Resources for the Metropolitan Washington Council of Governments serving 19 local jurisdictions in the Washington metropolitan area, Imelda is also a respected national leader in her professional field - human resources and public management.

A prolific writer, Imelda is the author of a 319-page employment guide, entitled *J.O.B.S – An Employment Guide to the Metropolitan Washington, DC.* In a very short period of time, she composed and produced over 20 songs and two CD albums. She was also the Executive Producer of her first CD entitled, ***We Saw the Best in You.*** She also composed a song entitled ***We are the Children of the World***, which has been translated into 17 languages. Nobel House Publishers in New York, London and Paris also published this piece in an anthology entitled *Theater of the Mind.*

An inspired book, ***Barefooted Soul***, is an inspirational compelling work Imelda finished in just forty consecutive nights. Through the words to describe her life's experiences Imelda's soul is expressed to all who read them. You see the reasons why Imelda has the stamina to deal with adversity, overcomes life's setbacks, understands the necessity for a spiritual connection, loves anything that life gives her and all those in her life. More importantly, the expression of her soul displays feelings, thoughts, actions for others to take into their own lives to help them deal with their own adversities and to use to be a leader, a success, a humble mentor. Her soul crosses all nationalities, religions, and races. It is the human spirit.

I have personally known Imelda for over a dozen years. I have been blessed to be a part of her extraordinary journey. Be a part of her life through the *Barefooted Soul* – listen to her heart songs and transform your own soul!

Jeffrey L. Snively, Vice President
First Magnitude International, LLP
Frederick, Maryland USA

Foreword

Michael C. Rogers

What you have in your hand is an extraordinary book and CD-Album package that conveys creative energies and an enormous undertaking by one woman whose talents and courageous life transcend into an inspirational journey of success. Reading this book is discovering another amazing side of Imelda Roberts. It brought back the time I met her in 2000 when I hired her to lead as the Director of Office of Human Resources Management of the Metropolitan Washington Council of Governments (COG).

Seeing Imelda then and now, I would never imagine she came from abject poverty. I would not even think of her as a maid, or someone who had gone through tough adversities, but somehow I also am not surprised. Discovering the other side of Imelda in her book, ***Barefooted Soul***, is indeed an affirmation of a courageous passionate spirit I have seen in Imelda all these years – a lady always ready to explore what this world has to offer. Seeing her today reminds us of the power of faith and confidence in what the human spirit is capable of achieving. Her success, transformation and remarkable personal breakthrough is a testimony to the innate abilities we have in each one of us waiting to be unleashed.

In February 2002, I personally presented to Imelda the COG Ambassador Award for ***"being a source of inspiration and hope beyond the boundary of COG"*** for an amazing volunteer project she did for victims and heroes of September 11th tragedy. With pride, this book vouched what Imelda is to me. Her book, ***Barefooted Soul***, is another inspirational book that will truly captivate you, let you get out of your own boundaries, and inspire your own world. It is a true yin-yang, which provides a powerful backdrop for two cosmic forces of energy in the life of Imelda. It is a tale of true triumph of the human spirit and despite all odds she rises up to prove we all can overcome life's biggest enemies and adversities.

More importantly, through her stories and reflections Imelda reaches out to provoke our minds and helps us see for ourselves through her life the other world we may not see through our own prisms – poverty, abuse, corporate depression, nasty politics, immigration and other destitution our world is experiencing everyday. She knows how to use her innate gifts to remind each one of us that we are children of one world, and as people we have to constantly ask ourselves … What would we leave behind to create a better world for those around us, and for our children?

The characters are real; the lessons are powerful and the social implications challenge current and future leaders to look beyond the daily status quo for the sake of the most destitute people, especially millions of victims of abuse and the more than a billion poor children in the world.

Read ***Barefooted Soul*** and listen to her heartfelt songs. This awesome book and CD-Album package is destined to touch lives and inspire spirits. Own it and find your own gifts to pass on to others and to our world! Enjoy the journey into Imelda Roberts' world and reap the benefits of what she learned along the way.

Michael C. Rogers
Executive Vice President, Corporate Services
MedStar Health

Introduction

***B**elieve in yourself and keep the faith within you. Believe that you have a special gift waiting to be discovered. It is up to you to unleash your innate calling.*

My Barefooted Soul
By Imelda Roberts (BMI)

I.
You'll never understand, until you feel the pain
Of my barefooted soul
Wanting to fly away
Fly away, fly away, till my pain goes away
This is the story of my barefooted soul.

II.
Come into my world of faith and hope
Mountains and valleys
River, lakes, and falls
The sun will rise; the rain will fall
Bright rainbows soon will glow
And an angel whispering hello!

Refrain.
"Fly away, fly away, singing praises to the Lord
And your barefooted soul
Can freely fly, fly away!"

III.
Sing a song to our Lord,
as He brings peace and grace
Hollow barefooted soul
With His love I'll be whole
He gives me strength and spirit
Fills my life with His bliss
Lifts my barefooted soul
With so much blessings, I adore!

IV.
He blessed my life with an angel
and soul-defining moments
Thanks to Thee for His love
I can now fly…

Repeat Refrain 2x
And your barefooted soul
Can freely fly, fly away!

My Barefooted Soul
By Imelda Roberts (BMI)

Barefooted Soul - A Journey of Faith and Dreams

For over 20 years, I have lived in America and, throughout these years, I have experienced the joy and excitement of being a Filipino-American and the pain and challenges that come with living my life in two different worlds. For almost half of my life, I have lived in a world quite different from where I was born.

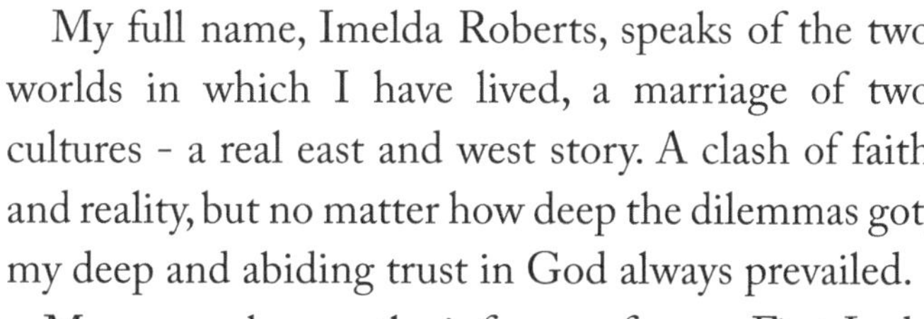

My full name, Imelda Roberts, speaks of the two worlds in which I have lived, a marriage of two cultures - a real east and west story. A clash of faith and reality, but no matter how deep the dilemmas got, my deep and abiding trust in God always prevailed.

My namesake was the infamous former First Lady of the Philippines who has made Imelda synonymous with owning 3000 pairs of shoes. A lot of times, my name was associated with this image. In reality, the name Imelda has its roots in the African and Arabic word, Imena, which means "faith and dreams." In spirit, this is who I really am – Imena, a journey of faith and dreams!

Through this book, I invite you to take a journey with me as I take a big leap of faith, and unveil my barefooted soul. Once and for all, I hope the "Barefooted Soul" will be a source of honest reflection as I reclaimed the very part of me I lost simply because I ignored it for so long.

From my childhood dreams to my epiphany at 50, to my soul-defining moments, join me and peek into the highlights of my life that have made me who I am today.

When you read the 40 soulful stories I wrote in 40 consecutive nights, I wonder if you will cry or laugh with me, be amazed, be dazzled or surprised at how a lady, less than five feet tall, has surpassed many tests of life. But, most of all, though my world is not a perfect world, I hope my life stories will inspire you to find your own spirit, uniqueness and your own perfect state of mind!

Come and take a journey with me ...

Will you see the failures I have made along the way, or the strength and resilience I have gained?

Will you accept me for a life's decision different from yours, or will you judge and cast a stone just because we are different?

Will you shed a tear when I break my shoes from the long tumultuous journey I have traveled, or will the wisdom and colorful perspectives it has provided me inspire your own world?

Will you laugh at me when my shoe is on the other foot, or will you understand we all make mistakes?

Will you discover the kindred spirit of companionship and true friendship, or find an enemy bitter with revenge?

Will you step into my world just because you envy me, or will you join me and be happy for, finally, I have reached my destiny?

Will you dance with me and celebrate what I have become and, in the end, will you see me as a Cinderella when my true love has begun?

Whatever it is, I do hope you will join me on my soulful journey that will transcend your own hopes and faith, and trust that a Supreme Being is with and in all of us.

Come and take a journey with me as I share my heart songs and the stories of my Barefooted Soul!

Together, let's discover our own inner gifts, life's lessons and indelible footprints for a better world!

Imelda Roberts

1 Epiphany at Fifty

"God has given each of you some special abilities; be sure to use them to help each other, passing on to others God's many kinds of blessings."
- 1 Peter 4:10 (LB)

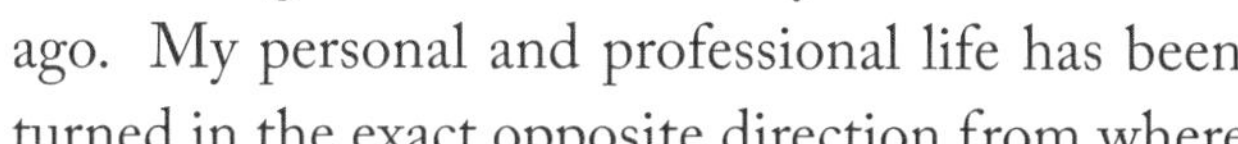

Turning the BIG-FIVE-O on October 3, 2005, was a big deal for me as I reflected upon how many years I have been in America and how much my life has changed since I migrated here over 21 years ago. My personal and professional life has been turned in the exact opposite direction from where I began in 1984. It seems as though it was only yesterday that my children Alberto and Andrea arrived in 1987 to join me. Today, both of them have grown up to become responsible adults with their own professional careers shaping their own life's journey.

At 50, I am ready for a new beginning and a more meaningful life! Joyful about exciting projects I plan to embark on in preparation for my retirement in a few years, I thought I had it all figured out. Where I'll be and what I'll do when I retire. I was in control of my career and where it would lead me. After all, my highly successful career in Washington, DC, the world's most powerful city, had been shaped simply because I visualized where I would be, focused, and acted with unwavering commitment and passion.

However, there was something inside of me that money, knowledge, success, or time would not heal. I call it my barefooted soul. For many years, it sat within the deepest part of my inner being, and its silence was slowly eating away at my soul. I was in denial, and I projected my own pain onto others.

I felt it through the stories I heard daily as I listened to people on the train waiting and counting their years to retirement with tales of woe about their bosses, their work and their unfulfilled lives. These strangers made me realize how much energy people waste doing things they don't want to do. Their stories pierced my hollow heart as I began to absorb and compare their stories with mine.

Sometimes I tried not to listen or I would go to what is called the "Quiet Car." Sometimes, I'd dream or sleep to pass the time inside the MARC train each day on my commute to and from Union Station. What a fitting name to describe the location where millions converge in this busy Washington, DC station each day to unite in oneness enroute to their place of employment. You can see the stress on many faces as they mindlessly walked hurriedly to reach their final destination. At the end of the day, as my train passed by the river dividing Montgomery County and Frederick County, Maryland, where I now live, the sound of the signal would instantly wake me from my slumber and remind me of a haunting question that permeated my being -- another day was over, and where had I been? As the train conductor announced, "Point of Rocks" – it made me think of a sedentary rock that symbolized the barrier to my once creative soul.

It had been years that my heart had been nagging me to do something to nourish my inner being. Tons of excuses plagued me and kept me sedentary. How did I have time for other big projects and the ability to execute with sharp precision and a targeted schedule? I never made any excuse on these big projects even if it meant working evenings or Sundays.

Through the encouragement of my dear love Jeff Snively and my long time friend Susan Vidal who lives back home in the Philippines, I made a gigantic leap of faith and renewed my passion for what I loved to do as a child – write! After all, the executive profile of the year written by Johnny Pecayo, which appeared in the *Manila-U.S. Times*, had sparked some emails that made me realize how far I had come in my life. In two weekends in early May of 2005, I finished four stories and a couple of poems for my book. I was very proud of my accomplishments.

MANILA ★ U.S. TIMES
SERVING OUR COMMUNITY FOR ALMOST 15 YEARS - SINCE 1991

An Open Letter From Johnny M. Pecayo,
Chairman, Publisher, and Editor-In-Chief, Manila-U.S. Times

May 6, 2005

Dear Imelda:

Your very impressive resume and super outstanding accomplishments caused a change in the Executive Profile of the Year (instead of the normal, Executive Profile of the Week). Indeed, it was the first time we went beyond the allocated half page for the featured executive profile. But there is a good reason for that. I wanted to capture the whole gamut of your working experiences, your inherent talents, and the connections you have established, including other personal achievements and to share them with the whole world.

What an achievement! Not anyone from our batch in San Miguel Corporation has done what you have accomplished after working from San Miguel Corporation. What you have reached is quite unique as far as those achievements outside of San Miguel are concerned.

Carry on and keep up the good work. The Filipino American community, the Philippines, San Miguel Corporation, your families and Circle of Friends as well as the Metropolitan Washington Council of Governments, I am sure, are very, very proud of you.

It is my singular honor to feature you in the MANILA-U.S. TIMES' Executive Profile of the Year. You deserve to be the role model for everyone!

Very truly yours,

Johnny M. Pecayo

However, for the next five months the book sat quietly, and my pen never moved to the next chapter. Susan never stopped encouraging me to continue writing. She threatened to charge me $100 every week if I didn't finish a few pages a week.

"Just one page a day while you are on the train," she told me. "You have an extraordinary story to tell, and it will inspire many people just as you have inspired me."

"But the next chapter is so emotionally difficult. It makes me cry just as soon as I start writing. It's a difficult chapter," I confessed to Susan and Jeff.

But deep down in my gut even though I knew I'd used this same excuse for more than 20 years, I found myself using it again. A few days after my 50th birthday, I sent a letter to my children and Jeff about my "new" plans.

I prayed each day to God for guidance, but I selfishly wanted my own way. Can you believe I even asked God to make me win the biggest Power Ball lottery playing that week? I reasoned with Him that I would be a good steward of my winnings, retire, and use the money for a good cause. Jeff and I even went to Las Vegas to celebrate my birthday at the Eiffel Tower Paris Casino with the silly thought that one of the slot machines would bring big fortune. Ha! Ha! My material wishes were not granted of course, and instead we ended up donating our hard-earned money to the casino owner's pockets and not a spiritual cause. But I understood why God did not listen to me, and I knew in my heart He had a better plan for me.

Paris Hotel, Las Vegas

I'll never forget the email my daughter Andrea sent me a few days later. Although she did not know who wrote the email, it was a perfect inspiration and a good reminder of what our purpose in life really is.

Isaiah 26:3, "You, Lord, give perfect peace to those who keep their purpose firm and put their trust in you." (TEV)

"In order for us to have balance, peace, and fulfillment in life, we have to discover our God-given purpose. Most people spend their lives trying to decide what they want to be and do some day. When in reality, we need to ask the One who created us what our purpose is. Only then, will life make sense."

Andrea's email continued with several beautiful phrases and then asked, "What do you love? What we love reveals the gift God has given us to fulfill and what we are called to do."

This made me smile, and I was immediately filled with the enormous urge to begin to write again and share my story with the hope that it would touch someone else's life. It brought back many happy memories of when my elementary and high school newspapers were filled with articles I had written. But I had never pursued my childhood passion for writing because my barefooted childhood was a time of survival, and food for the stomach was more important than quenching my inner desires.

A Perfect Revelation ...

Even though I have the time to pursue my childhood love, it's been five months since I've picked up my pen. I'm making many excuses once again...My life was filled with pain I don't think I can share...I want to share happy thoughts to make others smile. I even told Susan I would write something like "The Barefooted Child Goes to Washington." It would be fun to share happy and funny moments of my life as a new immigrant in the US, or even my encounters with well-known people and politicians. We even talked about the "many shoes" I've worn in my lifetime, and I could parallel it with my name Imelda. I could even write another book on employment.

After all, I was a published author of an employment guide that made its way to career offices and libraries throughout the country. It will suit my career background, I tried to convince myself.

But then, my daughter's email caught and touched the very core of my spirit.

> *"What makes you cry? Suffering of others makes me cry. Because I know the pain of loss, I have a ministry of compassion for those who hurt. Whatever makes you cry is what you're called to heal."*

I surely didn't know then who wrote these words, but I felt they were a perfect revelation for what I was about to personally embark upon. Like a flash in the sky, it was a radiant desire to unveil my whole being including painful secrets I have kept all these years. The time had come to cleanse my own barefooted soul. My daughter came to see me that night to give me a copy of *The Purpose Driven® Life* by Rick Warren. I knew then those quotes were from this beautiful book.

After several email exchanges with Susan, I decided it was now time to write. The next morning I was inspired by a morning hug from my Jeff. I felt his deep love and compassion as he whispered, "Now that you have finished writing the difficult chapter of your life, you can now move on and share your other great stories."

My children Alberto and Andrea also inspired me as they expressed genuine interest. My son had never paid attention to my BIG IDEAS and worldly projects, but this time Alberto was engaged.

Andrea started sharing what she thought would be a good cover design. The exchange between my children, though brief, was authentic and very special.

The spiritual flash that overwhelmed my being to use my abilities to help others and my desire to use this book to say thank you to those who have helped me along the way have been my epiphany at 50. I also have not been constantly faithful to my own God. My imperfect world and stressful life kept me busy, but despite of this, He has given me so much blessings and not one, but many angels. It is now time to tell the world my life is a testament to His unconditional love, and say "Thank You!" to all my angels who have touched my life.

The strong desire to do something purposeful in this new decade of my life along with the encouragement from my friends and especially my children are the reasons why you are reading this book today. I knew I had permission from my children, my friends and loved ones, whose lives are wrapped around mine to tell you not only my story – but also our story.

2 A New Day...

"Spiritual awakening is the recognition that you're not moving forward...that you are not living your best life. That's the moment to rejoice."
— Oprah Winfrey

On the night of October 20, 2005, I started writing again to heed this humbling call. I am overwhelmed by a sense of spiritual being. Somehow, my shame and vulnerability have been swept away by a new sense of sincere appreciation for what these frailties have truly given to my whole being. I know in my heart that my guiding Angel is with me in this journey as I write this book.

Now at 50, I still believe that my Angel has always been here protecting and guiding me. My barefooted soul wants to reach out to others who have been hurt by their loved ones and share that there is infinite hope awaiting all who have the courage to face up to life's trials.

In the midst of my hurried life, I eagerly whisper to the wind every now and then. How I hope to fill the barefooted minds of less fortunate young children so they will discover life's possibilities as I did. I smile to immigrants I meet along the busy streets of DC, give a little something to a homeless guy, and wish him a better life. I am heartbroken and disturbed about the war going on in Iraq and natural disasters that have touched people's lives.

But I am only one person who cannot take this whole world and change it as I envision it. It's a tall order no one human being can take on, but certainly our Creator can. In our own little way, I believe we can also make a difference.

Through this book and despite my imperfect world, I hope this new day in my life will be an opportunity to share that we have the power to change the course of our lives and our world – if we can think it, we can achieve it. It is up to us to turn the barefooted soul inside of us as an opportunity to define who we are as individuals and as people. It can be a moving force that destroys our own self and world, or it can be a positive energy that moves our spirit to unimaginable places where we can finally see the highest points in our lives and in our world.

The Barefooted Soul transforms my once dark secrets into a source of reflection, fuels strength from within me to break away from being a maid to life's daily syndrome of pain, stress, and misery, to finding the ONE higher purpose that will fill my inner soul.

Despite tragic and sad stories woven in this book, please allow me to share with you how I overcame them. In so doing, someone out there may learn from my difficult past. It is my innermost desire to tell you the most important lessons my life has to offer.

Despite the chain of poverty that impoverished the lives of my brothers, sisters and next generation siblings, I was blessed to have the love of my parents and the good hearts of my family who humbled me with their resilience, patience and endurance. It was the same core values that helped me overcome life's challenges and made me who I am today.

Despite the terrible life I endured in my young married life, I was blessed to have two children whose beautiful souls are a joy to my heart. The failures in my married life have been responsibilities I have come to accept. In the end, my frailties have become my strength.

Despite being college educated and having a great professional career in the Philippines, when I arrived in this country as an immigrant, I started all over again making meager wages as a babysitter and a maid. Through my labor of love and against all odds, I was able to prove that America is truly a land of opportunity. It is a place where I have reached the pinnacle of my career and have met wonderful friends and colleagues who have nourished our lives with the blessings of friendship, learning and human dignity.

So today, I heed to the Angel of the barefooted soul and continue my journey in true thanksgiving. This book is an expression of love to my Guardian Angel that gave me the infinite spirit to carry on. It is to all the other angels in my life who have touched my very soul. Thank you to those who lifted my heart along the way.

Through this book I wish to share my inner beliefs and the greatness of God in my life's trials and tribulations. Live my life through my stories, and when you do I hope you will feel my passion and see in your own eyes my reflections on important social issues that plagued my world. I believe this book has unraveled important lessons that challenge each one of us to reach deeply into our own inner soul, to find the special gifts within us, and look beyond to a world that may be different from ours. I also hope the Barefooted Soul inspires you to unleash your own innate calling and create your own legacy. It is a tall order, but the power of one human soul multiplied by many more would be an incredible force.

May the stories, moments, and the angel that guided my barefooted soul touch someone in the same way it touched my own life. May it inspire all immigrants seeking a new life and opportunities and in the end find abundance in their own lives. May it heal a woman or someone in pain as it healed mine. May our family's journey touch one child, mother and family at a time, and at the end may it have touched millions of barefooted souls!

Together, we can leave indelible footprints for a better world!

Celebrating 50th Birthday with Jeff

Las Vegas, the Sin City

Indelible *Footprint* In My Heart

Believe in yourself and keep the faith within you. Believe that each of us have a special gift waiting to be discovered. It is up to us to unleash our innate calling.

B***elieve.*** We begin our transient life on earth as a barefooted child with a blank canvas from which we can draw our own life's stories and lessons, and to leave whatever footprint we wish to leave.

Discovering our inner gifts and our purpose in life starts with our belief not only in our selves and our own abilities, but more importantly, the belief and faith that our Creator has given us special gifts. It is up to us to use them to fulfill not only our own material needs, but for the good of this world.

There is space for all of us in this universe. Others will be restless, unhappy, stressed, and lead a hurried life guided solely by worldly material compass; while others will find a balanced life fulfilling things guided by their inner spirits. Those who live a life in peace and in harmony with their inner gifts will leave an indelible footprint most especially in roads less traveled.

Remember the memorable childhood days and the child in you? Listen intently to silent hunches, and to the crisp laughter within you. Within these authentic natural moments lie your innate callings!

Let's take a stroll back to my childhood and rediscover the child in me!

We are the Children of the World

Aspiration

Aspire to reach a cherished dream and a great ambition. You are the architect of what you want to become.

I invite you to take a journey into my childhood days with this song and the stories that tickled my innocent life. "We are the Children of the World" will open your eyes to the real world of over two billion people living in poverty today.

The deep-seated emotions within me and my experiences as a barefooted child were actually the moving forces that gave life to its lyrics and melody. Thereafter, the song has been translated into 17 languages including Tagalog, the Philippines' official language.

As you read the stories in this chapter, may you think of the children of the world, their aspirations, and their future! We all can make a difference in their lives.

We are the Children of the World

We are the children
We are the children of the world
We sing before you
To share our love and hope
We are the children of the world
We are your future
But today our future depends on you!

While we play, other children are suffering
While we eat, other children are starving
While we learn about the world
Another child's mind is empty
Emptiness that kills the heart and soul

Our lesson of life is one that you know
We don't need to cry it loud
We don't need to say it all
But our life is shaped by what we see
As we look around
And see other children of the world

Whether born in America
Afghanistan or Africa
We were born pure and mild
We are molded by our world
So teach us how to live
Show the beauty of the world
Instill faith in God
And let us feel your love

Chorus:
We are the children
We are the children of the world
We look upon you
To make a better world
We are the children of the world
We are your future
Think of us –
We are the children of the world!
Think of us –
We are the children of the world.

3 A Prelude to my Lost Paradise: The Philippines

The beautiful nature and calm water that soothed my young spirit became my refuge. Welcome to the Philippines, my beloved native land and my lost paradise!

My childhood days were quite different from the life my children and I now live. My lost paradise is thousands of miles away from America, located in the Philippines, my beloved native land. This beautiful country of 7,107 islands and known as Pearl of the Orient, was a Spanish colony in the 16th century and ceded to the US in 1898 following the Spanish-American War.

The Philippines is a country rich in diverse traditions and history reflecting both Eastern and Western influences with Malay, Chinese, Indian, Spanish, and American ethnic roots. With over 160 dialects, Tagalog and English are common and official languages. Little did I know that this background would be greatly valuable as one day the barefooted child would leave what I thought was my lost paradise.

As a child, I played barefooted with tiny creatures in their natural habitat. My dainty, dirty hands swept the spiders from their cobwebs they had spun perfectly in the bushes. My wonder child would ask, "How can the spider weave this beautiful cobweb?" My curious, innocent being would invade its world and explore how the spiders would act and behave when imprisoned from its webbed world. I was tickled as I placed the spiders inside a matchbox. My eyes twinkled with innocent laughter as I watched them escape from the box onto a twig where they would hang on for their lives while spinning a sticky web. Then I would put them back in the bushes

in their original place so I could come back to find them later. In addition to the spiders, I would play with frogs that would jump up and down the flooded streets after a rainy day.

Dragonflies were my friends as well. I artfully mastered how to use them to prick the neighborhood bullies who said nasty things about me. Butterflies were my childhood fantasy. I was in awe as I watched their transformation from caterpillars into beautiful butterflies. "How did they do that?" I asked myself. One day it was a green, yucky, scary thing crawling onto the twig – and the next time it was brown with a cocoon opening like a very thin decaying leaf, then it became an absolutely colorful and fascinating flying creature. It was my dream that one day I would become a butterfly!

The animals living around me became food for my thoughts and creative soul as a child, but they would also serve as food for our hungry stomachs. For the most part, I watched birds with joy; I drew and painted a lot of them in school. But, I was also forced to watch and join my playmates with a slingshot made of rubber and twig used to hunt birds. The slingshot was a fatal tool used to catch the wild birds that would grace our dinner table. I picked snails in the farm to take home for dinner and eat just like you would eat escargot in the finest restaurants in the world. I used my feet to open the undisturbed sand by the river. I awakened tiny crabs we call "talangka," and in the end, the crabs I caught would serve as the best dinner our family would have that week. I watched fishermen lift and throw the net into the wide river from a "salambao," a wide raft made of bamboo used for fishing. I swam in the water and caught small fish using bottles. When this wasn't enough food, I remember at age seven running around with my barefoot muddy feet and twinkling eyes catching "hito" or catfish and "dalag," a breed of fish known for its delicious white meat.

I watched and called the chickens, "Coo – coo- coo!" I threw rice to feed the tiny chicks as they surrounded the mother hen. But when the next day came and old mother hen had disappeared, I could hear the grown ups saying, "Yum, yum, yum!" I played with frogs and then had to watch as farmers tied them together with bamboo thread, their feet hanging as they made their way to the wet market.

I ran around with turkeys as they waved their beautiful, colorful feathers. Their festive presentation is perfect for the role they play in making a special occasion grandeur than plain old chickens. Pigs, though awfully stinky and noisy in their pigpen, made the best "adobo," a recipe Filipinos are known for. The town fiestas with their loud celebration, drinks and delicious food were a perfect setting for "lechon," where the whole pig is roasted opened mouth with an apple placed inside of it, as if it were saying, "Eat me, for I have sinned!"

In the end, the big fat celebration would leave wallets empty as Filipinos' extravagance during fiesta usually overwhelmed the reality of limited finances for many of them. The temporary pleasures derived from this grandiose celebration, even if it meant breaking the piggy bank, were worth it. This tradition has been passed down from the deep-rooted influence of Spanish colonization in the 16th century.

I didn't have a dog living in our house growing up as a child. The only real pet that lived in our house was a swaying monkey who lived in the tree right near the stairways of our house. It used to amuse me as I go down the stairs. I also remember the "butiki," a tiny lizard looking creature that crawled in our ceiling, but no one dared to touch it since it looked like a praying mantis guarding our home.

Our games and entertainment were crude compared with today's world. No electronic gadgets, no cell phones, not even a regular phone or a television. Come to think of it, what would we do now without computers?

Our daily living was far different. No refrigerator, no dishwasher, no washing machine, or a beautiful soft sofa to rest on like a prince or princess! Our two bare hands, hardened by manual labor at a young age, were the tools we used to make everything in our simple life as magical and pleasurable as we wanted it to be.

God's creatures and simplest pleasures were what mattered most in my childhood. Though there were times my parents were not with me as a child, those who took care of me kept my barefooted childhood grounded, and they kept me laughing, smiling and strong.

The beautiful nature and calm water that soothed my young spirit became my refuge.

To me, 1950s to 1970s were so far different from today's world. It was a generation which I think 77 million baby boomers like I am look back to as a safer and simpler time.

For now, let me take you back to my own lost paradise. Let's see what kind of footprints I left behind in my younger years.

Welcome to the Philippines, my beloved native land and my lost paradise!

4 The Angel of the Barefooted Child

"Simple pleasures ... are the last refuge of the complex."
- Oscar Wilde, 11854-1900

My father, Miguel, was a businessman while my mother, Ana, stayed home to raise eight children, six girls and two boys. I was fourth from the oldest, but at a very early age, I managed to become independent. Growing up in a big family had its own share of happiness, chaos and waywardness. If there is one thing I remember crystal clear, it's my childhood days.

Perhaps it was the carefree life that made me live in a more spirited and independent way. Though my parents did not live with me during the week once I reached the early age of seven, I still knew they loved me. Perhaps it was my childhood Angel that protected and gave me happiness and hope despite my longing for my parents. Barefoot and walking in the fields where I spent my three years of elementary school, I had pure joy!

I distinctly remember living in the province of Apalit, Pampanga, three hours away from my parents who stayed in Manila to run our family business. They would come home on weekends, and I felt my empty space fill with joy when I saw them arrive and wave from the banca, a small boat that transported passengers from the other end

of the river. My elder sister Ate Baby and I lived with my grandparents, Apong Madong and Apong Maria, in a tiny nipa hut by the river. The floor was made of bamboo so when you looked up from below, you could see us walking up and down the kitchen or in the living room. The doors were made of dry coconut leaves. Despite the type of house we lived in, those times were safe and secure. My grandparents' house did not have modern conveniences. No television, no telephone, no refrigerator, and no stove. Apong Madong and Apong Maria worked like a team cooking in a makeshift "kalan" (stove) with three big stones and using wood and charcoal. The fresh vegetables, fresh fish and newly-pound rice were cooked using clay pots

Sometimes we were lucky to have fresh milk from the carabao to complete the day's meal. Eating together as a family was a ritual. Using our hands to eat the delicious food my grandparents prepared made it even more appetizing. The table laid flat on the floor, enough to sit and lay our legs sideways or in a crossed position as if you were meditating while eating. For each meal we gave our prayers for the bountiful blessings of nature from which we harvested our daily living.

I attended Cansinala Elementary School and walked to school several miles from my grandparents' house. It was rainy season half of the time I was in school. From May to September and in many other months of the year, it seemed the rain would never stop falling. When the rainy days came and the river overflowed, my tiny feet would ache from little pebbles that would stick under my sole.

Walking under flooded streets heavily weighed my body and feet as the water climbed halfway up my tiny body and seeped into my

my clothes. The chuckle in our laughter as several of my classmates and I would hold each other's hand side by side, formed a bond to prevent anyone of us from slipping away. As if wading in the flood was not enough, after school, I splashed my tiny hands in the water that Mother Nature poured generously so often in this tiny province. I would raise my face, let the rain touched my face and spanned around as if my playmates were the tiny raindrops. I would close my eyes and dream of my parents arriving on weekends with loads of "pasalubong" (gifts) from Manila, but instead, it was Apong Madong's commanding voice beckoning me back and shouting my name, "Imelda, get back home now!" that would dominate this moment's dream. I never saw my parents but I must follow my grandfather's order. I learned early on obeying my elders was a must. My dream of seeing my parents as often as the rain was at that time a dream.

I was told I was smart and was truly a joyful child, but I was also innocently rebellious and mischievous. I remembered being spanked by my first grade teacher for not following her instruction to write the alphabet on my paper. I learned how to write the alphabet and my name before going to school, so I was simply bored and wanted to get away from writing these letters over and over again. I refused to write the alphabet and told my teacher I did not have a pencil. When my teacher opened my bag, I had a dozen of them. She looked me in the eye and say, "Open your hands!" Before I knew it, the firm sound of the ruler smacked firmly creating a straight red mark in my tiny palm. I didn't remember the pain, but I heard loudly her commanding voice, "Don't' ever lie again! It's not good!"

The school I attended received rations of milk and other supplies from the U.S. government but I didn't really care which U.S. government agency it came from. All I cared about was to fill my empty stomach with delicious white milk hoping that my brown skin will turn white. I also heard it will make my crooked teeth straight.

Kids told me I was "maitim" (dark) so I thought drinking milk will make me less dark. I was also called "Apeng Daldal," a Filipino comedian known for his big two front teeth, so I was hoping with all my heart that drinking milk would help this too. Many times, I heard kids called me "pango" (flat nose), that I used to hold my nose firmly, until one day I hurt myself seriously. You might think these were all about being vain, and how cruel kids can be, but for me they were all part of growing up, innocent childhood play. Like a parable, each event has a moral lesson.

I didn't realize how much other kids' jokes affected me until I found myself getting into trouble. When asked to line up to wait until it was my turn to get a ration of milk, I pretended I was fainting to get everyone's attention. I got their attention all right, and I also got not one but at least two bottles of milk for my act. They figured I was really starving so the lady in charge of the ration hurriedly and generously gave me two bottles. I drank both bottles in a hurry only to find myself running around the bushes and banana trees to put it back where it belonged. My father laughed when I told him this story of my greed and how I paid for it. He laughed as he said, "You had a nature's call!"

I may have been amused by my own foibles, but one thing I clearly remembered was for every mischief I did, there was a punishment of some form. I learned early on that lying would get me punished, while greed, one way or another you'll pay, and sometimes it would take its toll through nature. Since then, I never lied to my teacher and followed the line as I was told. In all these, I also learned to live with myself, as I noticed my skin stayed the same, my nose was still flat, and my two front teeth were still crooked and big.

As for those who bullied and called me names, I had my own revenge. After all they were the same age range as I was.

The rule to obey was reserved for older folks. But I learned early in life that bad words hurt people's feeling just like they hurt me. So, I chose a more creative subtle way of revenge. As if nature was on my side, I would use it to get back to those kids who were mean to me. I befriended my enemy, and invited them to catch dragonflies with me. I would catch a dragonfly like a natural expert, hold it in its tail, and quickly let it bite the bully. As if I was destined to be a leader, I learned to turn my own enemies into my friends, and let them follow me. I would run away giggling while the bully ran after me feeling tickled instead of feeling pain. We rolled down the grass and chuckled as we looked at each other. By the time we finished our laughter, we were best of friends looking up the sky, as the dragonfly was set free!

I am not sure if my teacher would remember me now, but I sure remember her like the warm sun. Despite all my mischief, I felt, my elementary teacher, Mrs. Cunanan, cared about me very much. With her guiding hand, I was surpassing other kids of my age in school and my games were not the same. The influence of my elementary teacher was profound.

Her teachings also sparked other things in me. I was very creative with words that as early as elementary, I would write poems in the sand by the river where my grandfather's house stood. But her tempered and proper guidance would not take away my sometimes boisterous real spirit. As a barefooted child, my games were not the same as other young girls. I would catch tiny "talangka" (baby crabs) and let it go after it bit another bully. I would take a slingshot and with raucous laughter, I would climb the trees and shoot the fruits until it fell down from the tree. At times, I joined my cousins to shoot wild birds. I would catch snail, and patiently wait till its head starts coming out of its shell. Sometimes, in my naughtiness, I would get the snail from the trunk and leaves of the banana trees while its

sticky feet hesitated to go with me. Dolls were never a part of my childhood years. Other kids thought I was a tomboy.

I was barefooted and carefree… but my pure joy transcends the tall swaying golden rice stalks as I walked miles and miles in the rice field with sister Baby. We would follow my grandfather in the rice fields and watched until they harvested the entire hectares of land. My small feet were covered with mud and yet, we found joy catching frogs and putting them in a bottle. We would pick water lilies and remove the center bud to serve as our meal.

I knew I was more playful than my sister Baby. At a young age, I looked up to her and her beautiful face. She was more serious compared to my rugged nature. While my sister Baby was fixing herself, my grandfather would almost have a heart attack crying out loud for me to drop the long but slim field snake I found in our backyard. While my sister Baby would put powder in her silky face, I would have cuts and bruises and not even my grandfather could stop me from walking around barefooted.

When everything was said and done, there was one thing that brought back peace in my rugged barefooted childhood. Every Sunday morning after the rooster's made their morning cuckoos, the tolling of the bells summoning everyone to attend the church will follow it. My uncle, Tatang Simo was the caretaker of the chapel and together with my cousins we would all go to church. My grandmother, Apong Maria, would dress me up in a beautiful dress and shoes. For a moment, I was a little lady picking "sampaguita," a snowy tiny white native flower with a sweet scent. I would hold the flowers considered to be the national flower of my country, as delicately in my tiny hand as I entered the chapel and put them in an altar close to where I usually sit. Somehow, the pain in my barefooted feet seemed to disappear as I knelt and prayed. I learned early in my life that no matter how painful my barefooted feet were,

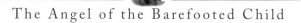

there was solitude in kneeling and there was comfort in believing in God and in our faith. There was no explanation needed on why I was there, and somehow I knew that Sunday was a time to behave.

Following the Sunday's mass, my cousins and I would go to our elders for blessing as we hold their hand into our forehead say, "Mano po!" (a gesture of respect). I found excitement changing my clothes, removing my shoes and running to play in the river. As a child, the river gave me a sense of connection to my inner soul. Many kids played and wade along the river. Although at times there were no older folks watching us, everything seemed okay. Everyone was safe because fear and obedience were our guardians. While other kids were playing around, I would find joy burying my barefooted feet in the sand while waiting for little water creatures to come from the disturbed surface.

But one day at the age of nine, this did not last long. My joy turned into boredom and as if the call of water was more powerful than the teachings of my grandparents, I went farther and farther until I reached the "salambao," a big wide raft made of bamboo used by fishermen to cast a wide net and catch plenty of fishes. I swam my way and would snorkel below the water to watch smaller fishes until I was hit by the "salambao." Gasping for breath from the water I swallowed and if my fate was not to die at the age of nine, I held on to the side of the bamboo raft. I found my body underneath the "salambao" as I held my head up and held firmly on the sides. All I remembered was watching up in the blue sky, and while the white water splashing strongly around my hanging feet created energy, I prayed, "God help me!" At that very moment, my two feet lifted up sideways as if my Angel was there to help me. I didn't need any further explanation, or need to recall all the other details. For I believed my Angel was looking over me. All that mattered was that I was saved. I found myself up in the "salambao" with the amazed fisherman asking "Are you all right?"

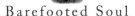

This day, my barefooted childhood experienced the miracle of abiding faith in prayers. I was alive and gleaming with joy to know that I would still see my parents who were struggling to give us daily food, my grandparents who raised me to be obedient and respectful, my teacher who taught me honesty and who saw the inner glow in me despite my mischief, and my Ate Baby and my friends including the bullies for shaping my rich early life. The bountiful nature that surrounded my youth was a landscape of resilience and resourcefulness, where material things were never an issue but the belief in God transcended our everyday living.

As if this day was a prelude to a new life, my parents came and announced that at last, our entire family would now live together in our own house in the city of Manila. Riding the same banca that I rode when I arrived in Apalit, Pampanga, at the age of nine – for now, I bade goodbye to this tiny province that connected my feet well into the ground, into the river, up in the sky and in the trees, in the fields and abounding nature, and to the tiny chapel where my knees bended in faith. I bade goodbye to my school with a name, Cansinala, derived from the word "light." To a young child's spirit, indeed, it was a light that guided my fragile years. All were witnesses to my carefree childhood.

Like the endless river and rainfall, my barefooted childhood was enriched by allowing even the tiny crabs, frogs, the snails, the lilies, flowers and all the simple pure joy to enter my very soul. For all these, I thank my Angel and my God for the simple pleasures that became the refuge of my barefooted childhood.

A Reflection of My Childhood

With no explanation, I know God was there,
And my special Angel, protecting me everywhere
With loved ones guiding hands and those who truly cared
My childhood was special and in early age I dared.
I dared to be myself, explored life with laughter
I reached out to nature and it filled my soul
My innocent spirit had a wonderful joy
It molded my being, as I enjoyed life more!
I dared to push the world, but with certain bounds
As loved ones guided my young fragile mind
I learned to be honest, and put my very best
I learned to love people, nature, and more!
I enjoyed simple pleasures of what this world brings
For life is but a journey no matter where I'll be
And if at times there was rain, this indeed I learned
The sun will shine again and bring warmth to my barefooted soul!

- Imelda Roberts -

5 Reflections of a Creative Soul

"Let early education be a sort of amusement;
You will then be better able to find out the natural bent"
- Plato, c. 428-348 B.C.

For now, my barefooted childhood has ended to give way to a new life. My family moved from the province to the city in Sampaloc, Manila, and it was now time for my sister Baby and I to join my parents and other siblings. The timing was also perfect as the experience I had almost drowning in the river, left a trauma in my childhood so strong I am still unable to reclaim the joy of swimming to this very day. The city was a perfect escape, but there was no sand in which to write my poems or thoughts. I found the city too crowded to run around barefooted and fancy free; there were no fields to walk in for miles and miles. I could no longer walk barefooted as the asphalted road would heat and burn up the soles of my feet.

I was enrolled in Legarda Elementary School, located miles away from our house. Enjoying each day's walk home with my classmates and friends, we would pass by Trinity Church along the way. As naturally as I adapted to the river and the quiet nature of the province of Pampanga, I adjusted very well to the noise in the city and my new school. Our new church was much bigger, and the paintings that graced the walls were very colorful. I would find joy staring at the saints as I prayed. As early as the fourth grade, I learned to make a living waking up early in the morning to help my mother sell delicacies in the muddy wet market of Blumentritt. As tiny as I was,

I charmed the buyers and would complete each sale quickly. After I sold out all my goods and waited for mother and sister to sell their wares, I would sleep inside the jeepney, with my muddy feet curled in a narrow seat.

As tired as I was, I was bursting with energy as I went back to school with barely enough sleep for my age. I was excited to discover my rich imagination early on. I wrote freely like the gliding slippery pen given to me by my father. I also loved sitting in his lap as he read the local newspaper. I used to read aloud with him. I would keep the used newspaper to wrap items bought from the market, and I'd read them over and over again. I was full of creative thoughts, and the music within my soul wanted to believe I had all the talents to be great and dreamed that one day, I would no longer have to go back to the muddy market to sell "puto" (rice cakes).

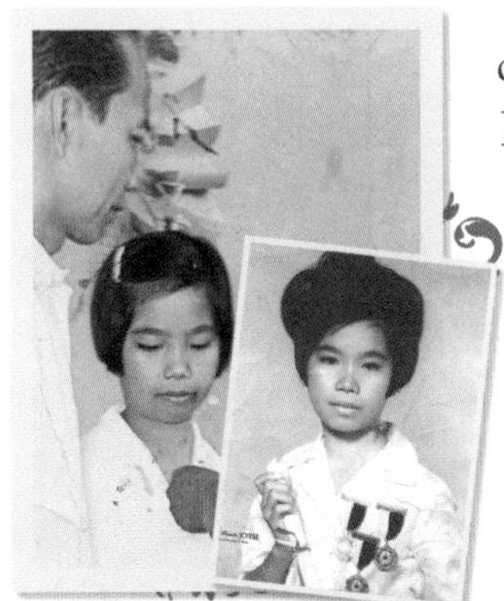

Recognition Day (1968) and Graduation Day (1969) at Legarda Elementary School

I joined the school newspaper. I joined the choir. I joined the band. I joined the theater. I even joined a singing contest and lost! But with all the amusement from being a part of these groups, it was writing for the school newspaper in which I excelled the most. It gave me great joy. I loved to see my name published as the byline read "By Imelda Roque." I was so prolific that I would write and write like there was no end. From the time I transferred in fourth grade to the time I finished sixth grade, my school newspaper was so filled with articles written by me that the editor was forced to use pen names! When I graduated from elementary school, I received numerous medals and several journalism awards including the Most Prolific Writer of the Year. My father went to school every month

to receive monthly certificates of honor for my outstanding grades. Although I transferred from the province to a more competitive and bigger school in the city, and my early mornings were spent helping my family earn a living, I graduated as the First Honorable Mention, or third in the entire school.

Although I graduated third from among over a thousand students that year, my father went back more times than any other parent because of my special recognition and achievements in our school newspapers and writing competition.

Despite all my creative talents and how seemingly easy it was for me to get excellent grades without the discipline of studying after school and the extra morning menial work I had to do before school, my greatest joy was playing with my new friends.

I must admit my slippery feet were my vehicle to my journey of a happy innocent young childhood. With no television in our house, I would sometimes climb up the tree with my slippery feet to the roof that overlooked my friend's living room. I would watch television from a guava tree sitting on a slim twig that swayed just enough across the tin roof to protect me from falling down to the ground. The television was positioned right in the center of the window, and it was a perfect place to watch my favorite shows, "Popeye, the Sailor Man" and "Casper the Friendly Ghost." For that very moment, I dreamed I was Olive Oyl, and Popeye was my hero as he munched the spinach that made him strong. I loved how he circled his hand

to punch Brutus, the greatest cartoon villain of all time, as he saved Olive Oyl from Brutus' drooling eyes.

I also loved to sing along while Casper's song was being played, and as if for that moment, Casper was indeed my friendly ghost. Originally developed by Joe Oriolo and Seymour Reit and made famous in the 1950s by Paramount, this cartoon left a powerful image as one of my best childhood friends. Endlessly, I would sing... "Casper the Friendly Ghost."

Kids like me grew up without expensive toys. Our toys were anything our imagination could create. I played with the monkey that swung back and forth in the tree by my friend's house. In the evening after dinner, I'd lie in the bed and put my hands together. It would create a shadow shaped like a dog, and I would make it move as if it were barking. There was no telephone either. Our minds were creative and resourceful - we improvised. We used two empty cans punctured in the middle and a long string would connect these empty milk cans. This would be our telephone and a means to talk to each other. As if it truly worked, we could hear each other's voice, and the echo would create laughter and joy in our innocent lives. We also played "patintero," a street game whereby we spread our hands to prevent our opponents from being able to enter our domain. We played "piko" using stones and our feet.

There was football and any other games we could think of including hide and seek. But there was something about me that was different. I did not play the girl's games. I have boys running after me not because I was pretty but because I would beat them in their games. I had rough features, and my face was covered with pimples. I didn't have any dolls or delicate toys. I did karate, horseback riding using a fallen tree, and I rode my bike. I caught spiders, put them inside a matchbox, and let them out onto a stick. They would run out and bump each other on top of the tiny stick. I enjoyed nature through my makeup games. The rain, however, was my ultimate joy. I was so excited when the rain poured, as it would create a puddle of water for me to play in. I would create paper boats or boats made of popsicle sticks. With my other playmates, we used the running flood to race our paper and popsicle stick boats.

One day, I did horseback riding using a fallen tree with my childhood friend, Dan. We teased each other until he told me I was like "Apeng Daldal," the comedian known for his big front teeth. I hit his hand. Then, he pushed me, and I hit my temple on the protruded twig, which caused me to bleed profusely. In return, I bit him in his face. I was rushed to the emergency hospital and was saved from the serious danger it may have caused my eye. I still have the scar on my temple that almost caused blindness. In the case of Dan, the big front tooth bite I gave him created just a tiny mark on his face. I sure don't know where Dan is now, but I remember him each time I see the scar from my childhood.

From all these mixed experiences, I maintained my sense of living a carefree world and my belief in myself. My world was filled with dreams I kept right inside my heart and my head. By then, everything was going well with my family. All my sisters, brothers and I had much bigger rooms. We also had a number of household helpers and a babysitter for our younger sister and brother.

My family's business was thriving with many salespeople getting their goods from my father's delicacy factory. I felt that many people surrounding our family and our business were helping my father. In return, my father was helping them, too. People would come from provinces to make a living in our factory. Somehow, my parents touched the lives of families who earned money through my father's business. In the end, just like what my parents used to do, they would go back home on the weekends to the province to take care of their children and families.

My sister's wedding day. Also in this photo is my father, Miguel Roque and Aunt Marta, my father's only sister.

It was during this time that my sister Baby married. My once buddy sister was no longer with me to walk to school. In the summer, my family would visit her and Kuya Dording in Candating, Pampanga. We also visited my relatives and Aunt Marta, my Dad's only sister. We enjoyed the annual fiesta, an extravagant celebration where, regardless of how poor you are, the feast was festive and everyone was welcome.

It was during this time that I would have liked to believe that my slippery pen was now ready to focus on writing and my selling days were over. It was now time to harvest the long days of work and that at last, my family had now reached heaven and that our life was now full. We were all doing well, and my family was thriving in their own right. My parent's business they worked for so many years was now providing a livelihood to many families. It was with pride that we were treated like queens and kings when we went home to the province. Many relatives and family friends visited frequently with tales of woe.

I clearly remember my parents extending help to those who needed it. I saw the joy and the pride my mother and father had in their face as they gave whatever they could to give to those they loved. There were plenty of blessings for me and my family. My parents never failed to give back!

This was a time for honoring my parents who worked hard for us and who generously gave to others. It was a creative time full of opportunities for me and my family.

Reflections of a Creative Soul

We are endowed with capabilities,
And endless rich possibilities
Unimaginable life prospects,
In borrowed time we must connect!
We have feet to walk and hands to dig
We have hearts to feel, a mind to think big!
Our spirit is our only limit
Our hurried life, it should not beat down the
Creative soul that is within us,
Waiting to shine, and be alive
Don't be afraid to reach and dive
Find your own glory and new heights!
For life is full of endless possibilities,
Free dreams, free joy, oneself to unleash
It's up to us to invent ourselves
With a sense of purpose, to be the best!
For when we reach our golden years
And we look back at our younger years
Our borrowed time, and transient life
Creative soul yearning to glow…
It will be asleep before you know.

- ***Imelda Roberts*** -

6 Invisible Youth

"Keep away from people who try to belittle your ambition. Small people always do that, but the really great make you feel that you, too, can become great."
- Mark Twain

I continued the joy of writing when I entered Ramon Magsaysay High School. I was among the top students who passed the entrance examination for a large well-respected public school. With long line waiting after me, I looked at the long list of students who made it. I slid my finger down each name and on the fifth was mine. I jumped with joy and left the long line of equally eager student applicants.

The ratio of students per class was over 50 students per teacher and there were over 30 sections. I was a part of the top group of students. I was privileged to be in Section One and a staffer in the school newspaper "Silahis." We were role models for others. I was in heaven as I fulfilled my education and the joy of writing.

But at some point during my high school days, my slippery feet that were once full of energy had stopped climbing trees. My legs started getting lazy because I was just watching television. This complacent lifestyle in this stage of my life unfortunately contributed to my slippery pen that stopped scribbling as if my creative life were at a standstill. Now in my late teens, I was transforming from my rugged childhood into a young lady.

By this time, my mother had her own group of lady friends, they played cards and gambled, and talked endlessly as they smoked long brown Alhambra cigarettes with the end of cigarette with fire inside their mouth, and they sipped coffee in between. I tried what my mother and her friends did with the cigarette, but never understood how one got pleasure while the fire was inside your mouth. It was a common way old people smoked cigars.

While in school, it was my father I grew closer with because of my interest in business. He was also there to get my certificates of honor almost every month. Just like him, I dreamed of owning my own business. At an early age, I had a keen business sense. I would sell delicacies from my father's factory and all the profits were mine. I earned my own money aside from my school allowance. My hands were overflowing with cash, and I didn't know what to do with it! I didn't want my sisters or brothers to see it, so I would put the extra money in a plastic bag and bury it under the ground. I enjoyed digging the dirt beside our house to hide my money, but I didn't like it when my Dad's rooster dug my treasure out. My mischief would bring smiles and joy to my father.

Disaster Strikes

The joy in our faces one day suddenly disappeared. I don't know exactly all the details except for a combination of many things including the stroke my beloved father had. I was heart-broken. My mother, who was a lifetime housewife, couldn't save the failing business. My siblings and I were all too young to understand what we needed to save the factory that fed eight children plus my parents. We had workers including family friends who took advantage of my fathers' supplies and other properties. My mother borrowed money from friends and relatives to keep up with household expenses. Ultimately, the house in which we lived was the price she had to pay in return for her debts.

As if there were portions of my life that were not within my control, my grades slipped away starting in my third year in high school at the same time our family business slipped down the drain. Although I continued to receive several awards in journalism, my academic grades suffered so much that I was moved from section one to section seven. I made several friends in this new section. Unlike the students in section one, this new group was more down to earth. They seemed to have more fun compared to the serious nature of the students in my original group. I had been an outcast in my first intellectual group, and in contrast, my new group of friends who were equally intelligent welcomed me. Perhaps the circumstances surrounding our lives had put us together in one place.

Imelda receiving journalism awards at Ramon Magsaysay High School during recognition ceremonies for winning several writing contests. (1972-1973)

Despite the setback, I continued school and made many close friends with my new high school buddies including Edith Lapid, my high school best friend. As a group, we took turns going to each other's houses. We rode the tricycle and sang Karen Carpenter's song, "Top of the World." It was our favorite song, and a witness to the dream that one day I would be on top of the world again. My resilience as a young teenager was once again tested and shaped beyond my control as my family's despair grew more and more.

At this point in my life, I never felt beautiful. I thought all my friends and cousins were pretty but not me. The mean words I heard from those around me, including those I cared about, pricked my heart. Some predicted I wouldn't finish school. As if our poverty was not enough, I was called "pangit" (ugly), Meldak," a combination of my name "Melda" and "pandak" which means short. Though I knew family members and friends who gave me these names did not mean any harm, somehow, this name-calling affected my teenage years.

Invisible Me

I was acting invisible. I had a crush in high school on this boy named Irvin. He was in my former section where I used to be among the top. I would pass by the room he was in and sneak in to see his face. But, being in section seven this time he would not pay attention to me I said to myself, "Forget this foolishness. This boy won't pay attention to you!" In the end I stopped my silliness and gave up on my feelings.

Then, there were other boys who at least liked me, including this tall intelligent boy named Edgar, the son of my English teacher. One day, instead of walking back home, I took a jeepney with my friend. There he was running after us. In his hand was a box and as the jeepney started its engine, he immediately gave me the white box. I remember him standing still, with a smile in his face as he waved goodbye and the jeepney drove away. Inside the box was a crystal necklace with heart pendant perfectly placed on top of soft white cotton. I smiled inside and I was happy to have someone intelligent like Edgar pursued me. But, in my head, I thought he was just joking so I also did not pay attention to him. I run away from him and never knew what happened to him since then.

I was so insecure, I dated only once during this time. I dated a handsome young man who lived a few blocks away from our house. A high school classmate introduced him to me. By then, our family life was in shambles. My young heart and my well being felt denigrated. I never felt any real excitement during my teenage years. Sometimes, when he'd pick me up from school, I would not show

up. In the gym located in the topmost part of the building, I would simply look down to see if he was there, and I'd hide. I finally went out with him to Luneta to celebrate Christmas night. I wasn't sure if our relationship would last so I broke up with him that night and said goodbye. I never saw him again.

I channeled my insecurity believing I was not beautiful so I acted like a boy. I rode my bike and raced with boys. To earn money in summer, I would convince my cousin who was a driver to make me a conductor on his long-bodied jeepney for a little money. Beckoning passengers to ride in a jeepney was a competition given the number of jeepneys competing for same passengers. If the jeepney was full the driver earns more money. My tiny young body with loud voice would call passengers to ride the jeepney. When two dozen passengers were all seated on both sides of the long seat facing each other, I would jump up the end of the jeepney holding on the bar. I would find joy being at the edge of the jeepney, holding unto the bar while half of my body was out swirling with the wind while the jeepney was running. Because of these joy rides in the jeepney, I sometimes missed classes and I was in trouble in school. My Dad was not there to teach me what to do – he was half paralyzed and could not even speak straight. I was devastated inside with no Dad to guide me.

I had my rugged streak-riding bike until one day, my uncle and oldest brother of my mother, Tatang Neo, scolded me and hit me with a broom for playing with boys and pushing my bike hard

against the fence. He asked me to go home and study. My mother cried and was upset. I was, too. But now I knew how much he cared about me. He taught me that school should be my priority. Perhaps he knew it was important for her sister's children to go to school because my mother's difficult early life might have been different if she had finished school.

I looked up to Tatang Neo's spirit. After all, his children were in school, and they owned several houses. They had a piano, which I used to tinker with when I visited their house on Christmas and other holidays. Their house was always full of people, and their dinner table was always full of festive foods. Most of all, I respected the discipline and organization of their lives.

But somehow, my teacher knew I was special. Mrs. Tiro, my school adviser in Ramon Magsaysay High School, paid a surprise visit. All of us were surprised. She spoke to my parents to tell them that I was a bright student and that I should really go to school and not stop. She probably knew something was going on and wanted to know why? I was glad Mrs. Tiro visited our house. It was then I realized people do care about me and that I should go back to school.

Listening to my mother talking to my teacher made me realize my parents were consumed with their own worries about our whole family on meeting obligations from the sickness of my father. I was awakened from my rebellious spirit. What was I doing? I was among the top students going down the drain. Thanks to my teacher who touched my heart and made me believe again! But it was too late.

If You Think It, You Become It!

By the time we knew it, our life as a family was upside down. My mom could not pay her debts so we were forced to leave the home

of our growing up years. I knew it was difficult for my parents, especially for my father to leave the house he built together with my mother for us eight children. It was devastating for everyone!

At that time, my father was incapacitated by a stroke. My older sisters found solace in marrying at early ages. We were still in a rented house in Sampaloc, Manila when I applied to go to college. Everyone thought I was wasting my time and the odds of completing college given our economic conditions seemed almost impossible. By then, my older sister had found a way out of hunger. She started her own business in Divisoria, a busy wet market in Manila. For several months while my life and school were hanging in the balance, I continued to live with my Ate Juliet where she rented a portion of my relatives' house.

In many ways, this chapter of my life was perhaps one of the most painful to reflect upon. The innocence of young life, the journey into my own world, and dreams shielded me from the pain of seeing my whole family become truly homeless. I had empty spirit so young to even fathom the impact of homelessness.

I was in denial. I pretended like nothing bad was happening and I slipped into a different world to challenge my own being. The young intelligent lady inside of me was gone for a moment. She got scared of dating and took her spirit somewhere else.

The bicycle kept my spirit in control of my life by bumping fence. My young body I hang in the balance of a jeepney believing I was strong and invisible and I could fly. I created my own self-fulfilling prophecy and tested a competitive world of boys I have never entered before. If you think it – you become it.

Perhaps it was this very same powerful mindset that gave me the courage and determination to reach further than before. The pain of loosing our home and the bullying was like a push of energy lifting me up and said, "Stand up on your two feet and do something!" It was my teacher, the voice of my mother, the sight of my father, and others who cared about me that woke me up before it was too late. I visualized myself going to school no matter what. In my heart I was destined to finish college!

Reflections of an Invisible Young Lady

While we can't blame anyone for the life we now live, to this day, I still cannot fathom the deep pain it caused my family for over 30 years. I wonder what would have happened to my other seven brothers and sisters if they had grown up in a better environment than the poor neighborhoods we lived in. My younger sisters and brothers did not have control over their destiny, and yet they were placed in harms way by the vulnerabilities of poverty in which their dirty feet stood for many years. I wonder what would have happened if people whose lives my parents touched, returned their kindness with generosity instead of greed. I wonder if the house in which we lived growing up had been spared by compassion, and we were allowed to stay – would this compassion have made a difference in our lives especially the lives of my brothers and sisters less fortunate than I am? Would over a quarter of century's struggle for them, and their own offspring had been prevented and spared from the chain of poverty? Would my life as rich as it is now be better if not for these events and frailties?

I guess it is impossible to answer any of these questions, or judge anyone who was part of this chapter. I could not blame anyone for any of these struggles. To me, our lives are but a journey so hard to understand and whose destiny is on the will of God. I simply thank Him for the lessons this chapter of my life has given me.

It is easy to blame others for our own demise, but we have to look deep inside ourselves to find strength. When our own lives slip away from the comfort and pleasures from which we are accustomed, it

is in this very moment when we realize how strong and resilient we really are! Those who are less fortunate will find solace with those who understand their plight for they, too, have lived the life. For somehow in their own glory, this someone will be God's instrument to lift them up from their homeless spirit and remember that despite poverty we can still be happy!

For the courage, resilience, and faith instilled in my very young heart, I had faith and dreams! I was also blessed to surpass life's tests and be a voice for those with impoverished existence.

It was this very experience and chapter in my life that inspired me to write the song entitled "We are the Children of the World" in 2002. It took me many years to openly respect and forgive the past, in order that I might honor the future. This song reflects upon my sincere and deep concern for children in my own family and throughout the world. Translated in 17 languages, it is my hope that this song will reach as many countries as possible to deliver my message of love and hope, especially for over a billion poor children in the world.

Imelda with classmates during her junior and senior years at Ramon Magsaysay High School. Together with her classmates, the tricycle and her favorite song "Top of the World" became witness to happy days and Imelda's aspiration that one day she would reach her dreams. (1972 - 1973).

7 Believe and You Shall Achieve: A Homeless Scholar Story

"The greatest glory in living lies not in never falling, but in rising every time we fall."
- Nelson Mandela

I never understood how all these things happened. In a blink of a second, my family was homeless. We did not have a choice but to stay with my sister in Binondo, Manila, a stone's throw away from Tondo, one of the poorest neighborhoods known for its Smoky Mountains. No, not your regular smokes, but the dirty soot that comes from burning trash in the landfill and eventually forms a mountain. It was the symbol of poverty surrounded by slums; a place for scavengers and young kids who picked trash for a living.

We still felt fortunate, and our consolation was we weren't in the Smoky Mountain itself. We lived in Juan De Moriones, in a room where all of us were packed like sardines when we slept. Except for my sister Baby, who was in Pampanga at that time after marrying her boyfriend, eight children along with my mother and father was a big family for a small room my sister rented together with their own children. We had more than a dozen lives living in a room as small as a garage.

My older sisters, Ate Pining and Ate Juliet, were ingenious and would not let losing our house starve us to death. They used their skills in cooking, set up a cooked food stall, and joined other sidewalk vendors in a wet market called Divisoria to earn our daily living.

They also sold anything they could during the day, in addition to selling cooked food for the laborers that worked in the evening. At that time, the place was a wholesale fishing and vegetable port in the evening. This was the place where retailers bought seafood, vegetables and other items to sell the next day. It was through this means that my family survived. Even my mother who was frail from the stress of poverty and my father half-paralyzed from the stroke did their best to help. Our life was a 24-hour ordeal - some worked in the evening selling cooked food, some during the day selling fruits, vegetables and anything they can sell. Most stayed on the sidewalk of Divisoria to sleep in a canvas lounge chair or a makeshift bed made of wooden boxes that were used to store fruits or vegetables.

The food stall was made of a pushcart the size of a dining table with storage at the bottom to hide pans, pails and other things. When all these contents were out and the night was busy cooking food for retailers and wholesalers that flocked Divisoria, the bottom storage doubled up like an eight by six feet space that gave a little privacy to my sleep. I literally slept inside this funky storage space instead of sleeping in the canvas lounge chair in the sidewalk where every human being who passed by our food stall would see me. Though noises and voices permeated my sleep, they would not match the young tired body in dire need of rest.

Despite an unusually difficult life, thankfully people liked our family's cooking, and our made up eatery was filled with people. It was a far cry from the days when our family had owned a real restaurant in Sampaloc and a delicacy factory. Our life in Divisoria was very different from the long gone days of my family's success in business. My father's stroke was unbearable, and it continued like a stroke that paralyzed our entire family.

Though I was no longer barefooted, the wooden clogs I wore were a perfect symbol for the place we lived. The wooden clogs were made

perfectly for a place that easily flooded and was very muddy. They were heavy wooden-soled shoes, with a strap usually made of plastic. It was an ingenious protection and one that I could easily clean. It protected my sole from the filthy mud that surrounded my life.

The streets were muddy and so was the Divisoria market. The smell, the surroundings, the darkness in the narrow streets and alleys were made for dark evil and big rats. The desperation was everywhere despite the great bargains you could get from this popular wet market. At times, when the narrow streets got flooded, the trash would float. The toads would jump up and down. The place where we lived was located a few blocks away from this market, and it represented poverty in contrast to the clean river I had enjoyed in Apalit, Pampanga and the dry, cleaner streets where I grew up in Sampaloc.

Lighting Darkness Through Hope and Through Enthusiasm

But, however desperate our lives may have been during this time, no one seemed to complain. All of us were too young to comprehend the poverty surrounding our souls.

Everyone seemed to accept our new house – a room with one bulb and three wooden steps with nail protruding down to the wooden platform just enough to land your feet without hitting the muddy ground. Our "second floor" was literally a wide windowsill, 12 feet long and four feet wide. The windows had bars, and the sill was about four feet above the floor of our room. This was my space where I studied, where the sun shined through the window or sometimes the candles at night would light my book as my young mind absorbed everything it could absorb. Along with the pots and pans lined up on one side, and pillows on the other, this space doubled up as the table, the kitchen, and anything we could use it for. The bathroom

was at the back of this old house. The kitchen where the food was cooked was in the hallway leading to this bathroom.

Regardless of this condition, I was full of hope and enthusiasm. No time for complaining, no time for heavy thoughts that would dampen my bright dreams. My crisp laughter and smiling face were my defense mechanisms that kept me going. After all, this was the time I started proving and creating my own personal breakthroughs.

I had just graduated from high school when all these things occurred. I had the opportunity to go to the finest state university, The University of the Philippines, but my family did not have the money for me to go there. I applied everywhere; walking many miles and feeling the pebbles go through my tired soles to find a school that would accept me for free. I was told a hundred times to stop this nonsense, as we did not have the money. Even my own cousin to whom I confided I wanted to finish college told me in a sarcastic manner, "You want to finish college and be a nurse. I don't think so. You don't have the money. Besides, you are not cut out for college and you will never make it," she said as her cynical laughter pierced my being.

I refused and said, "No, I am going to college, watch and see!"

I knew deep inside me I had the talent to make it. After all, my elementary and high school days proved I was a bright and talented girl. My teachers believed in me. Those who knew me back in our good days where I grew up predicted I would be somebody. It was these thoughts from my teachers and those who believed in me that kept me to go on.

I was blessed to learn about the only school in the country that provided scholarships for financially deserving students. I took the scholarship test and application, and by the time I knew it, I had been accepted in college! I did it and proved to those who ridiculed me that they were wrong. To get a scholarship at the Pamantasan ng Lungsod ng Maynila (PLM) (University of the City of Manila) was the beginning of a dream come true. My spirit soared high in the sky with the prospect that I had a chance to reverse my fate, our fate. It was a family's victory!

But being accepted in college was one thing. Sustaining my energy and the means to continue school was another battle. Just like my childhood days, it was another journey filled with perseverance, hard work, faith and dreams. It was a time of creating my own sense of self and overcoming any obstacles that came my way, including the deplorable conditions that surrounded our lives during this time.

My sister's house was too small to accommodate all of us. From PLM, I would just go home briefly to change my white blouse and yellow skirt uniform and then rush to help in the store until midnight. Though I was on a full scholarship and only had to pay miscellaneous fees of fifty pesos per semester, an equivalent of less than a dollar in today's exchange rate, I needed some money to buy food and other expenses. Working in my sister's store was the only way I could get my allowance for my food and transportation to school. From midnight to five in the morning, there were many nights I slept in a canvas lounge chair on the sidewalk of Divisoria, or if I was lucky I squeezed my tiny body inside the cart. Still tired and sleepy, I walked back home early dawn to my sisters' house, a few blocks away from the market to take a shower and go to school.

My weekends were spent selling mangoes and anything else I could sell, with a brief break to go to church in Binondo or Tondo. There were specific times that sidewalk vendors were not allowed to sell, but due to our needs, my family took a risk. We sometimes ran away from the police with "bilao" or round flat but wide containers made of bamboo that held our wares. With deep breaths and perspiration that soaked our tired backs, we would go back after the police had left us alone. It was an exhausting ordeal! There were times when my brother or sister would be unable to escape, and they would end up in the police station. But not even a fine and a day spent in jail with all their wares rotting would be enough to stop them from continuing to violate the time restriction imposed in selling in that zone.

PLM Conspiracy: We Believed and We Achieved

Nothing could match my intense desire to move away the mountains of poverty in our lives in order that I could finish school. I knew it was the only light that would take me out of this place close to the Smoky Mountains where children pick trash for a living. It became the symbol of our struggle.

My noisy wooden clogs made the sound of a child wanting her presence known. I walked high and proud, not minding the filthy conditions around me. No amount of poverty was enough to break my spirit. I consumed myself with school and other extra-curricular activities. I was in "balagtasan" (poetic exchange of wit) in Luneta, one of the biggest parks with an open auditorium with thousands of people watching. It was simultaneously aired in the radio and had a celebrity Vic Pacia, as the emcee. I felt very good to be with a popular man. I won several times and then Vic Pacia died and I was devastated. I won in other contests at school, and my grades were high. I was sent as a representative to student conferences in different places in the country. Each opportunity was a big deal for me as I discovered a

Imelda was the only student from the entire PLM that was sent to a Youth Leadership Training sponsored by the US Embassy. (Taken 1976)

new beautiful side of life and appreciated every moment of it like it was a breath of fresh air.

There were many of us who started together in college with the hope of becoming a nurse or something else. I was one of them, but I hated the laboratory side of this major, including the thought of blood. I also thought I would like to graduate in journalism given my writing skills, but I decided against it due to Martial Law at that time under President Ferdinand Marcos and his infamous wife, Imelda. There was a lot of restraint in our media during that time, and writers did not really make much money I was told. For economic reasons, I did not pursue what I thought would make me happy. In my second year, I was fascinated by courses in psychology and several options it would provide in my career - a choice between clinical, school and industrial/personnel management. They all sounded good to me. I had fallen in love not just with the courses but with my new friends I had gained in these classes.

Imelda with her classmates (BA Psychology, class of 1977) at PLM

By the time I reached my third year in college, there were only a handful of us. Our group bonded like Crazy Glue, nine girls, and one kind gentleman. We were close, and we were absolutely jolly and a little naughty bunch. We filled the libraries with our laughter, and we were asked to leave since we disturbed the other students who were studying. We ate together, played together and visited each other's humble homes. We went places since these newfound friends were more financially blessed than we were.

We even overcame peer pressure in terms of the clothes we wore. Thank goodness we had school uniforms. We also bought cloth in Divisoria and had our clothes sewn by the mother of our friends.

It was cheaper than buying ready-to-wear apparel. It was during my college years that my life was filled with exciting moments despite our financial hardship. My closest college friends Myrna, Abot, Edith, Josie, and two other girls in another course, Galo, and Zeny. All became godmothers to my future children. To this day, they are my friends for life.

By the time we graduated, there were only ten of us who majored in psychology. We were all in the top ten, a pride my classmates took as a major victory in our life. Academically, it wasn't really that difficult. What made it difficult was the life all of us lived as we struggled and juggled school with our daily living. Each of us has an inspiring story of survival to tell. Each of us wanted to prove to the world that we could overcome our plight. After all, the students in this school were selected for scholarship based upon their academic achievements and financial hardship. It was our common ground. It was here where I met my lifetime best friends. It was here where I affirmed that you do not need to be rich to be happy.

It was a perfect conspiracy among all those who believed in the power of education in our lives. It was in PLM that I proved without an absolute doubt that you can overcome poverty. It was in PLM that we believed and we achieved. It was in PLM where our professors/advisers, Josefina Limuaco and Laurie Serquina, were there to guide us along as if we were their children. We were blessed to have them in our lives. They too believed in us, and we achieved. Our friendship was also our strength. Together, we were a part of our young universe.

Our bright future and what we became now would speak of our triumph. All my classmates in college, as far as I know, achieved their own success with their own families living a happy life.

Our stories confirmed what Paulo Coelho wrote in his novel, The Alchemist...

"When you really want something to happen, the whole universe conspires so that your wish comes true."

Graduation Day 1977

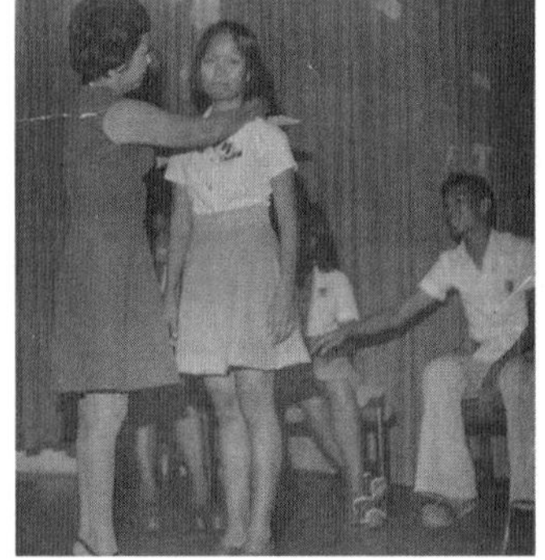

Imelda receiving a medal for scholastic achievement from former PLM President, Dr. Consuelo S. Blanco. (1977)

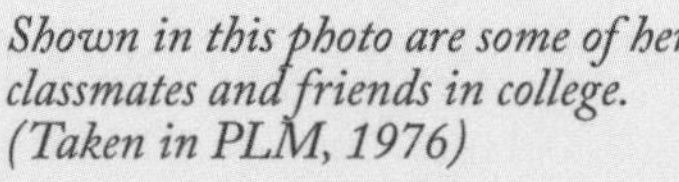

Shown in this photo are some of her classmates and friends in college. (Taken in PLM, 1976)

Despite extreme poverty, Imelda was one of only ten students who successfully completed a Bachelor's Degree in Psychology in 1977 from the Pamantasan ng Lungsod ng Maynila (PLM) through a highly competitive scholarship program.

Reflections About Children and Poverty

My journey as a poor child and a homeless scholar made me fully appreciate the plight of other members of my family, friends, and many other families I personally know who are still trapped by this economic social evil. But we are not alone. Our world is besieged by poverty and we must collectively act together as one humanity to help most especially over a billion children in the world who are living in poverty today. Other voices before tried, and just like many voices before them the passion fainted like a fog. The once poor barefooted soul in me wishes and hopes to revive a renewed passion on behalf of over a billion children in desperation and poverty.

If you think poverty is just in the Third World countries like the Philippines, Africa, and war stricken countries like Afghanistan, try visiting some of the worst affected states in the U.S. with highest percentage of poor residents relative to the state population such as Mississippi, Louisiana, New Mexico, and West Virginia. These states, including Washington, DC where I presently work and where 17.5 percent of its population lives in poverty, have the lowest incomes in the country as their conditions can be tracked, but does not account for the thousands of homeless roaming our urban cities. As in most regions around the world, poverty tends to be concentrated due to various economic, geographic, or demographic traps.

It is shocking to consider that the United States, the richest nation in the world, and hardly the most populated, can afford to see its citizens and most especially its children in poverty. Recent poverty in the United States was at its worst between 1980 and 1985, at the time I migrated here in the United States in 1984. Since then this condition only improved slightly. In 2004 and based upon the US Census data, of the 73,277,998 children under 17 years old living in the United States, up to 18 percent of them live in poverty. With over 13 million children in impoverished conditions, the U.S. ranks

second to Mexico of industrialized nations with the worst child poverty rates that at times exceed 20 percent as reported by UNICEF. {www.unicef.org.} Likewise, the 2004 Census Bureau also shows that even the most powerful city in which I now work, Washington, DC, has not escaped this harsh reality with 29.6 percent of its child population living below the poverty line.

Though true that government, religious and humanitarian groups have always been the healing missionaries of the impoverished, it was rarely, if ever a collective effort. With specific economic interests dictating where and to whom our attention is given, billions over the years have been forgotten in destitution.

Others before me ignited the passion on the plight of the invisible population of our country and the world. Michael Harrington's book "*The Other America*" inspired the nation's leaders like J.F. Kennedy and L.B. Johnson to declare a "War on Poverty" in the 1960s. Reaching back to F.D. Roosevelt's new deal, programs such as expanding Social Security, among other public welfare and health programs were implemented. The War on Poverty has been fought since America's great depression, but War itself, such as WWII and the Vietnam War diverted the hearts and minds of those who could help.

Though the threshold of the poverty line is often highly debated in the U.S., there is no denying the millions of children dying from poverty every year around the world. As economist Jeffrey Sachs indicates in his book the *The End of Poverty*, if the news media would report on the alarming rates of poverty-stricken deaths every day, we could transcend their isolated coverage into true awareness. A study from UNICEF has estimated that nearly 30,000 children die every day because of poverty and is largely overlooked when the worst affected regions cannot communicate their needs.

Of the 2.2 billion children world wide, half of them live in poverty,

with up to 640 million of them living without adequate shelter, safe drinking water or health services. These children, if not orphaned by disaster or tragedy, depend on families that live on less than a $1.00 a day.

The World Bank Group Annual Report 2004 and the study commissioned by United Nations Development Programme (UNDP) provide the objective realities of the world we live showing 2.8 billion or half of the world's population living on less than $2.00 a day. Just imagine the 850 million people that are hungry and undernourished as shown in the World Food Day in October 2005 report. Worst, just imagine the reality of the report from the UNICEF State of the World's Children 2005 - Childhood Under Threat, showing a billion children living in poverty. Picture the lives of children in developing countries where one in three children has no adequate shelter. Feel the thirst of one in five children unable to drink clean water. Put yourself in the body of one in seven children who does not enjoy essential health services. The resulting incidence of diseases and high mortality rates affecting our world's children should put big powers in the world to shame for not taking enough action to save our children.

If you think these statistics are not real, my family and I are living proof of what poverty can do to our spirits. Though I was blessed to overcome such poverty, I am among the lucky few in comparison to a billion children who unfortunately did not have a chance to speak their voice and rise above the bondage of poverty – a bondage that pulls one generation to another as more human souls besieged by this curable disease, until finally they are left to die.

The staggering numbers reported by reputable organizations made me believe we as people have failed to cure one of the roots of many evils in the world – taking care of the poor children of the world. Sometimes, I think we truly live in a hypocrite world...

If our world spends billions of dollars on weapons to kill enemies of war why can we not spend the same passion and resources in saving children's lives? If we treat children with compassion instead of neglect, we teach them the cure against hatred and bitterness. Ultimately, we teach them how to care and to grow as responsible peace loving citizens.

If we can spend billions of dollars on diseases that would take years and years to find a cure, why can we not cure the curable disease of poverty? The poor children of the world are right before our eyes. We know that food, water and shelter can nourish their body and minds, and yet we left them behind for the sake of scientific breakthrough. Though medical breakthroughs are essential even for unknown diseases, and so is curing the known disease of poverty.

If we spend billions of dollars in games and recreation, paying big bucks for sports and entertainment, why can we not spend a portion of these monies towards helping the poor whose only request is for us to give them the cost of a bag of popcorn to live a day or two?

If we spend billions on "pet projects and programs" that are based upon pure politics and in most cases not even essential to our existence as a nation and as a world, why can't our world leaders and politicians collectively come together as one leadership to combat the true world-wide social problem killing our own children?

If powerful countries like America want to truly stop the war on terrorism, we must start with taking care of our children. Poverty brings about desperation of the heart and spirit. Poverty robs children the dignity to rise above such indignant circumstances. In the end, these are the same young people that are likely to be vulnerable from terrorists and other evil who fray and corrupt young minds.

I am reminded by what Mahatma Gandhi said,
"If we are to have real peace, we must begin with the children."

Having lived in the richest country in the world had provided me an opportunity to take advantage of its rich resources. Though I am only one voice, I am a living proof of what compassion and vision for the poor can do. On behalf of more than a billion poor children, the barefooted soul wish that we could find vigilant cures to a disease that plagued my young world.

My parents living with my sisters, nieces and nephews in a rented room in one of Philippines' poorest neighborhood. (Taken 1970-1984)

To earn a living, my family became sidewalk vendors at Divisoria since early '70s.

8 In Honor of My Father: San Miguel Early Lessons

"I'm doing all this stuff not to gain a reputation, not to just to be known by my colleagues to be effective but it's because of you. It's people. I care about you. I care about your life and God called me to accomplish His work but His work is focused on people."
- Apostle Paul

In my lifetime, every position I've ever held I did with love and exuberance. From selling mangoes, seafood, delicacies and cooked food as a sidewalk vendor in the muddy streets of Divisoria and Blumentritt as a student, to a supervisory human resource position in my early twenties in the Philippines' largest multi-national corporation, my career life in my native land was an enviable position. After all, thousands each month flock to apply for a job in San Miguel Corporation, a huge conglomerate of over 30,000 employees with over 100 facilities in the Philippines, Southeast Asia, China and Australia. As a producer of three percent of the gross national products at the time I was there, working for San Miguel was an honor. I was hired even before I graduated from college, and my life was never the same again. It was San Miguel that lifted me from poverty, and for this I am forever grateful.

"Working in San Miguel was like honoring my father Miguel"

I was only 21 years old ready to graduate with a bachelor's degree in psychology from Pamantasan ng Lungsod ng Maynila (University of the City of Manila), when I became a student intern at San Miguel.

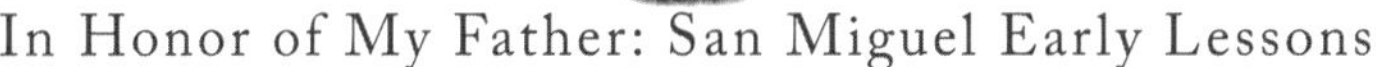

My class adviser and professor, Dr. Josefina Limuaco, a graduate of Stanford University, orchestrated my internship in the Testing Unit Recruitment/Human Resources Division that began in November 1976. I reported to a lovely lady named Haydee Albayda who guided my early life at San Miguel. Two months before graduating from college I was offered a full time job as a psychometrician and was responsible for test administration to thousands of applicants. Haydee left the company a short period thereafter, and I have never seen her since then. Professor Limuaco kept in touch with me, but I have not heard or seen her for many years. My young life was held firmly in the palms of these two kind women. With their gentle hands and warm guidance, they released me like a small fish into a big ocean steadily swimming on a voyage I had never been before. My life was nourished with love, confidence in what I could do and exuberance – the most important lessons of my entire career.

This number one company in the Philippines in existence for over a century and Southeast Asia's largest publicly listed food, beverage, and packaging products company was a witness to my humble beginnings and my early professional growth. From a student intern to head of Sourcing in the Human Resources Division corporate wide recruitment, the major business lessons I learned from this company have guided me to this day.

The first lesson I learned in being a part of this company:
Find and invest in a great company and you will look and feel like somebody!

It was also in this company that I discovered the rich opportunity of what other people can do to our lives. At an early age, I was surrounded with highly-skilled, educated people from the finest schools in our country. I was an outcast as I saw the kinds of lives my colleagues had – most came from well to do families and the best schools in the country. But I was blessed to have in our department the most fun loving people. My life was field with friends, a long list of friends too many to list down.

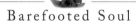

Once you find the right company in which to invest your career, the second lesson I learned: Surround yourself with great people who can do a great job and at the same time have fun. You will nourish your mind and your heart. With great people around, you will look and feel great yourself.

San Miguel was a very progressive company filled with big thinkers and big ideas. From big ideas, they executed and marketed the best selling brand products in the entire country. It was a monopoly that was hard to break. Though you worked very hard, the company invested hugely in its human resources with benefits unrivaled in the entire country. From 13 to 14-month pay bonuses, to cavans of rice, and other perks even for low ranking employees, no wonder why San Miguel was every college student's dream-come-true career. The Campus Recruitment Program I was responsible for gave me an opportunity to see the depth of admiration San Miguel had in the Philippines. Long before organizational development and human resources information systems were heralded in other big countries, San Miguel was pioneering these processes, investing in its own management training and development, high tech human resources information system, and recruitment strategies measured not only by the quality of the people brought in by the time and standards agreed upon in the entire company. It was truly a world-class company. The Human Resources Division where I worked was highly regarded, and it is here where I learned early in my career the power of human resources. It was also here in my early twenties where I got involved in strategic issues affecting the current and future state of my company.

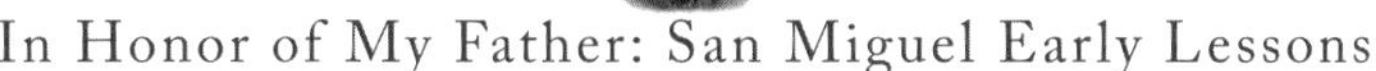

Vision, mission and goal setting, standards, retreats and other big thinking processes that separated the highly successful companies like San Miguel from those that were not. Big thinking was my next big business lesson.

My bosses who I considered my mentors were a big part of my success. David Santos, Odette Jimenez, and Ricky Bunuan – all were witness to my young life eager to learn under their tutelage. Without them knowing it, the impression they created to this day I remember. Odette was a woman I looked up to as she exuded so much confidence and knowledge in her field. Her long black hair and beautiful smiles were the lasting impression when I think of Odette. My interview lessons on executive recruitment were among those I learned from her. Her ability to deal with highest level of officers while I get nervous even just simply interviewing a chemist with her was amusing to watch. Along with other ladies we exchanged a few ladies talk including buying shoes from Susan.

On the other hand, David was my direct boss and he was actually the first person to hire me as an intern along with Haydee. When Haydee left, he gave me a chance to lead the Testing Center. He was a kind gentle boss, but he left and transferred to another position within SMC and after this we rarely got connected. His help and compassion at the time I was new with my roles as intern and psychometrician to this day I will remember.

And Ricky, my friendly boss was one of the most people-oriented person I have ever seen while I was there in SMC. He was promoted to replace David so his transition as our new boss was relatively easy. He had the biggest smile and a warm voice. He was the person who trusted me to head the sourcing and testing program including the SMC's nationwide Campus Recruitment Program. Together, with my other colleagues like Auring, Connie, Agnes, Claire, Susan, Zeny, Noel, Joyce, Galo, Ruben, Mario and others, Ricky formed a perfect team. But just like I did, he left the Philippines a year after I left. I finally got connected with him while they were living in New York and before they moved to Canada.

Aside from the lasting impressions, my mentors and supervisors gave me this most important lesson from them –

Learn from those around you – from those you can model behavior you wish to aspire to, especially from your bosses and mentors you highly respect. Open your mind to the endless possibilities more experienced people can bring into your life.

Indeed there were lasting friendships and many lessons San Miguel gave to my young life. My father, who died a short time after I started at San Miguel, would have been the proudest person to see my professional growth in the company. Working in San Miguel was like honoring my father Miguel, a businessman, who inspired the entrepreneurial spirit in me at a young age, who taught me hard work, dedication, and faith in people -- even those who may be considered my enemy. I learned how to quickly maneuver in a world different than my own. It was my father who taught me the "politics" of relationships as he grew his business. The bankruptcy of his business after his stroke also taught me a big lesson: Nothing in this earth is infinite except for the knowledge you gain, memories of those we love, and the good deeds they leave behind.

It was the knowledge and good spirit of my father that I took with me. I was always smiling, laughing and having fun with my co-workers. Every minute of my time with San Miguel was about people and for the wonderful people who surrounded my young career. With love and exuberance for what San Miguel has positively done to my life, it is the same with my father. Working there allowed me to honor my father Miguel and put into practice much of what he taught me.

Imelda with late Richard Sotelo, VP of HR (seated with necktie), and her friends and officemates eating together on lunch time.

Imelda with some of her friends and officemates at SMC.

Imelda administering tests to job applicants.

San Diego Reunion - 2005

Reunion with SMC friends in the Philippines - 1999.

Reunion at National Cathedral, Washington, DC - 2000

Aspire to reach a cherished dream and a great ambition. You are the architect of what you want to become.

A***spiration***. From childhood to adulthood, our life is a constant search for something that will fill our lives - from simple to complex, from mundane to challenging, from small to big dreams. Our life's aspirations and dreams fuel our existence not only for the short-term but also for the long haul.

Aspiration breaths life into our dreams and inner desires. Aspiration gives spirit to our vision. Without aspiration, our life will be at a standstill and may lead to complacency. We may find doing things mindlessly over and over again, until one day we found ourselves far behind from where we want to be.

But, how do we know if our aspirations are in harmony with our inner calling?

And what happens when you worked hard to reach your goals and something took over your dreams?

Will the castle you built in the sand be blown away by the strong wind, or would it strengthen you to aspire for something better?

When you aspire with all your heart and soul, no amount of disappointments will kill your spirit. When your aspiration is grounded from the very core of your being, all the way to your bare feet, no amount of pebbles pricking your bare soles will stop you from walking forward until finally, you reach your destiny.

Did I live up to this key lesson? Let me share with you my toughest moments and tell me what you think?

Secret Lies, Secret Stories

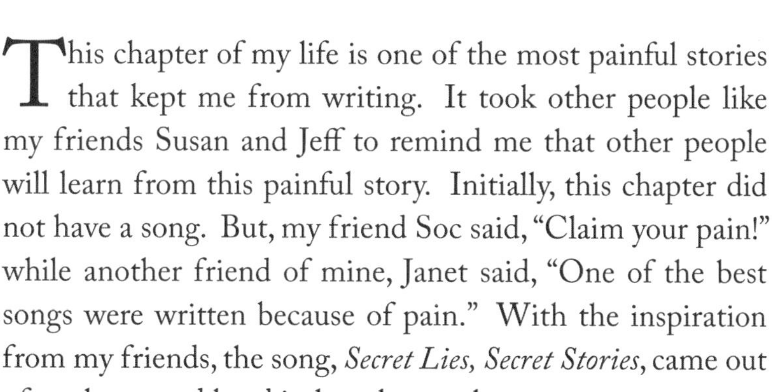

Resolve the issues of the heart and the mind as best as you can. The longer problems and pains linger in your life the more they pierce deeply into your heart. Claim your pain, and let your soul gain peace and strength from within.

This chapter of my life is one of the most painful stories that kept me from writing. It took other people like my friends Susan and Jeff to remind me that other people will learn from this painful story. Initially, this chapter did not have a song. But, my friend Soc said, "Claim your pain!" while another friend of mine, Janet said, "One of the best songs were written because of pain." With the inspiration from my friends, the song, *Secret Lies, Secret Stories*, came out of my heart and head in less than an hour.

Once I started sharing, the pain I kept for years was lifted from the deepest core of my inner being. A wellspring of creative energies trapped inside was unleashed. Words began to flow from my heart. It was a liberating moment as my secret lies... secret stories were finally revealed!

Secret Lies, Secret Stories

I

Do you have a secret piercing into your life?
Loneliness and pain, kept you awake at night
Secret lies, secret stories just within your sight
Dark secrets in your heart only you can see the light…

II

Do you have a secret from past life, gone by days?
You tried hard to forget, but in your mind it stays
Secret lies, secret stories just won't go away
But, don't you hate living your life this way

Chorus

When it's time for secrets to finally say goodbye
In your heart you'll find courage lifts you high
Secret lies, secret stories we can't forever hide
It's time to let them go,
Smell the rose and to life say, "Hello!"

III

Time is too short, to live in the dark
Heavy load you have will keep you leaning back
Secret lies, secret stories don't let them hurt your heart
Resolve and claim your pain, peace in your heart you'll gain!

Repeat Chorus and III
Yes, it's time to let them go,
Smell the rose and to life say, "Hello!"

Secrets of the Barefooted Wife

"In the depth of winter, I finally learned that within me there lay an invincible summer."
- Albert Camus

Everyone in my family including my friends and co-workers in San Miguel thought I led a perfectly happy married life. Many did not know my humble beginnings. I was a joyful, fun- loving, giggling person on the outside, but this was in complete contrast to my inner soul. I kept my pain from everyone; this barefooted soul kept my heavy heart from telling the truth about my married life. In a country of 87 million people of which more than 80 percent were Catholic, marriage was a sanctity that could not be broken, except in cases of annulment.

I never had the joy of feeling what it was to be a young lady pursued by other young men. Boy was the first one who paid attention to me while I was in college and earning my allowance in the muddy streets of Divisoria. He was several years older than I was, and he swept me off my feet at a very young age. In my heart, he was the only man who would pay attention to a poor ugly person like I was. For the attention he gave my innocent life, I gave my commitment to love and marry him after I finished college in 1977.

My scholarship and education was no match to the harsh environment and its impact on my young, innocent life. Boy was shrewd and made sure I got married to him; he took me to Pasay, a city outside where we lived and where we were secretly married a year before I graduated college. By the time I finally realized the life commitment I had made to this man, it was too late.

I gave my life and love wholeheartedly to Boy, and we got married in a church ceremony after I graduated. I had simple pleasures and pure joy with the birth of our two children, Alberto who was born on August 21, 1978 and Andrea who was born on November 11, 1979.

My life was complete because of them. I added Grace after Andrea's name to symbolize the grace God gave me for allowing me to have children. Experiencing motherhood at a young age including almost giving birth to Andrea in a taxicab were unique memories I fondly treasure as a mother.

The joy of motherhood was a stark contrast to my life as a wife. Somehow, our lives as husband and wife grew apart as my career took off successfully. The truth is my husband and I were no longer in the spirit of loving each other "till death do us part" when we separated in 1983. Despite our lack of love, we were still married in the eyes of the community that told us we had to stick together no matter what. My friends and co-workers saw a different me. They would never guess how broken my spirit was. I would laugh with them, share beautiful stories, jokes, music and friendship. Not even my family or best friends knew that every laugh they gave me nourished my dying soul. To this very day that I wrote this chapter in this book, the details and secrets of my barefooted soul have been kept within me. Why you ask? To protect myself from living this pain again.

The Dark Secrets Looming My Young Life

I have been great at hiding from my very own darkness and lies that engulfed my young married life. I knew I made many mistakes as a young woman, wife and mother. But I knew as well, God had forgiven me for my frailties. The guilt we allowed to touch our lives was not healthy, and the sacrifices women like I endured were stupid. But sticking with my husband, despite my broken heart, was following God's will and my faith I told myself many times.

I served my husband and kneeled to take off his dirty shoes from the mud that surrounded our own living. I would hand wash his shirt from the puke of his own drinking habits. I wiped off his

body with a hot, wet towel and removed the dirt encrusted on him from lying half dead in the gutter. I'd do anything to take away the stinking smell of alcohol. I made love to this man even though my heart was ripped by my own failure to save my own soul.

Six years into our marriage, we got separated for almost a year. He abandoned my children and me for another woman and his work. It was too much for me to endure.

I sheltered the lives of my two young children and worked hard to give them a decent home. I focused on my thriving career; making extra money on the side by selling anything I could sell to give them a decent life. Without my children, family and friends, I would have lost all hope. It was a period of almost one year of separation, but as far as I was concerned, he abandoned me long before, beginning on the day I first became pregnant.

I didn't really know what was inside of him, but the slow and nagging pain he caused my tiny human soul made me feel I was unworthy of trust and respect. He fought with me right after we came from our wedding. He was jealous since my boss was "chatty" as he called it during the celebration party at my house. He accused me of having an affair with my bosses. He would even get jealous when he saw me in a jeepney, a public transportation where passengers were seated side by side. My insecure heart would never dare to even think of another man, but his jealousy was killing me. He said, "You know I am jealous because I love you!"

But then he also cursed and threw things at me for no apparent reason including an electric fan and bottles of beer. He threatened my childhood male friends with a knife that came far away from the province of Pampanga to see my father who was paralyzed by the stroke and was living with us at the time. He used nasty words to my parents as they tried to protect me from him. It was only after many years that I learned he had a child older than our son. He projected his own adulterous sins to me, and I accepted them as my own. This person I once loved did not really love me. He was a real bastard and made my young life a living hell!

But I wasn't strong enough to tell this to his face. As a woman who was raised Catholic, to be submissive and compliant to your husband was a way of life. I survived any way I knew how. I lived a life of deceit, protecting him over my parents. I was in denial and enabled his abusive behavior. I told everybody he was a nice person and how kind he was to help my sisters and brothers in Divisoria, where he helped them earn a living through the seafood business at his work. I prostituted the truth in exchange for the daily food he gave to my poor family and to me to raise our own two children. I was an accomplice as he hurt my parents.

My father left my house to go to Pampanga while he was sick. What troubles me greatly is that I never had a chance to ask for my father's forgiveness for forsaking him. My father, who loved me so much, died of a stroke in our relative's house instead of my own. I was overcome with guilt and shame. My young broken heart was too hurt and dying to even cry, "Help!"

A Test of Faith

I never blamed or questioned God but took this as a test of my faith. I grew closer to Him during this time, and it was my faith in God that kept my hope alive. I found solace attending Christian events and going to church. After endless soul searching, I thought the best answer to my barefooted soul and emptiness was to reconcile with my husband. I wanted so bad to give our family another chance, to be together and to save the sanctity of our marriage.

I was doing very well in my career. I had saved some money, and I was able to buy my own real estate property by myself in the Brookside Subdivision, a new development located a few miles away from the corporate office where I worked. At the young age of 27, this was a huge achievement.

Despite my achievement, my heart was empty. I never failed to worship God and talk to Him. I attended the mass with Pope John Paul II when he arrived in Manila, in the early part of April 1984. With thousand of worshippers wishing to see and hear the Holy Pope, I was a tiny soul in the midst of crowded Luneta, an open park in the City of Manila, blessed to experience this once in a lifetime spiritual experience. At this very moment, I felt alone with God despite the crowd and the noise surrounding me. I simply surrendered and prayed for the chance to explore other places where I could find another future for my children. The next day, my prayer was answered. I was granted a visa to the United States. I felt blessed and empowered. I learned how strong I was without a man by my side. I knew in my heart God would never leave or forsake me.

My husband and I had grown apart long before the dreadful summer day in April 1984, but because I hid the truth, no one knew this day would ever come. The evening of April 22,1984, Boy came to see me, and we had a serious conversation. Despite his accusations that I was leaving for the United States with a lover, I did not see the signs that my life was in danger. I was downright stupid and agreed to reconcile with him. Though I already had a visa and could practically leave him, I felt the obligation to put back our family in order before I left for the US. My plan was to leave the end of May.

The next morning, April 23, 1984, my children and I woke up early. Andrea was too tiny to go along with us so I left her with my sister Juliet in Binondo. Alberto and I took a pail and broom and went by the market to buy materials to clean our new house.

Boy was with us, already drunk, but I felt everything seemed okay. I wrote a check as a down payment to the house and cleaned the

house with a joy in my heart. Though it wasn't the best looking house and neighborhood I envisioned for my children, it was the start of reconciliation and living together as one family again. After we finished cleaning, Boy said, "By the way, I have to go to the warehouse of Ninang Edith." I didn't know that our godmother in our wedding had a warehouse near our new house so Alberto and I went along. We rode the jeepney and walked inside this big lot full of "tiklis," containers made of bamboo used to haul seafood and other goods. There was a shanty house at the end, and there was a narrow dark warehouse far away from the warehouse where he took us. He said the caretaker lived in the shanty house, but to me it looked abandoned.

He left Alberto outside the door by the window and before I knew it, he hit my face several times with his strong fist and blood and saliva came out of my mouth. He shouted like a mad maniac and as if he was not satisfied, he smashed a gun into my shoulder as I wept for my life. I fainted and all I remember were the eyes of my son peeking through the window as I shouted, "Please don't hurt me!" Inside I prayed, "God, please help me!" I awoke lying on a bench that stood witness to his brutal hands. Gasping for a breath, I was filled with emotion; fear for my life, but I had enough strength to beg for my life. He was standing up looking down on me as my consciousness came back. I remember him murmuring and cursing like a mad man and then he pointed the gun at my head and said, "You are leaving for America with your lover and you can't fool me. You cannot leave me. I will take you to Visaya! I will kill you if you ever try to escape."

I knew in my heart that if he had his way, I would live a life of asylum in my own country. Visaya was the province South of Manila, far away from my family and where he was originally from. It was a secluded island difficult to reach by regular transportation. It was

his way of controlling my whole life. Either way, deep inside me I said, "I'd rather die than be with this man."

But then I heard Alberto pounding the door. Boy was disturbed by Alberto's knock. He opened the door and I saw Alberto crying. My child hero was standing up and my soul was awakened to save not only my life but also my son's. How could a man I was almost ready to forgive for abandoning us had the nerve to put my life in his hands, let alone allow his own son to see his abuse? I knew a devil had engulfed the spirit of this man I once loved. I played with this devil to save my soul and to give a new life to my children. At that very moment, I was awakened from a long nightmare and realized I could never love a man who committed an unspeakable barbaric act on a body he did not create. Only God can take this soul He created. I needed to save my life so I lied to this brutal man and said, "I love you and never meant to desert you. That's why I agreed for us to be together again in this new house we just cleaned."

I gasped for breath to save my life begging him, "Please take me to the hospital. We can just tell other people I fell on the stairs while cleaning the house. No one will ever know what happened today. I will not tell anyone. Please take me to the hospital," I repeated. "I promise, I will not go to America. You can take us anywhere you want."

I begged him as I prayed deep inside for God to save me. I don't know what happened next. All I know, my prayers were answered. I was in the emergency room of a hospital being wheeled to save my life.

But my ordeal that had started at the break of dawn was not over. I dreaded the night that was about to come alone with this man when everyone else in the hospital was asleep.

An Angel: A Messenger From God

Boy was watching me like a hawk and would not leave me with anyone. I did not get a chance to say a word to the nurses or doctors when they came to check me. I tried to find help, but he watched every move I made. I feared for my life and my child so I kept quiet and played the drama he wanted people to believe. Several hours passed and finally Boy fell asleep at the bottom of my bed while Alberto was beside me. It was the moment I'd waited for. It had been about 12 hours that I had been held "hostage." I walked slowly out and saw a janitor in the hallway cleaning. While walking towards the bathroom, I pulled him quickly inside and whispered, "Please, sir, have mercy on me. Please, God, please help me! My husband will kill me. Please call my mother. She doesn't know where I am, and my husband is planning to kill me."

I quickly gave the phone number to him, and the janitor vanished without telling me what he was going to do. I feared he was not going to help me. Without him, I don't know what would have been. I surely don't know his name. But he was my angel that day. Just like what an angel means in Greek, he was my messenger. The lanky janitor whose name I do not know acted as my messenger to protect me from further physical danger.

The next thing I knew my mother and my eldest sister Ate Pining arrived in the hospital while Boy was still dead asleep, as the long day and alcohol in his body knocked him down. My mother almost fainted when she entered the door to my room and saw my swollen black and blue face and arms. She started crying as if she had lost her precious daughter, and said, "Oh my God, what happened to my child?"

Despite my bruised body, my spirit lifted with unimaginable strength. I grabbed my Mom, and whispered with firm commanding voice, "Don't cry Mom, please stop crying or else Boy will wake up!

He is going to kill me." I pulled off the IV out from my hand and despite blood squirting all over my hand and shirt, I pulled Alberto, my mother and sister and said to them, "Hurry, let's go!"

Barefooted and covered with blood, I ran away in the speed of light with my Alberto in one hand and my Mother in the other. We ran down the stairs, giving one last minute instruction for my sister Ate Pining to pay the hospital bill. In a few minutes Boy was rushing down after us. My sister Pining hid under the hospital reception desk when she heard footsteps hurriedly going down the stairs and saw Boy coming down awakened by the commotion. I frankly don't remember how I got to my uncle's house in an instant, but it was clear in my mind, my own husband wanted me dead or alive. To protect my mother and my sister's life, they went back to my sister's house in Binondo and kept my secret from him. Since he did not see them rescue me in the hospital, they pretended they did not know anything.

For the next 24 hours, he hunted me down. He went around houses where he thought he might find me. He went to my sisters' house and took my things and packages for my friends to take with me when I planned to visit the USA in late summer. He ripped off my clothes, took my suitcase, and took all the right sides of each pair of shoes leaving behind the left sides.

My mother took my son and me to my Uncle's house in Sampaloc, Manila where she thought Boy would be afraid to go. But she was wrong. He went there and for fear that their lives would also be in danger, my relatives pretended they did not know anything either and that they never saw me. I hid inside the pigpen when he came to my uncle's house that night. It was a night of sheer terror.

The following day, we learned from my sister Boy had gone to Pampanga to hunt me down there. This province was about eight hours away. This gave me a chance, to go to Juan de Moriones to

see my family and little daughter Andrea one last time. I also left Alberto there with the promise that I would come back soon. I said goodbye to my family and hid in a temporary shelter for my own safety.

My friends and officemates in San Miguel finally learned about the tragic events. It was my friends, Agnes, Susan and Zeny who helped me hurriedly get airline tickets to the US. My friends wept with me as they saw my face and swollen body imprinted with terror that only my faith in God allowed me to endure. Because of my injury, I was taken to Fort Bonifacio Military Base, where a sister of Zeny, a military employee, sheltered me until such time I was ready to fly and escape, never to come back again for many years.

A Barefooted Wife's Reflections

The day I almost lost my life to the man I once loved was the day I was set free from the guilt of my own religion and from the abuse I endured in my young life. Our God told us to save the sanctity of marriage and to forever hold each other till death do us part. I thought I had failed Him on this one, but I know now that God did not tell His children to allow those who invade the life He has given us to be violated, let alone by the man you once loved and faithfully served. It was the most crucial dilemma in my life, but the barefooted soul I was once was no longer bare, for deep inside the failures and vulnerabilities of my young life prepared me for the years ahead. I have many blessings to thank for if not for these traumatic and barefoot days – the blessings that overflowed to me, and my family.

As I recall escaping from the hospital barefooted, I was blessed to have the Angel of God who protected me not only during my barefooted childhood days but also during this traumatic horrible ordeal.

Reflections on Marriage, Abused Women and Divorce

"The wife's body is not the husband's own body, but it must be loved like his own body."
- Pope John Paul II

There had been many studies with regard to abused women and divorce. The Bureau of Justice and American Psychological Association statistics show that 95 percent of abused spouses are women, and that one in every three women experience abuse. As someone who lived such a terrible experience, these statistics are real.

Unfortunately, I believe those who are in poverty are more vulnerable to abuse. In fact, studies from organizations such as the National Organization for Women cite the reports of abuse are a much higher in low-income homes and even higher when the male is unemployed. Though the causes of abuse can often derive from financial woes, the true motives are too numerous in finding readily available solutions.

In my case being in a violent relationship was something that no one would ever think would happen to me as I kept the shame within myself, did not seek help and almost died from failing to save myself. Even an educated woman like myself was not saved from the abuse and controlling behavior of the man I once called my husband. Though I was blessed to escape this terrible ordeal, the impact of this

on society, including healthcare, crime, poverty, isolation, as well as on children can be devastating despite available therapies.

It took over 20 years for me to realize I should not be ashamed to tell the world in order that others may learn from my past. Thankfully, here in America, there is an increased awareness and the mobilization of women's rights have created shelters and support for those brave enough to overcome what hinders them from escaping abuse.

To even dress the term as domestic violence hides the gruesome fact that four women die everyday from murder or assault by an intimate partner. The National Organization for Women {www.now.org} cites this as a statistic from the FBI, adding that this number reaches far higher than the death toll of even the Vietnam War. Studies show that because 95 percent of victims are women, they are 10 times more likely than men to be victimized reinforcing an age-old gender dominance in society.

The emotional and physical aspects of abuse are, like our bodies and minds, inextricably linked. One form of abuse can quickly lead to the other and emotional or verbal cruelty is no less damaging than physical harm as it can go unnoticed for years. As the National Violence Against Women Prevention Research Center has revealed, there is no act or indication of abuse too small in prevention. Insults, humiliation, blame, coercion, suspicion, threats, intimidation and depression can all be a sign that a partner may become abusive. {www.ncdsv.org}

There are now well over thousands of victim assistance services and prevention programs in over 22 countries. Though as long as abuse statistics continue to climb, crying out a need for protection, something as delicate as violence in the home must be addressed wherever possible.

A promising step came in 1994 when President Clinton signed the

Violence Against Women Act into Congress putting over a billion dollars into programs for legal action and research.

There is nothing closer to perfect irony as this very bill signed by Clinton forced him to pay restitution in a harassment case filed by Paula Jones. The act has since been renewed twice by the U.S. Congress and though debated as to its true effectiveness, is better than government negligence towards the problem.

Divorce

One of the most important legal tools to escape an abusive relationship is divorce. Except for annulment cases, divorce is not available in the Philippines as a largely Catholic country. It was the American justice system that gave me the opportunity to say "No" to such as inhuman treatment through an uncontested divorce. Though divorce is against my religion, I know in my heart my own God would agree with the step I took. For anyone to be trapped by the binds of marriage when they are in harm's way is a wrong no state nor religion should inflict.

This of course is the upside of something that has become tragically common in fairly recent years. The last census to collect accurate data on divorce in the U.S. was in 1990 with 1,182,000 that year. The next decade divorce rates in the U.S. fluctuated between 4.7 and 3.8 for every 1000 of the population {www.census.gov}. It has actually dropped slightly over the years, but so has the number of marriages. There was also a study published in the Oklahoma Bar Journal in 2004 that revealed almost 43 percent of first marriages ended in divorce within 15 years. Women tend to file for divorce more often than men and a European study found that the leading causes of divorce were infidelity or affairs, family strains, abuse, mid-life crises, addiction and workaholism.

There are a great number of people who believe that a vow before

God and family is inviolable. Divorce has been accepted religiously for centuries, especially when the vows those partners profess have been broken. Likewise, annulment has been allowed for grounds like fraud, bigamy, mental illness, and other causes where a valid marriage in the eyes of the church could not be established. For example in the Catholic Church, "psychological incapacity" ground has been a part of Canon law or the law of the Catholic Church where marriage may be declared null and void and "declaration of nullity" established based upon this ground.

However, it can be said that today's culture, especially western culture, has allowed a misuse of divorce catering to lazy attitudes of commitment. Perhaps the biggest affects are felt when children are involved, but when a marriage struggles blindly it may put the child's happiness at stake as well.

As in my case, I certainly could not tell you how my church would view the steps I took against my ex-husband but marital abuse and physical danger inflicted upon anyone reminded me of what Pope John Paul II said,

"The wife's body is not the husband's own body, but it must be loved like his own body. It is therefore a question of unity, not in the ontological sense, but in the moral sense: unity through love. "He who loves his wife loves himself" (Eph 5:28)... The union of husband and wife in love is expressed also by means of the body."

- Pope John Paul II
L'Osservatore Romano, September 6, 1982

Resolve the issues of the heart and the mind as best as you can. The longer problems and pains linger in your life the more they pierce deeply into your heart. Claim your pain, and let your soul gain peace and strength from within.

R***esolution.*** Relationships are perhaps one of the most challenging life's issues we would come across in our lifetime. But, nothing is more powerful than the will to live a full life. Our hearts and minds are capable of anything including finding resolutions to the most difficult and challenging problem we encounter in our lifetime… be it in love, money, or life itself.

There are times resolution is simple. There are times it may just mean communicating and making things clear with the involved parties. But, there are times it can be a life's dilemma haunting us. It may also mean changing our whole life and going to a strange space and time we have never ventured before.

Whatever it is, claim your pain! Keeping them inside for too long will keep you from moving forward. Not resolving problems and keeping pain from within hurts you more than it hurts the other person. It keeps you from welcoming a new life... a new horizon.

Positively looking at the present and the future involves freeing yourself from the agony of your past. Resolve, move on and welcome a new frontier! I did.

A path to success was forged through America's freedom...
the triumphant spirit of the human soul,
and generous loving angels that surrounded my life.
Welcome to my new frontier...
The United States of America!

America, Land of Liberty, Land of Opportunity

Enthusiastically perform whatever you choose to do in life including difficult life's tests; it fuels the heart to greatness.

The heartwarming feelings and inspiring stories shared with me by immigrants I've met in this country, the new freedom and endless opportunities following a terrible ordeal, along with my relatives and friends who welcomed me in America, inspired me to write the song "America, Land of Liberty, Land of Opportunity." Just like millions of immigrants ahead of me, my days as a new immigrant were days of dreams, awe and enthusiasm for the so many opportunities that lie ahead.

May the stories in this chapter remind you of the triumphant spirits of millions of immigrants who came before us and helped build America to what it is today.

America, Land of Liberty, Land of Opportunity

America, you are the land of the free
America, you are the land of liberty
Throughout the world you're viewed
As the land of great opportunity
A proud home for those who love true liberty!

You open your door to immigrants
From far away across the ocean
Irish, Africans, Spanish or Asians
You are home-sweet-home
to multi-nations.

Refrain
America, you are the land of liberty
There is no place in your home for tyranny
America, you are the land of opportunity
Where every man, every woman deserves equality

Throughout centuries, you stand for peace
But you'll fight the war to protect your freedom
You raise your flag proudly, proudly in the sky
You show the world liberty will never, never die!

America, you are beautiful and colorful
With various religions guiding your soul
America, you are the land
of dreams and liberty
Where every man, every woman can live freely!

Repeat Refrain (last line 2 x)

10 A Prelude to My New Frontier: America

"America will always be a beacon of light for the oppressed of the world."
- William Denis Fugazy

For seven years, I relished every moment I spent at San Miguel Corporation. A sudden turn of events was no match for the joy I had while working there. My life was turned upside down by a tragedy that engulfed my whole world, and the next thing I knew, San Miguel was now my past.

It left a strong imprint in my young soul; the strength I carried from it as I fought for my life took me across halfway around the world with my spirit intact and my hopes bright for a new beginning. The next thing I knew I was in America – one of the richest countries on earth. It is the third largest country next to Russia and Canada in terms of size, and the third largest country next to China and India in terms of population. Considered the world's most powerful nation, America is the extreme opposite of the Philippines in terms of economy marked by rapid advances in technology, low unemployment and steady growth.

You would think this would be great! From the Philippines to a rich powerful country of America – why would I complain? After all, I

have dreamt of going to America and seeing the Statue of Liberty. It was the most prominent figure I have about this country. I also grew up watching movies of Robert Redford and listening to singers like Barbra Streisand. But, the circumstances under which I was forced to leave no one but me could heal. My heart was heavy leaving my beloved native land, a happy successful career at San Miguel, and most important my two children. But, coming to America I must say was one of the richest journeys of my life. It was through this new frontier I found courage, hope and dream to start all over again for the sake of my children's future.

My new world was also a freedom-loving country with rich opportunities and a promise of equal opportunity regardless of race, gender, nationality, and even religion. And just like other Filipinos and immigrants ahead of me, it's up to me to seize every opportunity life has to offer in my new world.

Filipinos in America

America is founded upon the very spirit that we Filipinos carry with us the promised land of opportunity. One of the most ambitious groups in the country, it has been documented by writers before me the perseverance and determination of Filipinos as they climb the economic ladder of success without compromising a community rich in values. It is no wonder in 2005; the United States House of Representatives passed Hawaii Congressman Ed Case's resolution "honoring the centennial of sustained Filipino immigration to the United States, a resolution that provides richly-deserved recognition of the incredible contributions of a people and culture which has personified the very essence of our American experience." The 2006 centennial celebration also honors the first fifteen Filipino laborers who were recruited and migrated to Hawaii in 1906 as sugar workers or "sakadas." Thereafter, their contributions paved the way

to continued migration of skilled workers in the years to come.

It must be noted however that Filipinos started coming to America long before the sugar workers in Hawaii. While still under Spanish rule, immigrants from Luzon Island arrived as early as 1587. Within the seaports of the Louisiana territory they became a driving labor force at the very start of the settlement of the New World.

As the U.S. expanded its conquests beyond the Pacific, a colony in the Philippines started a new wave of immigration along with the Chinese and Japanese. We Filipinos have forever maintained our identity and strong family ties, but have long been the invisible majority of immigrant groups. Mexico may have the largest numbers of U.S. immigrants, but they have only to cross a land border. Crossing great distances by boat for centuries and even further still between 1981 and 1996 we Filipinos in America were the second largest group of U.S. immigrants.

As did many ethnic groups of early America, Filipinos ahead of me struggled years of prejudice to gain acceptance into the sanctuary of the American economy. Between 1929 and 1935 a rash of racial conflicts affected the immigrant communities of California due to fears they were taking jobs. Mobs of hundreds resorted to violent acts against an otherwise peaceful migrant population. The tensions eventually led to congressional action in a 1935 Repatriation Act that tried to block immigration from the Philippines. It went as far as limiting the amount of laborers hired and restricting service in the U.S. military. That changed quickly in 1942 when up to 10,000 of them fought during the Second World War.

With the largest concentration of Filipinos in any state in America, matters of geography made California the port of entry for immigrating Filipinos, but Hawaii, the state with the second largest number of Filipinos, was the stepping-stone for many on the journey. Possessing agricultural roots, the first immigrants to the island became an asset to the sugar plantations. Their experience, determination and willingness to work at low wages brought thousands to the plantations, but many returned to the Philippines during the Great Depression years. Some early migrants managed to explore as far as New York were there is a thriving community today. Several thousand even established a knack for fishing the extremely cold climate in Alaska. Most of all it was the farmlands of California, Arizona, Utah, Colorado, Montana and the Dakotas where their skills flourished.

As they worked the lands of the west, building communities and laying the foundation for future generations, years later an Immigration and Nationality Act opened even more opportunity. A need for medical professionals brought hundreds of thousands of Filipino families to the eastern U.S. boosting a decade long population boom. This boom after 1965 welcomed many new immigrant families, but also reunited loved ones with those that had made the leap before them.

It would be a great disservice to consider early Filipino immigrants as only the laboring masses. Additional to the influx of professionals after 1965 there was also the Pensionados Act of 1903. For many years following, the Pensionados ventured to the U.S. as scholars supported by the government of the Philippines. Whether an intellect, a farmer, or a fisherman, Filipinos embodied the very essence of America's history and it's future.

As of 2005, there are over 2.3 million Filipinos in America, the second largest Asian group next to Chinese, who have followed the steps of millions of immigrants from different countries and be a part of the American dream. With highly marketable Filipino talents and skills, it is no wonder that teachers, nurses, doctors, and other highly skilled workers are being recruited from the Philippines to fill the scarce workforce needed by many employers in America.

For now, let me take you back to how I started in this freedom loving country as I continue the historic tradition of hard work, perseverance, tenacity and the belief in the American dream displayed by millions of immigrants ahead of me.

Welcome to my new frontier, the United States of America!

Washington Monument District of Columbia

Statue of Liberty, New York

The Golden Gate Bridge, San Francisco, California

Historical Sources: Census Bureau website www.census.gov, The Philippine History Site, www.hawaii.edu, Understanding Persons of Philippine Origin, By Sheila de Torres www.buffalo.edu, A Century of Challenge and Change: The Filipino American Story, Smithsonian Institution Centennial Commemoration website, http://apa.si.edu/filamcentennial/

11 I Left My Pain in San Francisco

"Climb the mountains and get their tidings. Nature's peace will flow into you as sunshine flows into trees. The winds will blow their own freshness into you, and the storms their energy; white cases will drop off like autumn leaves."

- John Muir

April 26, 1984, was a new beginning. It coincided with my father's birthday. It was a tumultuous journey, but I knew in my heart someone was with me throughout it. Could it be my father, whose name was similar to Saint Michael, the Archangel who led the faithful angels to defeat the hosts of evil and drive them out?

Just surviving an ordeal where I almost lost my life to the man I once loved made me believe "the great prince who standeth for the children of Thy people" was with me all along.

My father's love was with me as I traveled to a new world where I've never ventured before. At age 28, it was my first time riding an airplane. As I leaned my tired swollen face in the window looking in the bright sky, I saw a glimpse of my father, "Don't worry my dear child – a new world awaits you! Your courageous heart and your beautiful smile will rule. Keep smiling and be happy," he told me.

My humble beginning in this great freedom loving country, stripped of my loved ones, my success and education I had built over the years in the Philippines had been temporarily suspended. I knew I must begin to climb another mountain just like I did in the Smoky

Mountain of Tondo. The difference was this new one was a snowy white mountain, cold but very beautiful! It was another perfect metaphor for the loneliness of leaving my children behind for the sake of their future. The overwhelming view of the Golden Gate Bridge with the foggy sky enveloping its peak was a signal to great opportunities that await those who can pass the chilling test. The busy streets of San Francisco were filled with Americans, Asians and other peoples of the world busy minding their stores or touring this beautiful city. With a tiny smile on their faces, they were somehow reassuring me, "You'll be fine! Don't worry." San Francisco was a witness to my humble beginning. It was my port of entry.

I arrived in San Francisco with just a few clothes in my suitcase. I joined millions of new immigrants with the hope of a new beginning. My heart was pounding as the Immigration Officer asked, "How much money do you have?" I composed myself and answered calmly, "Two Hundred Dollars."

Despite my heavy heart and the still painful ache from the abuse I had suffered in the past three days, a new door was opened as the Immigration Officer said, "Welcome to America!" and stamped my passport and signaled "Next" to another person behind me.

I walked through the room packed with people. As if the words "welcome" did not sink in to my still dizzy head, I was confused and disoriented from the long flight and my nervousness from my recent horrible nights. I asked the lady in a soft voice almost afraid, "Ma'am, would you kindly tell me where the Immigration Office is?"

The lady answered in an equally soft voice pointing to the door I just came from. She smiled and said, "You just passed it!"

My legs almost collapsed as if my heavy load had been taken out of my whole body. I was ready to jump with joy for finally I arrived safe in America! I saved myself, I saved my soul, and I saved our future.

I landed in a seat with a telephone above it, sat my back against the wall and dialed collect to call my sister's house. "I am now in America," I said with a smile in my voice.

There were tears on the other side of the phone, but there was laughter and joy, too! The voices of my two little children, Alberto and Andrea, filled my heart with hope as we said, "Goodbye, and I love you!"

Leaving my own country straight from the hospital, to a military base, to the airport, bound for San Francisco as my port of entry without kisses and hugs from my own children and loved ones back home awakened the deepest strength I've ever had to have in my soul. I carried on with a big smile to cast away all the negative energies that surrounded my being! My educational background and my illustrious career in the Philippines' largest corporation was deliberately set aside – this was a reality I came to realize as I stepped in San Francisco, my port of entry.

My first order of business was to buy a camera in a nearby gift store. Silly at it may sound, it was my way of saying to myself, "Enjoy this new world!" It was my first possession that witnessed my early days in the streets of San Francisco curiously walking in a new world I had never seen before. I stayed in a hotel and only slept a few hours that night. With hardly any sleep, I left San Francisco with a renewed spirit and a positive attitude.

The most prominent thought in my head was -- I must overcome all obstacles. This was a time of survival with no time for pity, no time to cry, no time to even think about the tragic events of my past. I pushed in the very deep core of my bone the pangs that pierced my inner soul and let it stay in the dense solid matrix of my body where the pain would lay silently and in secret for many years. I left my pain in San Francisco and locked away my secrets as I headed to my final destination - Washington, DC.

12 An Immigrant's Story in the World's Most Powerful City

"Dreams are illustrations ... from the book your soul is writing about."
- Marsha Norman

Washington, DC, the nation's capital was beaming with tourists at the time I arrived in what used to be called the National Airport, now Reagan International Airport. Though it was late in the afternoon when I arrived, the spectacular site from above overlooking the Potomac River, and glimpse of the historical buildings including the Washington monument and the US Capitol building were signals to the serious nature of this city. After all, this is the seat of this country's government, politics and power. Its facade was quite different compared to San Francisco's vibrant almost eclectic feel. It was springtime, a cool fresh air touched my skin and I caught a beautiful glimpse of tulips and cherry blossoms. It was also Easter week, a resurrection of life and a new beginning.

Welcoming me on my arrival on April 26, 1984, was Ate Carmen, my first cousin, and Kuya Tony, her husband. Following this long trip, my other cousins, Ate Ligaya, Kuya Digo, and Kuya Vincent, all of whom I had not seen for many years welcomed me with open arms. I also met for the first time Ate Carmen's twin, Ian and Sean. It was heartwarming to see them all.

I was grateful for this new day in Washington, D.C., a city bordered by the states of Virginia and Maryland. It was a region that was full of life and prospects for career opportunities, cultural events and a haven for tourists and immigrants. With open arms and an open mind, I was thrilled with this new journey, just like millions of immigrants who have come before me.

I was like a little child as I appreciated a McDonald's hamburger when my cousin Kuya Digo took me there the first time we met in Springfield Mall, Virginia. The comforts in my cousin's house -- from a microwave to their beautiful sweet smelling home were a haven to my tired body and soul. My cousin Ate Ligaya was kind enough to welcome me into her apartment near Dupont Circle. Together with Ate Carmen, she showed me the basics, from using appliances to riding the Metro to buying lottery tickets. It was my beginner's luck in lottery that amazed them the most. I won more money during my first few months than they ever had! I won enough to send for my children in the Philippines!

With Faith and Perseverance, Nothing is Impossible

Of course the sheer coincidental luck of the lottery was not the key to how I survived in this big city. I used the nation's capital as my own capital for a new life, and I stood firmly in the belief that it was a symbol of freedom and democracy, not only to the world but also to individuals like me. Survival was the name of the game, and I played it like a pro. Every moment was an opportunity, and every opportunity brought me closer to my final destiny, which was to finally break my bondage from my abusive ex-husband and get my children to America. This was my mission.

This mission was not easy given my humble beginnings in the nation's capital. I was fired from my first job as a temporary babysitter/maid that I had desperately taken with an employment agency. This was May 1, 1984 - five days after I arrived in America on April 26, 1984. I needed a job – whatever job – and I didn't have time to waste. Though I had money from the sale of my property in the Philippines, I had to work to pay for the lawyer I hired to get my divorce from my ex-husband.

I was referred to work as a temporary babysitter and a maid to a millionaire family in Foxhall Road, Georgetown. I took this temporary job, planning to last for one month, but I lasted a week. I washed the children's clothes and placed them in the dryer. The sweaters shrunk, and the white clothes turned pink. There was no excuse and before I knew it, I heard Mrs. Miller saying to the temp agency, "She is a very nice person, but she does not know anything about the house. She just ruined the kids' clothes!"

A few days later, a lovely blond curly-haired lady, named Mrs. Marks, met me at the corner near the Safeway Store in Chevy Chase, Bethesda. As soon as we met, I knew this would be a person who would teach me and forgive me for any mistakes I'd make as a housekeeper/babysitter. Their house was located in Chevy Chase at that time, and in a few months they were moving to a huge mansion in Potomac, near the house of Sugar Ray Leonard.

They were a Jewish family who took in a Catholic maid and made me feel like part of their family. I ate with them. I vacationed with them in Delaware, Ocean City and other places. Not once did they introduce me as their maid. I was a part of their family. They even went so far as to sponsor my immigration papers a few weeks after they hired me. It was this family who helped me get a lawyer for sponsorship and to file for divorce. In six months, (October 1984) the court of the District of Columbia ordered my uncontested divorce from my ex-husband. I achieved my first goal despite overwhelming odds.

Feeding the Stomachs of Dignitaries

At almost the same time, I was offered a job by the Embassy of Australia to work as a domestic assistant at the residence of the Ambassador of Australia on Cleveland Avenue, Washington, DC. The diplomatic visa was important for me in order that I might get my children into the US. Hence, though sad to leave the good family of Mr. and Mrs. Marks, I resigned without telling them about this new job. It was difficult to say goodbye to a family that treated me like their own. By then, they had already moved to Potomac, Maryland. I helped them move and clean. Out of guilt of leaving them, I also found a Filipino replacement to take over my job.

My next stop was working for the Embassy of Australia working for Hon. Sir Robert Cooke. The salary was decent, and with free board, lodging and tax exemption, it was a much better opportunity than being an administrative assistant for a small company. It was here where I met some of the most beautiful immigrants I've met on my journey.

There was George, the butler, and his wife Maria who did the laundry. As a butler, George had his own house on this big lot surrounded by a beautiful garden. His whole family lived there free, while they owned another house somewhere else in Maryland. Santino, from Italy, also lived in the same compound with his family, even though they also owned properties. Two other Filipino ladies worked there, and one of them was named Sally. We took turns helping with household chores and other needs of the Ambassador and his family. Living free in a very nice house, in a huge lovely compound, and in one of the most expensive neighborhoods in the city was indeed a blessing. This place was a witness to my first snow in America and many other memorable moments as an immigrant in this country.

As a group of immigrants, we thought we were all blessed. We

were treated very well with decent salaries and allowance, free room, lodging and great friendship among immigrants who supported our interesting but somehow lonely lives. Most of the people I met appeared to have come from good families in their own countries. Each of us was busy writing letters back home, saying just enough to brighten our families back in our native land, and assuring them we were okay. At times, it was half-truth. We figured not telling them everything was okay. We kept any negative aspects of America within us and just shared our positive experiences. We didn't have time for pity. We were here to make a living - period.

There were also many funny and light moments in the Embassy. There was Irvin, who was from Jamaica. He said he was a singer and worked as manager in a club in Jamaica before he came to America. He would hum and sing while doing his chores. During break time, we all congregated in the lounge area and watched the afternoon soap opera. In between, we would share stories about our lives.

Irvin would add, "I just wrote a letter to my mother. I told them not to worry. I am doing well, and I got a job as a floor manager." He would laugh and in his Jamaican accent he would say, "But I never told them I was a janitor." His laughter filled the room as he emphasized being a janitor is the same thing as being a floor manager. "I cleaned the floor, and that's how I managed the floor," he chuckled as he described that back in Jamaica he was a real floor manager and singer in a big club in his hometown.

In my case, I simply wrote to my family and friends that I was doing well working for the Ambassador, and I had a diplomatic visa. No more and that was it. No need to tell all the pitiful stories those highly educated immigrants go through to start a new life.

Though I know this was just another step along the way, I was happy with my new group. We laughed about funny things that happened in our work, including seeing the Ambassador mistakenly eating a beautiful cream soap lying in the kitchen counter, thinking it was a piece of white chocolate. In a more amusing but not disrespectful way, we found every opportunity to fill our empty lives with something to liven it up at the expense of the people who employed us.

Santino, the Embassy's chef, would share Italian stories as he cooked the finest food for the ambassador's guests. At times he would throw a piece or two of the appetizer as he asked us to taste his culinary cooking. George, the calm collected good-looking butler who looked very respectable in his black suit with gold trim, would bring his own Greek cooking including baklava, while his wife Maria sang while she ironed clothes. Sally, another Filipina, was like my boss, and deep beneath her harsh façade, she had a generous heart. She had been working in the Ambassador's residence for many years. She was my teacher as I learned the detailed art of setting fine tables for dignitaries, taking care of the plants in the atrium, turning down the bed in the Ambassador's bedroom, and other personal errands for the Ambassador and his wife.

George taught me how to serve like a pro -- from wine and appetizers to main dishes and dessert. But I was never good at serving a formal dish. The serving dishes were too big for my tiny hands. I was good at putting name cards right in front of the plate and fixing the beautiful fine linen and expensive silverware used in the table setting.

Outside the Embassy, I had the opportunity to meet other immigrants since we visited each other's houses on weekends and vacation time. There were doctors from other countries who were now in the U.S. cleaning laboratories at hospitals or working in low paying research assistant jobs. Former supervisors and managers were now waiting tables, cleaning rooms in hotels, babysitting -- doing anything they could to make money. I wondered why Americans

were not available to take some of these jobs that paid better in a lot of ways.

My time as a new immigrant was a time of learning and child-like innocence. I was in awe just going to Safeway to see how they scanned the groceries I bought and automatically give you the total price for a cartful of items. We did not have that kind of technology in the Philippines at the time I left. Back home, I did my shopping at the wet market where shopkeepers kept their money in their pockets, and vendors used a pencil and paper to add the amount you bought.

Though English was my second language and my training was considerably very strong, being in America taught me a whole new appreciation of English. I heard more words than I'd ever used in my entire lifetime in my own native land. I interchanged words. In Safeway, I asked for bunion for soup instead of bouillon. I pronounced words differently, and everyone seemed to ask, "Say it again, please." I would repeat what I said and only after the second time would my words be understood.

My camera, my first priceless possession I had bought upon my arrival in San Francisco, took many pictures as I captured people I met and places I visited, including get-together parties of other immigrants and Filipinos. Shopping was not reserved for the regular office workers. We went on shopping sprees, hunting for bargains and sales to send back home as gifts when some of our friends would go back home to visit. I accepted additional cleaning jobs on my days off to be able to send more money or remittances to the Philippines to sustain the life of my loved ones and my children. It was a regular obligation more important than our own needs. My life as a new immigrant was a sacrificial time when our life was not completely our own.

But just like in previous days, I now marveled at how much

patience, endurance and sometimes tolerant we had become to enslave ourselves for the sake of those we dearly loved. No one complained, and in fact, all were content and happy it seemed.

Though I had one of the most humble jobs in Washington, DC, I took it as an opportunity. After all, working for an Ambassador was a big deal – we got to eat the left over food, the same food the US Secretary of State and Secretary of Defense, other ambassadors, dignitaries, government officials and reporters ate. I would stand and wait patiently, holding their long coats, which were far heavier than my petite structure, could carry. I'd open the doors with a smile in my face as I looked up to most of them. I was less than five feet tall, and most of our guests where like giants looking down on me.

At any rate, I was honored to work at the Australian Embassy under two Ambassadors. Following the term of Sir Robert Cotton, Ambassador FR Dalrymple came from their tour in Indonesia. I continued to carry on other domestic tasks and to serve food for the important people who made major decisions that affected not only their countries but also other countries, including my own.

Imelda with George, her favorite butler. Taken inside the Embassy of Australia Ambassador's residence. (December 1984)

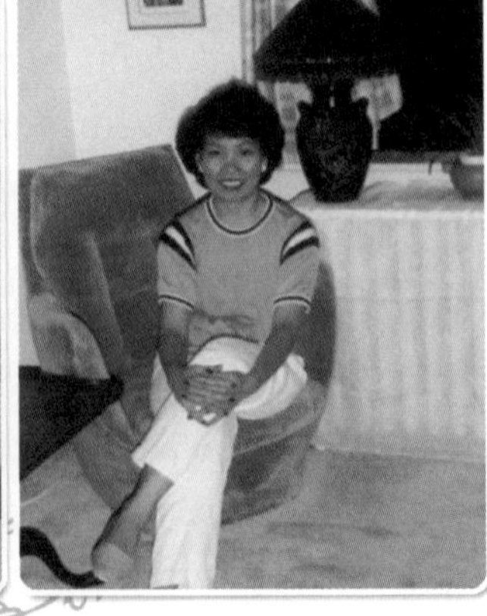

Imelda's room in the Embassy (1985).

Awakening My Homesick Soul: My Children, My Strength

It was around 1985, a time when Philippine President Ferdinand Marcos, his wife Imelda Marcos and their children, were in a state of expulsion from the Philippines. I was in the same room serving dinner to the dignitaries, government officials, and the discussion was about my country and our deposed Philippine President. I remembered very well Senator Richard Lugar in that conversation and taking a phone call.

Though the shooting of the late Philippine Senator Benigno Aquino occurred on August 21,1983, his assassination dominated the news, with President Marcos accused of plotting his political opponent's sudden death. This conversation in the Embassy of Australia reminded me of the struggles my country has been experiencing for quite a long time even before Benigno Aquino was killed.

But my children were still there in the Philippines, and the pain was becoming more unbearable. My life was filled with dreams as well as some nightmares of the past that kept haunting my soul. It was like a book clearly drawn forever in my heart and mind that no amount of time can heal.

The night was long and I filled it with long distance calls to the Philippines to hear my children's voices. When the time was over, I would lay at night restless. No days were left empty. I filled every moment with activities that would keep my dying soul from giving up. The thought of my children was enough to awaken me as my tired body succumbed to the hard physical labor of being a domestic worker. I looked at a photo sent to me by my sister as Andrea and Alberto where on the phone talking to me. Their beautiful faces comforted me at night when I would be awakened by a nightmare and terror of the past.

I prayed for more strength and wished for an angel to fly them over to America and for a soldier of God or a knight in a shining armor to lift me up.

Reflections:

As I reflect on my life as an immigrant in my new country of America, I learned the importance of humility of spirit, tenacity, and opening ones mind to the opportunities that lie ahead despite struggles and challenges. This state of mind allowed me to conquer instead of surrender. It allowed me to live than simply survive.

Though I had to start all over again, I was truly humbled by the opportunity this country has given me. I was a stranger to this land, but I was welcomed with vast opportunities, but it was up to me to seize them. Though my initial journey as an immigrant involved physical labor, perseverance and hardship, the belief that this country can be a true place for liberty and freedom nurtured my being. Though there were lonely nights I was kept awake by the thought of my loved ones I left behind in the Philippines, the bursting fireworks of independence from the slavery of my own marital past and the future of my children awakened my inner being.

It was my responsibility to my own self and to my children, orphaned by the circumstances that surrounded my marriage, to overcome a nightmare, to dream and believe there would be a new life for all of us.

I must say with absolute certainty that those people who surrounded me with the gift of kindness, understanding, compassion and hospitality made my journey easier. My young heart, though still aching from the past, experienced the gift of friendship from my relatives, new friends and immigrants I met along the way. They were not dreams, but real people drawn in my soul as I moved on and explored the land of liberty, the land of opportunity.

For being a part of my journey, thank you!

13 In Search Of...

"Go and tell my servant David, this is what the LORD says: Are you the one to build me a house to dwell in?... I have been moving from place to place with a tent as my dwelling."
- Samuel 7:1-17 (NIV)

As if an appointed time had come to meet my knight in shining armor, a twist of fate changed my future the night I met David Roberts. Meeting David was heaven sent, but for a moment I felt like I was losing my mind even considering falling in love after the scars of abuse my first husband had given me.

"What did you say? You are marrying again?"

"Oh no, not after what you have gone through! Are you stupid? Are you crazy? What the heck are you thinking? Haven't you learned from your mistakes? Have you lost your mind? Besides, your job in the Embassy allowed you to get your children, and you can stay in America for the rest of your life. You don't need a man to ruin your life again!" These words swirled through my head as I relived my days meeting and marrying David Roberts.

Though my lonely heart was vulnerable, finding David Roberts was one of my biggest blessings in America. His name David in Hebrew means "the beloved one," and indeed he was.

"David served God's purpose for his generation. A man after my own heart." - Acts 13:36 (NASB)

I wasn't out searching for a man the night I met David. My days off from the Embassy were spent earning extra money, including cleaning the house of Randy, a very nice senior American and a friend of my cousin Ligaya. I was focused on cleaning Randy's bathroom and making it as clean as I could when he said to me, "You really should take a break and at least meet new people and have some fun."

He told me places to go for free without spending a lot of money. He figured I needed a life instead of cleaning bathrooms during my days off. Perhaps he saw me talking to the commode as I made it sparkling clean. He probably knew there was nothing fun about doing this job on Sabbath Day.

With other immigrants and friends I met, and with the help of my relatives, I did start having a life. We went out and had fun just like any other people. We went dancing, going to friend's house, parties, taking turns to cook, went to church, picnics at the park, shopping and buying lottery tickets in between. Though I did a lot of dishwashing after parties, I was filled with gratitude for the temporary joy meeting people gave my lonely heart. These joyful escapades sustained me as I did my chores in the Embassy.

It was almost a fluke that I met David that Saturday night. I was supposed to go meet another friend in Georgetown to have dinner, but when the phone rang, my insistent senior American friend invited me to attend a party at the Hyatt Regency. I said, "I can't. I have dinner plans tonight with my Pakistani friend." Hearing the insistent voice on the other side, "But this is free, and you will enjoy it! Besides, this does not happen every night!" So I called my Pakistani friend and cancelled my dinner.

I asked Tess, a Filipina friend I'd met through my relatives, to accompany me. So there I went in a red and black dress with a little makeup, which I had not put on for a long time. Tess and I took a cab to the Hyatt Regency in Arlington instead of Georgetown. In my own naïve way or perhaps fate, we walked inside this beautiful huge hotel in Arlington. As we entered the ballroom, the place was beaming with lots of people dancing, drinking, talking and just having fun. The sign said, ISO Parents Without Partners. I did not know what ISO meant, but we went inside anyway. Only after the party was over did I learn ISO meant In Search Off – literally a party for people in search of love, partners, boyfriends and girlfriends! Oh my! Though that was the case, I felt like Cinderella, and it was one of my most memorable evenings in a long time.

Meeting David that night was special. I was charmed by his beautiful smile and gentlemanly way. Before the night was over, I felt like I had known him for years. He lived in Arlington and worked for a government agency. That night was followed by an intense courtship. David asked me to breakfast the very next morning! He visited me in the Embassy, took me to places I'd never seen including Nova Scotia, Canada, Maine, West Virginia, Ocean City, New Jersey, Delaware and much more. He swept me away with flowers, notes, cards and many little reminders of how much he loved me. Each day with David was a breath of fresh air consoling my lonely heart from my separation from my children.

In two years from the day I arrived in America, he proposed, and we got married in a simple civil ceremony in Arlington and had a very lovely reception with very close friends and relatives at the Gangplank Restaurant, a boat restaurant on the Potomac.

After a few months of living in an apartment in Arlington, we bought a house. This was a dream come true for me who had been living in the Embassy on weekdays, with my cousin in Dupont Circle on weekends, and with other relatives in between holidays. David in

my mind answered God when he asked,

"Are you the one to build me a house to dwell in? ... I have been moving from place to place with a tent as my dwelling."

The house we bought was far from Washington, DC. It was a huge five-bedroom house on over an acre lot in Stafford, Virginia -- quite different from the small room I had lived in at the Embassy. As a result of this move, I left my job in Washington, DC and got my first recruiting assistant job with a newspaper company in Springfield, Virginia. Still far from our new home but much closer than DC.

At this time I started living the American way. I learned to drive many miles to work instead of walking one floor down to serve the Ambassador. I got my first speeding ticket driving towards 95 North worried about getting late to work in just a couple of weeks after I got my driver's license. I paid taxes from my income instead of being tax exempt. My net income was less than when I was working in the Embassy, but that was okay. It was re-entering my real career and my profession. Besides, the love David was showering upon me made it all worth it! My life was coming together. I had a new job, a gorgeous new house and a wonderful new husband.

So what started as an ISO was really in search of a new life and a new beginning. My prayer was answered. To me, David was a soldier of God and my knight in shining armor. The love that David Roberts gave me from the moment I saw his gentle eyes and charming smile were the best gifts a barefooted soul could ever ask for.

Our house at Hope Street, Stafford, VA

Memorable Photos with Dave Roberts

Imelda with her husband, David Roberts. Taken with friends and relatives at Gangplank Restaurant, January 1986.

Wedding party at a boat restaurant in Washington, DC.

Party time with David, friends and relatives

Honeymoon at Nova Scotia, Canada

Snow plowing time at the Roberts' driveway at Stafford, Virginia one heavy winter time

Enthusiastically perform whatever you choose to do in life including difficult life's tests; it fuels the heart to greatness. Enthusiasm energizes our soul and brings positive hope into our life's journey.

E***nthusiasm***. Just imagine how you would feel doing something without enthusiasm. Are you bored, tired, distressed, unengaged, unhappy, or do you have this nagging question, "What am I doing? Why am I here?"

We are where we are and we are doing what we are doing because we choose to do so. We have the freedom to choose regardless of extreme circumstances we come across our life.

With enthusiasm, each step we take could be filled with positive energy. The more positive energies we have, the more we are bound to reach our ultimate destiny in harmony with what will make us happy.

Whatever you choose to do in life, the key to not just surviving but living life is to enthusiastically take each day and each task as a part of your journey. Without enthusiasm, negative thoughts will nag your daily living and pull you down more than keep you moving.

When we are faced with a situation beyond our control like sickness or death or when we are forced to do something, we still have the choice to keep a glimmer of hope within our hearts. The most successful people, including everyday heroes, welcomed life and challenges with hope and enthusiasm.

You Are Our Hero: In Honor of David

Forgiveness

Forgive even those who hurt you. It is in forgiving that the pain and agony within your heart finally finds peace.

David Roberts (1984)

David Roberts, my knight in a shining armor, gave his love to my children and me. He swiftly took us into his arms, and we lived together as a family for seven years. We will forever honor his short life on earth.

David died of cancer, holding my hand just as I finished singing "Amazing Grace" in the hospice wing at the Veterans Memorial Hospital in West Virginia. Though he left this earth six months from the time he was diagnosed with cancer of the esophagus, he is alive everyday in our lives. David was our hero and the soldier of our lives. He will always be my children's father.

David was first a hero who bravely fought in
Vietnam and served America
David was a loving friend and a husband to Imelda
He was a father who showered laughter to Andrea and Alberto
And forever we honor him, for he was our angel, our real hero!

Written in 2001 following the tragic events of September 11th, the song "You Are Our Hero" was inspired by my enormous feeling of loss of those who've kept us safe. The lyrics of this song were woven from how I felt about David and other heroes who gave their lives to all of us. The melody I heard in my head was clearly a marching sound in honor and remembrance of the true soldiers of our country. It was especially written with thoughts of David, for his courageous journey as a soldier, and for his beautiful spirit and love.

You Are Our Hero

We won't forget the life you risked
We won't forget the courage you gave
And in our hearts, you are our hero
We will remember you, forever more
Forever more - we will remember you
You are our hero!

Refrain
For you hold us safe in your hand, in your heart
While you fight the terror that we faced
Your heroic deeds will not be forgotten
You inspire us and
make us proud of you!

We honor you for what you've done
We give you praise
for unselfish love
Your bravery we won't forget
We will remember you
Forever more -
Forever more,
We will remember you
You are our hero!

Repeat Refrain

You are our hero! You are our hero...

14 A Reunion of the Barefooted Family

"Faith is the strength by which a shattered world shall emerge into the light."
- Helen Keller

My life in America had gone through almost three cycles of spring, summer, fall and winter and I was extremely overjoyed. What else could I ask for? I was Imee to David, and he was my Dave. My shattered and once broken world was beginning to emerge as one beautiful heaven. My faith was constant, and with it I saw my life blooming like bright dandelions welcoming spring. My mission, though at one time an impossible, arduous task, was almost within my reach. The faith and beating hearts of two people in love made it all possible.

Spring was a perfect time for the salvation of the barefooted family; the process to get my children from the Philippines began in springtime of 1987. My two beautiful children, whose love kept me strong, were still living away from me. Bringing them to America would complete my life. I begged Dave to help me get them! And he did. We sold the house in Stafford and made a little money to buy another house in Woodbridge. With our finances in order, we showed the government we could afford to support them. Dave filed a petition in the Immigration Office to get our children, and in less than a few months, they were granted residents' visas.

For almost three years, my connection to my children had been through long distance phone calls made through my sister. I cherished a photo of Alberto and Andrea talking to me on the phone that had been taken by my sister. It kept my spirits high. I talked to them regularly, and my telephone bills were high! AT&T should be rich by now! Telephone bills were our largest expense next to our mortgage payment. The voices of my children and the connection to my family were all worth it and kept me going.

I should have had the courage to go home and take them with me personally now that they had a visa. However, I was still having nightmares of my past. I did not have the strength to face my demon. Dave was also afraid something would happen to me should my ex-husband learn I was back to get our children. Though he had essentially abandoned them all these years, we played it safe.

Northwest Airlines had a program whereby they would assign a stewardess to accompany Alberto who was nine and Andrea who was turning eight. So we arranged for the children to be escorted by a stewardess at each major stop so we were assured they were safe. When they landed at New York we got a call, and in a few hours, they were in Dulles Airport in Virginia.

We were so excited! Their rooms on the second floor were all decorated with new furniture. Understandably, Dave was a bit frightened since over night he would become the father to two grown up kids he had never seen before. He overcame his fear, and we proceeded to the airport. Dave and me, my friends and relatives, Ate Carmen, Kuya Tony and their son Sean, all went to welcome my children. Just like my

Taken at Dulles Airport 1987 during the arrival of Andrea (7), and Alberto (8) in America.

arrival, Ate Carmen and her family were there to welcome my two children who I had not seen for three long years.

My excitement and mixed feelings were inexplicable. I could hardly breathe while waiting for them to come out of the narrow jetway connecting the aircraft to the airport terminal. It was a different time back then without security risk because we could go all the way to the arrival gate and meet passengers inside the airport.

My hands shook with anticipation! I peered nervously down the narrow walkway. Soon all my empty sleepless nights would be replaced with smiles, happiness and seeing my children emerge like beautiful angels.

Finally, as if in slow motion, two tiny souls came walking down the passageway hand in hand and accompanied by a stewardess. Alberto wore a suit, and Andrea was in a pretty pink dress. I was wearing a bright yellow dress as I welcomed both of them with teary eyes. As I hugged and kissed them, their weary, fragile faces looked brighter. I hugged them in my arms, never wanting to let them go. I introduced both of them to my relatives and to Dave. It was a beginning for all of us as a family.

Alberto and Andrea's early days were memorable, amusing and fun. I pray they never forget their first timc going to school, their first Halloween, their first birthday party, their first snow, and all other fun things in between that nourished their young lives. We made up for the time lost not being together.

It was also a time for learning the English language. I'll never forget Andrea saying, "I am colding." Alberto and Andrea were both in "English as a Second Language" classes, and their progress was phenomenal. Within a couple of months, they spoke better English than I did!

This was also a time for Dave and my kids to bond. He took the time to show my children the real essence of being a father. He paid

attention to them, and he nurtured them with his love. He made time to play and have fun with them. He was there for them, giving them guidance and teaching them as needed. David was their "Dad." David was our hero. Our shattered world had become brilliant and filled with peace and love. It was a whole new world beckoning us as one family!

Reflections:

Our days as a family were memorable with photos marking every aspect of our new life together in America. My children's journey was my journey. Their photos speak of how far we have traveled and illustrate the many blessings we have acquired along the way. Words cannot express the joyful feelings of a mother now united with her children. The photos below reflect upon how blessed our lives have truly been. May they speak a thousand words, a reminder and a memory for how David has changed their lives, our lives.

Memorable Moments with Alberto and Andrea

First Year in America - Alberto and Andrea (1987-1988)

Saying Goodbye to Our Hero

"The bitterest tears shed over graves are for words left unsaid and deeds left undone."
- Harriet Beecher Stowe

David Roberts was a child of God whose life on earth was spent in a meaningful way. He gave us love, and he left us with a peace in our heart that we will forever be indebted. The detail of my life with David is a book by itself. This chapter of the Barefooted Soul is about honoring what his life has meant to my children and me.

Though his life on earth was cut short by a devastating cancer, I know he is at peace with His Creator, and his spirit lives in our hearts. Even on his death my children and I felt his presence. After the funeral, we went home and a black butterfly was flying around the rose bushes in front of our house. It reminded us of Dave. And then, the butterfly landed right in front of our doorstep. Andrea and I kneeled to the ground to touch the butterfly. An awesome feeling went straight into my being as it stayed for a moment as I placed it in my palm. Andrea said, "It's Dad!" And then we let it to go and fly - just like the song David wanted to have in his funeral, "Fly Away."

There were a lot of great stories about Dave that now I wished I shared when he was alive. But, it is not too late to share to the world the legacy he left in our lives. Let me share with you a letter from my heart I wrote on the day Dave died. The pastor read it right before the American flag was given to me honoring his service to America.

No amount of words can explain the profound sadness and tremendous loss I felt as he left us on this earth. But then I realized that a peacemaker like David would surely be in Heaven.

"Blessed are the peacemakers, for they shall be called the children of God."
- Matthew 5:9

A copy of this letter was placed in his casket for him to take into his next life and for him to know the impact his life has made on the thousands he touched.

David Roberts' Lessons of Life

I've known David Roberts since 1985. I know him in a very special and intimate way as his friend, wife, and a real Dad to my children. We will forever keep David in our hearts and thoughts for the unconditional love he has given us. Even in his last hours, he made us feel very special and very loved. We feel very fortunate to have him as a part of our lives. For this, I cannot let him leave this earth without saying:

"David, thank you so much for the true love you gave us!"

To me, his passing is truly a personal lesson of life! It is a lesson of love, forgiving, and making the best of what we have in our life. But most especially, it is a lesson of courage and strength.

My last days with David were a rediscovery of what a beautiful person he truly was. Sometimes in our lives we get caught up with so many daily challenges – we forget there is so much beauty around us that we fail to see the beauty of those people we love. Sometimes, it takes death, or when one flies away that we then catch a glimpse of how truly beautiful they are! David's life and death has been about finding courage, love and beauty in the midst of life's challenges ... and that is what David is all about.

Despite his cancer, he has brought joy to me and to my children, his children. I am sure he did the same thing with his family and others close to him. Despite mistakes I made in our lifetime as husband and wife, he unselfishly said, "I love you." Despite the pain that I may have caused him at some points in our lives, he was quick to say, "There was nothing to forgive!" Despite the pain his cancer had brought to him, he made jokes, shared laughter, provided hope and clear direction on how to accept God's will as he cast his faith upon Him. He even chose his own gravesite to rest. How many of us can take on such an enormous task? David can and David did!

I truly would like to remember David for the love, beauty and joy he has brought to me, our children and to all those around him.

David, I will especially remember you as a soldier of God as you touched our lives with your strength, love and lessons of life! I will keep you in my prayers as you fly away with amazing grace to a new journey filled with peace and everlasting love. I will hold you in the palm of my hand and in my heart until we meet again!

To his dear friends and loved ones, may David's lessons of life inspire you as you continue to keep him in your prayers!

In Loving Memory of David C. Roberts, Jr.

Forgive even those who hurt you. It is in forgiving that the pain and agony within your heart finally finds peace.

Forgiveness. David's lesson of life was like my father's lesson. Forgive even those who hurt you. It is in forgiving that the pain and agony within our hearts finally finds peace.

Perhaps, this is one of the most difficult lessons I have to live up to - to forgive those who hurt us. However, as human beings we all make mistakes in our life. Compassion for others especially those who offended us, or did something terribly wrong to us is quite hard to give.

But what is the price of not forgiving? Would you want to carry the heavy load of every mistake people that affected you? Would you find peace in your heart carrying a heavy burden, while those who may have offended or hurt you have moved on with their lives. Would you rather live with anger and hatred, or would you rather let it fly away?

Our Creator, and my heroes and angels like David and my father, Miguel left behind an important lesson - when we forgive, we inherit the most powerful path to bringing unconditional love and peace on earth.

With love and peace, we can fly away, and finally feel free!

With love, David's story is sincerely dedicated . . .

To 8,744,000 U.S soldiers who served on active duty in the Vietnam War from 1964 to 1973, and to over 58,000 soldiers who died or were classified as M.I.A. (Missing in Action) during this war.

To individuals afflicted by cancer and other fatal diseases. The American Cancer Society reports an estimated 570,280 deaths in 2005 due to cancer alone. With over 1.4 new million patients in the same year, cancer is the second leading cause of death in the U.S.

For more information about this devastating disease,
visit *www.cancer.org*

Fly Away, Soar Like an Eagle

Optimism

***O**ptimism is an onward bound positive energy that lifts the spirit and where one sees and finds opportunity in the midst of difficulties. It is the light despite darkness, it is the smile within sadness, it is the laughter within our soul, and the wide wings that make us fly and soar against the wind.*

As I look back on my humble beginning, many very good things have happened. Although my journey was rough at times, one thing helped me persevere. I had the instinct to choose which direction I would take, and which path I would pursue relentlessly. Like the eagle, where I was really did not matter, learning to fly against the windy sky to reach my targeted destination was an instinct I seemed to have mastered. The optimism, focus, passion and energy I put into every dream were the main ingredients in how I overcame my toughest plight. What Eleanor Roosevelt said is ingrained in my heart,

"The future belongs to those who believe in the beauty of their dreams."

I truly believe when you envision something for yourself and work towards that vision with all your heart, dreams do come true. Who would have ever thought I'd reach my perfect career destination and survive what I have been through! My life and professional journey have been a story of abiding faith, dreams and thanksgiving for those who trusted and believed in me.

In reflection, the secret to my professional success was actually based upon seizing every opportunity, labor of love, exuberance and appreciation for every little thing that comes my way. My son Alberto put it this way: "Every little hard step helped me to labor up the hill. Before I got to where I am today was simply a process that prepared me for a bigger role." My son was right. Every step I took was an opportunity to bring me to where I am today. Every job, no matter how odd or humble, I accepted with love, awe and enthusiasm. In the end, my victory was sweet and felt like an eventual triumph of good over evil. It was a labor of love and a legacy to God.

This chapter of my book focuses on my career and finding my own place in the sun. It was a time when several opportunities knocked, and with an eagle eye, I snatched and took the right opportunity to fly away. I was blessed with many opportunities, which I call my first leading breakthroughs. My success in my career life is also a testament to what Charles Darwin said, *"It is not the strongest of the species that survives, nor the most intelligent, but the one most responsive to change."*

It was my career life full of dreams, positive thinking, discovery, passion, making the best out of what I have, and never giving up my dream that inspired this song -- ***Fly Away, Soar Like an Eagle.***

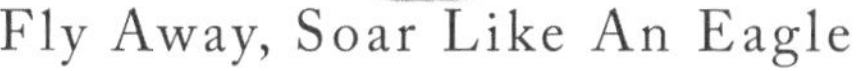

Fly Away, Soar Like An Eagle

When you hope and dream,
a new world begins
When you freely let the soft wind
touch your skin
You open your world
to life's great pleasure
Seek and discover
your own true treasure
In an endless world you're free to explore
Fly away, fly away, & soar like an eagle!

Follow your passion and don't give up
Amazingly soon you will rise to the top
Follow your heart and fly away
Fly away, and soar like an eagle!
Don't let a minute pass you by
Don't let despair break your heart
and cry! This is your world
Fill your world with hope and joy!
Freely dream... dream, Fill your world
With dreams and hopes!

Refrain
Fly away, fly away
and soar like an eagle
Fly away, fly away
and soar like an eagle!

Reach out for your star
and see what it brings
Spread your wings
Let the world see your dreams!
This is your world
Fill your world
With dreams and hopes!
Fly away, fly away
and soar like an eagle.

When you share your hope to the world another hope begins
When you freely let your loved ones feel your dreams
See the beauty of the world through you
You'll never know, others' dreams will come true!
This is your world, Fill your world
With dreams and hopes!

Repeat Refrain (last line 2x)

"Fly Away, Soar Like an Eagle," reflects upon my successful journey in a highly competitive job market in the world's most powerful region. , Washington, DC region. The words and melody speak of my triumphant career journey. But please, don't think I did it all by myself.

I hope you will learn from this journey in as much as I learned a lot from my mentors, colleagues, friends, bosses and my career angels. May the next stories inspire you to fly away and soar like an eagle!

16 First Career Breakthrough

"Develop success from failures. Discouragement and failure are two of the surest stepping stones to success."
- Dale Carnegie

Please don't think for a moment that I was a babysitter, a maid, and domestic help to the Ambassador and all of a sudden I soared high and became an executive right away. Just like the eagle flying high in the sky, I had stops along the way, before I landed in my most perfect setting. In my case, my career flight was indeed a process of learning, discovery and a true journey of spirit, which included some unpleasant necessary stops, but most importantly, a series of breakthroughs.

Back in the Philippines, I had my own secretary so I never learned how to type. I was told typing was a necessary skill in America. So while I was in the Embassy, I bought a small portable typewriter and enrolled in an evening class at Sanz School in Dupont Circle, Washington, DC. I took my first typing lessons and learned my first word processing skills using Wang computers. My investment paid off. Soon, I was ready for the corporate world again. I applied, took a typing test, and there you go – I got a job! I did not hesitate for a moment to find out what was needed to help me re-enter the career I loved even if it meant starting from the bottom all over again.

I was hired as a Recruiting Assistant with a medium-sized military newspaper company in Springfield, Virginia. It was my first entry into the corporate world of America. I took this entry-level job because I knew it would give me a chance to go back to where I left off in my career in human resources. I was the only Asian employee in the human resources office.

For over two years, I worked very hard in this company to prove what I could do. When Daphne, my colleague who acted as my direct supervisor/mentor moved to another job in Prince George's County, the Recruiter's job she held and the next step to my current position became available, I applied for it. Sadly, it was my first rejection. Even though I had more education than what the position required as well as the knowledge of the internal processes of the company, not to mention seven years experience from the Philippines, I was passed over for the promotion. The job was given to an outside applicant, an American woman who spoke Spanish. I was informed this language skill was helpful for a Recruiter's job, even though the job announcement never mentioned this need.

I was firm in my belief that I could have done this job but for the life of me, I never understood why I was passed over. I felt betrayed. My hard work had not paid off. I had been insulted by cultural questions, and I was hurt not just for myself but also for my own kind. I felt Asians would have a difficult time breaking into responsible professional positions given the stereotypes and reality of seeing many Asians in low-level positions during this time. Many were clerks, administrative assistants, and a lot of Asians were in some sort of business. They worked in dry-cleaning businesses, restaurants, retail stores, and other small shops, but they rarely were hired for professional positions. Perhaps it was this feeling of unfairness to the assumed "soft spoken and compliant" nature of my race that pushed me out of this department to explore other options. I felt my accent also contributed to my rejection as I was asked to repeat my responses to the interview questions.

As hard as it was to leave the career I loved, I could not stand the thought of working for someone who did not respect or value what I had contributed. I requested a transfer to the Research Department. Though my job in this department was only for six months, it gave me new ideas, which included doing my own research on companies that might give me a better opportunity. I learned a lot from this short assignment. My boss Perry took me in as his administrative assistant, and he gave me a great deal of support. It was in this position where I first learned how to do database work. For this, I am thankful to him. Though Perry was supportive, research was really not my field.

I couldn't be happy in such a place, and I knew it would affect my productivity. I also would not let such an experience stop me from attaining what I knew in my heart I could handle very well. I felt the rejection was an insult to my race, education and my seven years of supervisory and human resources experience in the Philippines' largest private corporation. I took to heart this rejection and channeled my negative feelings in a very positive way. I was only 29 at the time, and I wouldn't accept being boxed into a career. I was not happy where I was so despite terrific support from my boss Perry, I took my career somewhere else – nowhere. I resigned without a job!

Writing and Publishing My First Book Expanded My Universe

I was fortunate and blessed to have a husband at the time who truly understood my ordeal. With Dave's support, I resigned from my job and decided to research the entire employment process. I poured my heart into researching companies, the government and every organization in between. I scoured countless books in the library on the "American" way of recruitment, selection and employment. Home computers were not popular at that time,

and almost everything was done manually. Despite this, I finished the project in record time and guess what I learned? Pretty much nothing! I had done the same recruitment processes for seven years in the Philippines' largest corporation! In fact, some of the processes I had experienced were more exhaustive, cutting edge and right on target with what American organizations were doing. Hence, in no time, I reclaimed my expertise!

Expert I was – as affirmed by those who reviewed my book! In less than four months, I finished researching and writing a 319-page career book entitled "JOBS: The Employment Guide to the Washington, DC Metropolitan Area." I was confident my book was one of a kind, and there were no similar books that were as comprehensive as mine. My book was reviewed favorably by the Library Journal. I was in career fairs and was invited to community colleges. My book was self-published but because of the good reviews by this premier magazine for the library and publishing industry, my book made its way to career offices in various universities and public libraries. Independent book dealers took my book including big ones like Baker and Taylor. Though self-publishing was not a lucrative business, I sold out of the first printing, and it became the best investment I'd made in my career. At age 29, I was a published author!

Researching, writing and self-publishing a book by myself in less than four months was my first career breakthrough in America. Landing a professional job in split seconds was my needed bonus. Being a published author expanded my universe. Book dealers were now distributing the book, but my desire to land a job in my field was stronger than ever so I focused and applied the strategies I wrote about in my own book. Though I did not have a job during the months while I was working on my book project, in no time, I got

several interviews and job offers.

The Georgetown University: Affirming the Value of Education and Reputation

Given the great reputation of Georgetown University, I accepted a position as Employment Officer in this highly esteemed university. I recall my first learning lesson at San Miguel – "invest in a reputable company, and you will feel like somebody."

Imelda worked in the Human Resources Office located at the Healy Building, Georgetown University (1991)

Indeed, Georgetown made me feel like I was somebody -- especially meeting new and wonderful friends. It was in Georgetown University where I met my first true best friend, Farimah, a lovely lady from Iran whose outside beauty reflected the depth and love of her inner soul. I also worked with two other ladies I will never forget. Katalin, a tall lovely lady from Bucharest who eventually became one of my friends and Pat Connelly, my supervisor and first career angel who hired me for my first professional position in the USA in the field I love. Together, these three women gave me tremendous support not only in terms of my career, but friendship and laughter during my early days in the professional world of America.

Imelda with Farima, her best friend, at Georgetown University during President Bill Clinton 1993 Inaugural Ball.

It was in Georgetown where I met some of the most interesting people in my journey as an immigrant. It was here where I realized how many well-educated immigrants come to America and give up their education and previous career in search of a new beginning. There were veterinarians working as lab assistants, doctors working as research assistants, and nurses working as nursing aides. All took their jobs to heart with a positive view that the labor of love they provided to this great reputable institution would in the future bear fruit.

At Georgetown, I once again began to appreciate the value of an excellent education. Although Georgetown's tuition fees were among the highest in the region, it was well worth the investment with such famous alumni as President Bill Clinton, and the President of my native land, Gloria Macapagal-Arroyo.

Georgetown opened my eyes to how fortunate I was to have completed my education in the Philippines without having to pay tuition fees. Without this, I would not be in a position to take my journey into this great university.

Reflections of an Asian Minority

Though the experience at the newspaper company was not positive, it challenged me to look deep inside of me and take a risk. We must be bold and hold on to what we believe within ourselves. Getting out of a situation I was not happy with was one of the best steps I took in this stage of my career. In retrospect, I am thankful that I did not get the Recruiter's job after all. Without the rejection, I may have affirmed loyalty to those who promoted me and stayed there as long as they needed me. A door had closed when I was denied this promotion opportunity, but in the end, a wider door welcomed me into a whole new world of professional expertise and excitement.

Most importantly, I feel that we as individuals, including new immigrants and minorities in this country, do have a say in our future! It was this experience that motivated me to look inside of me, find my strengths, and allow myself to explore other opportunities

without fear or compromise.

As I reflect upon the experience I had with my job with the newspaper company in Virginia, it was actually the first career that awakened my soul as a professional Asian minority living in America. It made me wonder how many other Asians like myself were wrongly questioned on cultural issues that had nothing to do with job performance. Asians have the talent and capability but the prejudicial view of being "quiet and compliant in nature" is a setback that sometimes limits ability to assume higher professional and leadership roles.

Though many things have happened during the last 20 years, including increasing my salary 25 times my pay as a maid, the emergence of Asians as the highest percentage of minorities who earn above the median national average salary and among the most highly educated, a lot more will need to take place. Asians are less visible in many areas of American culture compared to other minorities. From movies, books, government appointments to corporate boardroom executive positions, I wonder when the day will come when more Asians stand side by side with other races in this country. It will be a victory to a woman minority's soul whose heart was once hurt by prejudice!

First Government Post

Working for a government allowed me to give thanks to an institution that gave me a chance to pursue my education. No longer was I at the mercy of the government.
- Imelda Roberts

With just me earning a living, two children in school and a mortgage, the lure of a better paying career was hard to resist. Though I truly loved the people and friends at Georgetown University, working for the university along with two other part-time jobs to sustain our expenses was quite challenging. Working as an Employment Officer at the university during the day, patient service rep in a hospital after work, and working on weekends on another part-time job was very exhausting.

Arlington County Government came knocking at the right time. I needed a financially attractive and equally challenging position in a location much nearer to our home. Located directly across Key Bridge and the Potomac River coming from Georgetown and Washington, DC, Arlington County was a culturally diverse and densely populated county with over 3000 employees at the time I was hired. My timing was perfect. It was a county experiencing tremendous growth, and a leadership phenomenon was sweeping the local government world.

Applying for a job with the local or federal government was very challenging, and at times it tested my patience. My keen desire to break into a government job at Arlington County was so intense that I applied not once but twice for the same position. I was told I needed to apply twice for the same position, when the first candidate who was offered the position turned it down. I remember applying and going into another panel interview with Ray Vanneman, other panel members, and representatives from the Arlington County Personnel Office. At the end of the interview, I was very confident I would get the job this time. My persistence paid off, and I got the job! It was here in Arlington that I started a career in government; I was in my early 30s at the time and now in charge of human resources services for the Department of Public Works.

Working for a government agency allowed me to give thanks to an institution that gave me a chance to pursue my education. No longer was I at the mercy of the government. After all, my education in the Philippines was made possible due to the government program at PLM for deserving but financially needy students. Though I was no longer in the Philippines, I felt working for the Arlington County government was honoring government institutions that had given me a chance as a young student.

Friends at DPW

With other Arlington County staff during a fashion show, Asian Heritage Month

Department of Public Works (DPW) Picnic. (Photos above taken in 1992-1993)

My experience with Arlington County was truly fulfilling, and it made me happy and equally challenged. Who wouldn't be -- I was surrounded by men! It was challenging from this point of view, but even though the department was comprised mostly of men, I stood out and had a ball.

The people I worked with were among the most professional and authentic people I have ever met. I had tremendous respect for my bosses, Ray Vanneman, Ken Hook, and Sam Kem, all of whom were very supportive and allowed me the opportunity to shine and contribute to the department. I was blessed to have Ray as my direct supervisor, and he gave me his full confidence and allowed me to grow. He even sent me to Georgetown University where I finished an advance certification in Organization Development while working for the county.

It was also here that I met some of the finest professionals and truly authentic friends I have met in America. First, there was Mary Din. Mary was from Cambodia and both of us clicked together like we were sisters. We had a lot of happy times together and secret ladies' talks. I also reconnected here with Tony Barcelo, a former colleague at San Miguel Corporation back in the Philippines. His presence in Arlington made my first few months feel like I had been there for years. I also met other good friends like Robert Froh and Paul Culver. My cousin, Ligaya, also work there as an added bonus!

Aside from a warm camaraderie of many other friends and colleagues in the Administrative Services Division, what I learned from Arlington County was an affirmation of many values of progressive organizations. It was a time of change when I was there. It was this first change that gave me an opportunity to learn many things that impacted not only our department but also the entire county.

The leadership buzzword at that time was called High Performing Organization or HPO. Arlington was going through values-based changes and alignment of systems and procedures in support of these values agreed throughout the country.

The change processes I experienced in Arlington County, along with the Organization Development classes I was taking at Georgetown

University, were coming together in perfect harmony. What I learned at Georgetown, I immediately applied at the county. My career was going very well. By the time I knew it, I received several superior performance awards, including a countywide Superior Performance Award given by the County Manager for accomplishment in diversity, safety and systems alignment in support of the county's mission, vision and values.

Despite being rejected for a higher job I applied in another department within the County, the continued confidence of my bosses and colleagues within DPW was heartening. In addition, I was also given a consulting role in publishing, working directly with Ron Carlee, the former Human Services Director and now the County Manager for Arlington County. It was another opportunity where I learned my strengths in publishing and computers. Though I was already a single parent by then, my family, friends and career in Arlington County filled my life with many blessings and lasting relationships.

Receiving Superior Performance Award from former County Manager, Tony Gadner

With DPW staff and Sam Kem, former director of Public Works receiving Saftey Award

Friends in Arlington 1991-1993

New Angel in My Life

It was a happy time but a new chapter was being written as Jeff Snively, a new angel came into my life. His entrance catapulted my world into a different place. In no time, Arlington County was a part of my past as he took my life into another career transformation I did not expect.

18 First Management Post in the Charm City

Enoch Pratt Free Library is a library for the rich and the poor, regardless of color – a library that was a gift to the City of Baltimore by Enoch Pratt, a philanthropist whose love for the poor touched my very soul.

While enjoying my career and friends at Arlington County, unbeknownst to me, my career was being written in a different place by an angel named Jeffrey Snively. I first met Jeff at a seminar we both attended, and we had lunch together after this. On the week of Valentine's Day he invited me for lunch and the next Saturday, he visited me in my house in Woodbridge, Virginia. In a heartbeat, his blue eyes charmed me! And so another chapter in my life began!

Enoch Pratt Free Library
Cathedral Street, Baltimore

My prince charming was also my career angel and he was my number one fan when it comes to believing in my abilities and what I have to offer. He was amused that I had researched, wrote, and published a 319-page book all by myself in four months. He couldn't believe I was a maid once in my lifetime, though honest to goodness, he swore he'd never have me do his laundry. At the time Jeff lived in Columbia, Maryland, which is very close to Baltimore. So when he saw a position for Chief of Human Resources and Volunteers Services for the Enoch Pratt Free Library in Baltimore, he quickly cut the ad out and gave it to me. Our long distance relationship was probably taking a toll on him I said to myself.

Though I wasn't really looking for a management position far away from Virginia, Jeff's encouragement was hard to resist. I took another leap into unchartered territory. I pulled out the ad I'd kept and put my heart into the application. The lure of Charm City and the prospect of working for the Enoch Pratt Free Library, one of the oldest free public library systems in the country began to grow on me. By the time I knew it, Jeff and I were going around Baltimore.

The Organization Development course I was taking at Georgetown University at that time was also breathing more life and energy into my busy career. It gave me renewed self-confidence. I was re-energized. My spirit and confidence were growing like crazy, and the more I was exposed to diagnosing difficult organizational issues as a part of our team project, the more I learned my strengths in dealing with people, organization and management.

My supervisory experience in San Miguel reemerged and reaffirmed. Finishing an advanced certification in Georgetown under the finest management and organization development teachers and mentors gave me a new vibrancy. Not to mention my classmates, all of whom were in senior management positions in different companies and government agencies in the region, gave me a strong perspective that proved highly beneficial in my new journey in which I was about to embark.

I also started reading about Baltimore and learned as much as I could about the Enoch Pratt Free Library where the position was available. I prepared myself and did my very best to impress them with my knowledge of the city and human resources. I applied in August and in October I was interviewed. In no time, I was hired into my first management job in November 1993.

Thanks to Carla Hayden, Executive Director, and Gordon Krabbe, Director of Administrative Services and Finance, for their vote of confidence. I was also grateful to Robert Hillman, the Chair of the Board of Directors of Pratt at that time who did the final interview with Carla. After my meeting with both of them, I was hired.

I was fortunate to come to this great institution and to be a part of a new management team led by Carla Hayden. Carla joined Pratt at its Director in 1993. I was hired a few months after her. My high regard for her, including the people I met during my interview, convinced me to take an unchartered place far away from Woodbridge, Virginia. Though I read some negative news surrounding the firing of the former Director of the Library, I saw beyond any negative publicity and was able to grasp the true beauty of this great institution that has served the Baltimore area since 1882. It is a library for the rich and the poor, regardless of color - a library that was a gift to the City of Baltimore by Enoch Pratt, a philanthropist whose love for the poor touched my very soul.

And my instinct was absolutely right! It was at Pratt that I met some of the finest people I have met in my career. The projects were challenging, and I had a team of staff who were all engaged. Most importantly, I had the full support of my bosses who allowed me to implement creative, fun and challenging programs.

Getting the job at Enoch Pratt Free Library was the beginning of a management and leadership journey that would change my life and career for the better. It was a tremendous responsibility to run not only its volunteer services but also its entire human resources programs and services affecting 28 branches all over the city of Baltimore.

Together, we accomplished a lot for the library including several leading edge projects and highly energizing moments with staff, including the Self-Sustaining and Team Approach To Renewal Program that provided the Human Resources to focus on its current state and plan its future aligned with the library's overall mission. The series of focus sessions revived energy among the staff in a library system plagued with difficult challenges like the imminent closing of library branches, budget shortfall, and negative headline

about the former director of the library.

It was also in this institution where I was given the confidence to facilitate the strategic planning process along with senior management team and branch managers. Carla and Gordon gave me their support and encouragement to conduct numerous processes including future search conference, board retreat, and other processes at the time the library was experiencing tremendous challenges. It was at Enoch Pratt Free Library that I was given the liberty to be a part of shaping its future and in the end, I was proud to have been a part of the library's revival and Carla's legacy.

Following the strategic planning process I led and facilitated, the library produced its Strategic Plan heralded as an instrument for future funding. Indeed it was a living document that those I left behind took to heart. Following its release, additional funding by the City of Baltimore was released. Other financial commitments were made including I recall $28 million in funding from Maryland General Assembly on facilities improvements for this great institution. Carla graced the newspapers so many times including winning the *Library Journal's* Librarian of the Year.

I loved this job so much that I would even work on Saturday, take my children to events in the library and work late into the evening. One time, I worked almost up to ten in the evening and wound up getting locked in the stairwell in between two floors of the main library. I knocked and knocked, and then put a notice under the door so anyone who might still be there could open the door for me. Thank goodness Debbie, another hard working librarian, was there to help.

There were many librarians in this network who loved their job just like me. After all, the Pratt Library was well known in the country for many things, including SAILOR, the hub of the public Internet service in Maryland.

As a pioneer in the Internet, the Pratt Library was among the first libraries in the country to do their websites, a project I was privileged to be involved with. Due to my seemingly quick knack in technology, combined with human resources and volunteer services under my department, several Pratt staff and I designed and conducted the first public Internet training for Maryland residents. It was during this period that I brought in experts to teach other staff in the library to become trainers. One of the most successful training programs we conducted was the Technology Train-the-Trainers Program. It was a program that prepared staff to not only learn how to teach the public the use of email and SAILOR, but also to learn important strategies in training adult learners. It was one of my most touching experiences.

The Technology Train-the-Trainers Program in my mind touched a number of staff like a caterpillar that bloomed into a beautiful butterfly. It was this program where administrative staff, who never had training or experience in standing up in front of the public, took the courage to join us in an intense three-week program. This was followed by an actual simulation, which then culminated in the library's first technology training for the public. The memories of this training program were shared in a heartwarming graduation reminiscent of our school days when we freely explored the most creative part of our being. I now treasure the photos given to me in memory of this special endeavor.

Aside from the warm friendships I gained in this great institution, it was humbling to work alongside a woman Executive Director like Carla whose contributions to this great library were revered by others in leadership positions throughout the nation. It was not a surprise she later became the President of the American Library Association, the oldest and largest association in the world.

It was Carla who touched my spirit as a woman trying to find a leadership place within an organization. Her conviction, dedication and leadership in this organization are a true legacy. I was a part of a journey in Pratt's revival and it was an honor for which I am truly grateful.

Memorable Happy Times at the Pratt Library

Carla Hayden, Executive Director, Enoch Pratt Free Library

Imelda in a Peggy Sue attire during the launching of the Library's Strategic Plan -- Back to the Future. With John Richardson, Facilities Director.

With her staff at Human Resources and Volunteer Services, and Gordon Krabbe, Director of Finance and Administrative Services

Imelda dancing with other Pratt staff during a Holiday event

With her former staff, Eleanor Brown, receiving flowers from the staff for the Technology-Train-the Trainers Program

19 My First State and Technology Post

"Dreams are illustrations... from the book your soul is writing about."
- Marsha Norman

My career at Enoch Pratt Free Library gave me further exposure in technology. It was in 1994 when SAILOR, Maryland's Online Public Information Network was born with Pratt Library as its home. It was the introduction of SAILOR that made Maryland the first state in the United States to offer statewide Internet service to its residents.

Though my first exposure to technology was the Wang class I took in 1985, my passion and keen interest in technology really started when I did research for my first published book. Somehow, I envisioned a job information network and so I titled my company Job Search Information Network and drew an illustration and a logo of a computer in the middle of a map of the USA and used this in my career book. That was in 1986. A few years later, it was a dream come true.

The Technology Train-the-Trainers Program, designed to be the training ground for teaching staff and Maryland citizens about the Internet, gave way to other volunteer opportunities. By the time I knew it, I was asked to serve on the State of Maryland Governor's Information Technology Board (ITB). It was here that I worked closely with Major Riddick, Chief of Staff of Governor Parris Glendening. I was a frequent speaker in committee meetings, and beyond this, I was given other statewide projects including the creation of the first website for the Maryland Technology Showcase, a statewide gathering of major technology companies in the region.

For three straight years from 1995 to 1997, I was the person who designed and programmed this website. I was also in charge of what was called the Maryland Techno-Van Project with funding approved by the Maryland General Assembly. Though this project had funding in place, and a big media event was held in the Governor's Office in Annapolis, it did not materialize due to lack of passion from those agencies that first partnered with this project. The continued lack of interest on who would run the project from a state agency (remember I didn't work for the state) contributed to its final demise. But such things happen in technology. Some ideas die and some flourish. My involvement in the highly successful Maryland Technology Showcase and my contributions to the Diversity and Equal Access to Technology in Maryland gave way to three consecutive years' of recognition from then Governor Parris Glendening. To my young heart, it was an honor.

Since then, I've given my free time and expertise on a volunteer basis to further hone my technical skills. I've created several other websites for private and government agencies. I've been asked to speak to groups from other states, and I was one of the few speakers in the National Organization Development Association to speak about "Connecting with the World through Technology." My experience in technology gave way to my role in the City of Frederick as the cabinet official in charge of technology for the entire city. From DOS to Windows, to fiber optic and a full-blown web presence at the time I left Frederick, the city went from the dark ages of computers to the 21st Century.

There is so much to learn in the ever-changing technology. One thing was sure, the power of technology and the ability to leverage and balance it with projects involving people and human resources gave way to some of my most memorable winning moments in my career.

Imelda Roberts with Parris Glendening, former Governor of the State of Maryland, state employees, and members of the Maryland Information Technology Board during an annual recognition award. Imelda was a recipient of the "Vision and Dedication in Technology in Maryland." for three consecutive years, 1995–1997 for her volunteer efforts and contributions in access and equity in technology.

On a volunteer basis, Imelda was the person who designed the first website for the Local Government Personnel Association, the National Forum for Black Public Administrators, and several other organizations. Today, she continues her volunteer efforts doing websites for organizations she cares about. She has also started human resources projects benefiting the general public.

First Cabinet Official Post

"True pilgrimage changes lives whether we go halfway around the world, or out to our own backyard."
- Martin Palmer

The thought of working directly within a local jurisdiction was exciting, so when I saw a position advertised reporting directly to the Mayor of the City of Frederick I applied for it.

It seems I was attracted to positions with organizations experiencing big changes. From the HPO changes in Arlington, to the revival of the Enoch Pratt Free Library, and now the City of Frederick's personnel challenges. The city was also experiencing tremendous growth. By this time Frederick was the second largest city in the State of Maryland in terms of population.

Working in organizations confronting change and major challenges is the kind of job that truly excites me because it is a learning environment. I would rather have these kinds of challenges than to just come in and do nothing but maintain existing programs and procedure already put in place with no sign of progressive and continuous learning. I get more excited being able to help with strategic issues. I enjoy making an impact in organizations that need my expertise in creating new systems and processes, change management and organizational development. In so doing, I believe I make a difference in the overall strategic direction of the organization.

Come to think of it, even though I read about several personnel incidents in the news as I researched the City of Frederick as a potential employer, this did not detract me from pursuing a career in a place where my family and I wanted to live. My children and I would all benefit from the move -- I would be working ten minutes from home so we could spend more time together; Andrea wanted to attend the new high school in Frederick. Alberto was in the University of Maryland so our move would not impact him. The position would be challenging and one in which I could contribute my expertise.

These were my primary considerations. The financial side was also attractive to a single parent like I was. So I applied and got the position! As soon as I gave my acceptance speech during a morning press conference with the City Mayor, the Frederick News Post afternoon edition carried a front headline with my photo in it. The local television and radio stations played the news, too. It was the beginning of my real public life.

I was hired by then Mayor Jim Grimes on January 3, 1998, just in time for his inauguration following his commanding reelection bid for the second term. Working with Mayor Grimes was indeed a humbling experience. He is a millionaire and a mayor – one would think that must be scary! But in all actuality, Mayor Grimes is one of the most humble and down to earth persons I have ever worked with. Despite what he has accomplished in life, he is a dedicated public servant who went out into the city to mow grass and clean the streets from snow for citizens even if he did not need to. I found the mayor to be very personable and easy to get along with. I also saw that he sincerely cared about the City of Frederick and each and

Happy New Year 2018

every citizen. Despite his financial status and business success, he went on to become a city mayor and serve the City of Frederick for an income I personally would not even consider. His heart was in all the right places.

In a short time, I began to see Mayor Grimes' sincerity for the City of Frederick, a place he called home almost his entire life. It was not too long before my working relationship with the mayor became a perfect union. There was mutual respect on both our parts. As Director of Human Resources, he allowed me to make decisions that positively impacted the city employees, including a first salary and benefits study costing over a million dollars. Because it was the first study ever been done in many years, there was media interest in it.

Though this was the case, the Board of Aldermen approved the study unanimously. Within six months, there were many positive changes within the human resources division. Several employee relation cases were addressed. As a result, I received the Outstanding New Employee Award after less than six months of employment. It was a heartwarming award, one that I truly relish. After all, it was the city employees who nominated me for this award given during the Maryland Municipal Week. It was on the news as the start of positive media coverage for the mayor.

Imelda receiving an award from former Mayor Jim Grimes as Outstanding New Employee for positive contributions in bridging employee and employers relations issues in the City of Frederick. (May 1998)

This was followed by several other winning moments for Mayor Grimes, including the highly successful Unity with Momentum Program, a citywide program that engaged the staff of the City of Frederick to take part in shaping the City's mission and vision. I was pleased to be a part of this exciting time. In less than six months I was promoted to become one of the cabinet officials as Chief of Human Resources and Administrative Services in charge of human resources, information technology, payroll and other administrative functions. Being a woman and in the Mayor's cabinet team was indeed an honor.

In 1998, City of Frederick Mayor Jim Grimes appointed five cabinet officials including Imelda Roberts, as Chief Administrative and Human Resources Officer. With her in this photo – left to right: James Graham, Chief Public Information Officer; John Leisenring, Chief Financial Officer, and Mayor Jim Grimes.

Besides human resources, I also led the technology transformation in the City of Frederick. From DOS to the Internet to fiber optic technology never seen before, the City took a gigantic leap into the 21st Century technology. In a few short months my team accomplished goals that had not been met for years. This was made possible through the expert hands of my staff, most especially by Scott Kishimoto, whose technology expertise at a young age is quite phenomenal.

Though I worked late in the evening including Saturdays, I did not mind it. I loved my job. It was a commuter's dream job – since it was only ten minutes away from my house. It allowed me to go

home for lunch and pick up my children from school. My staff was comprised of highly talented professionals: Jeanne, Angie, Maura, Bobbie, Dan, Scott, Jeanne Nakamoto, Jodene and Joyce were a group of individuals who worked diligently in this high-pressured environment. Though we had many challenges and lots of things to accomplish, for the most part, we were a perfect team.

It was here in the City of Frederick that I first directly worked with elected officials. I had great relationships with Aldermen Meta Nash, Joe Baldi, Bill Hall, and Blaine Young. Having their support and confidence, along with Mayor Grimes, meant a lot to my department and me. I was given the opportunity to be involved in major issues affecting the city. From strategic planning, city reorganization to a whole array of human resources, technology and administrative functions, in my mind it was a dream job.

Imelda delivering speech in one of the public meetings in City Hall at the City of Frederick. Also in this photo is Alderman Joe Baldi. (1998)

This dream job translated not only in promotion for me but awards for my staff and the entire city. In just over a year, the outside world was celebrating the contributions human resources gave to the city in a short period of time. Our HR Team, comprised of a small but dedicated staff, came away with not one but four awards in the Local Government Personnel Association, including the first HR

Team Award ever given by this 40-year old professional organization and the highest management supervisory award to me. The photo that speaks of this award winning moment was captured in several newspapers.

The City of Frederick human resources staff received four out of nine award categories from the Local Government Personnel Association during the 12th Annual Personnelist of the Year Award Luncheon honoring the "best and the brightest," and recognizing outstanding achievements benefiting local governments.

While the outside world was celebrating our accomplishments, a powerful force beyond my control was taking place. In no time, a challenging journey that would test the very core of my professionalism put me to the test on a roller coaster ride.

First Political Nemesis: An Officer and an Alderwoman

"Nearly everyone can stand adversity, but if you want to test a person's character, give him power."
- Abraham Lincoln

My acceptance speech when I took the position at the City of Frederick was prophetic; this job was not just a job change. It was a life change! Though I expected being a political appointee included some amount of exposure to the media, I did not expect the negative way in which I was portrayed. My public crucifixion started with a simple thing, and to this day I still cannot fathom it. The hatred it created in one alderwoman against me was so ingrained that it was recorded time and time again through negative news about me.

The City of Frederick City Hall

At this point I was already a cabinet officer at the City of Frederick. I was a five-foot tall petite officer, and the alderwoman was double my size. The controversies publicly played in the media were also beyond my control. A negative force was taking over that engulfed my last year with the City of Frederick. It was a political nemesis whirling in my head.

Though I respected the alderwoman and had consistently complied with requests that came into my office, giving out personnel information is bound by my own professional ethics. My office provided her the salary information she asked for, but not the family

medical and maternity leave information of a particular employee. When she insisted, I channeled it through the mayor. In my mind, I felt strongly that I could not violate an employee's personnel information. Beyond the salary, which in the public sector is an open book, anything that pertains to a specific employee's personnel record is completely confidential. Besides, there was no authorization from the employee to release this information. I really cannot understand why a legislative official would take a strong interest in the personnel information of a specific staff member anyhow. Her reasoning that she needed the information to serve the public was beyond me. I think this behavior oversteps any reasonable bounds. I stood my ground, and however true to the ethics of my profession, my action was taken in the wrong context.

Going against those who were in political power put me in a lot of trouble. Though in my mind I did my job and was doing the right thing, this alderwoman had a fatally strong point of view that to her merited news coverage and destruction of my soul and my reputation, including putting my family's livelihood at stake. Her threat, "I will get Imelda fired if she thinks she can cross me" was perhaps the beginning of the uncivil behavior that engulfed city politics.

The next thing I knew the January 28, 1999 headline in the local newspaper said, "Alderman: Officials Blocking Information." I was the bad guy featured in the local newspaper. The headline said I denied her public information she needed to serve the public. Given my respect to the confidential nature of my role, I never spoke in detail to the news reporters. I simply said I followed protocol and existing human resources regulations; the Chief Information Officer confirmed this was the case. I thought this was the end of it.

I was dead wrong. It was just the beginning. Between the alderwoman and the media, I became their ping-pong ball, being hit in the face with negative news that would not even deserve a news space in places where I used to work like in Arlington, Baltimore or the State of Maryland. But in the City of Frederick, despite the internal nature of my projects, I was a headliner.

Since then, controversial news clips overtook my City of Frederick award photos scrapbook. Angie, my administrative assistant, was obviously affected by all she'd witnessed. One day she wrote an editorial published in the Frederick Gazette entitled, "Flunking the Test of Character's True Measure," referring to how she had witnessed the rude behavior and character of the alderwoman when the public was not watching. She could no longer tolerate what she was witnessing and exercised her freedom of expression. She believed the alderwoman was really out to get me; she was on a "war path and Imelda better not cross it." Some people's arrogance and egos overtook their rationale thought.

I admired Angie for her courage and energy! She was petite and less than five feet tall but her vibrant personality, courage and beautiful spirit were bigger than the tallest mountain in her hometown of West Virginia! Soon after she left the City of Frederick to focus on her family and care for her children. She preferred the quiet life in a huge cottage built for her by her husband back home compared to the noisy chaos and nasty politics enveloping her life in the city.

Many employees and people outside the city gave me their moral support. It was this support that enabled me to keep going. Others who took this as a more "political" issue between the mayor and this alderwoman gave their two cents in the matter. "You have clout," some said. "You are now in the important circle in Frederick, and that's why you are on the news and getting editorial space in the local newspapers!" What a perspective. Though I did not really like what was going on and did not buy what they were saying, the moral support of folks around me helped me get through these rough times. I tried to ignore the negative news and focused on my work!

Though these controversies did not affect my work, and in fact we got several awards during this period, including approval of all recommendations that positively changed employees' lives, the ordeal was unbelievable. It was like a never-ending drama played in the media, and I was the villain.

My courage came in the form of protecting my profession. Not speaking against anyone in the media, however good my intention, was perceived as guilt. Who could blame the media for seeing only one side? Sometimes we get persecuted for doing the right thing and for our silence. But in my case, I did have many angels who spoke for me, the officers, the City Mayor, the employees and even the President Pro-Tem. Though I did not solicit help from them, they spoke up for me. I abided by the confidential nature of my job and did not give the media what they wanted to hear.

Though I was living just 10 minutes from where I worked at Frederick City Hall, the political climate beseeching my career was hard to ignore. Being a political appointee, and the thought of not having a job after the election, was more than enough to make me think about looking for a job somewhere else. Realizing many things beyond my control were happening in the City of Frederick and elections were looming on the horizon, I sent my resume to a job hunter in response to a position with the Metropolitan Washington Council of Governments in September 1999. In less than a week, I got a call for an interview from the headhunter.

What a great timing! It was the beginning of a more positive time in my career. In early November I was offered a job. The regional scope serving 18 jurisdictions and the financial reward were hard to resist so I accepted the position.

Getting out of the City of Frederick was not only good for me but also good for the city. My high salary was a waste of taxpayer's money with productive time exhausted by facing up to this alderwoman and

the media. After I was offered the job, I gave my resignation to Mayor Jim Grimes. Both of us were on leave that second week of November. I was off to celebrate my daughter's 20th birthday and to do other personal errands in relation to my new job. Since both the Mayor and I were both on leave this particular week, we agreed to announce my resignation when both of us returned the following week. Besides, my resignation would be effective almost two months from my notice.

Despite our plan a final nasty goodbye news headline blasted the entire community: "A Cabinet Officer Resigns Without Telling the Elected Officials." Obviously this was not the case. The news said we could not be reached for comment. Of course, the Mayor and I were out on leave. When the City Mayor returned, he quickly issued a press release to address all the news that surrounded my resignation. This time, I broke my silence. It was now my time to speak and once and for all confront this dark controversy surrounding me for so many months.

In a crowded Board Room in City Hall, I finally had my day. I spoke about the issue in a very objective manner. On November 15, 1999, my last speech included these words:

> *"No employee not even public officials should endure false statements that harm their reputation and character. A responsible journalist role is to report the facts and not to create an illusion, most specially one that potentially harm ones reputation... Even a newspaper, an individual or public official should not be cavalier in their use of free speech, and potentially abuse other people's rights...*
>
> *As for the public information issue, so highly publicized in January to March this year, ... the issue was not just simply about salary information but an employee's rights to personal privacy with reference to her Family Medical Leave. In my opinion the articles*

on this matter is another example of misleading and incomplete story. It is important for the actions of the Government to be reported to the citizens, but at the same time protecting the rights of its employees. I hope the Mayor, the Board of Aldermen, officers of the City of Frederick, County officials and employees will be vigilant in not letting harm to occur to any employee in the future.

I will leave the City looking forward to a new great job in this coming new year. I hope you will remember me based upon my spirit, character and integrity which I will bring with much stronger than when I first arrived here in the same room exactly two years ago. I thank everyone who provided their full support and confidence during my two-year tenure with the city."

When my speech was over, a standing ovation and big applause ruptured into the air. Everyone was clapping, which warmed my frozen feet and hands numbed by the callous political power that knew nothing better than to hurt my soul. Only one person did not budge, did not clap and did not stand. All by herself the alderwoman sat alone while the others were clapping wildly. As the crowd cheered, my heart said, "It is all over Imelda. You can now move on! A more illustrious dream job was waiting for me back in Washington, DC."

My son was right again when he said, *"When someone hurts you Mom, a bigger job was ahead waiting for you!"*

Reflections on Valuing Power

"God give us the grace to accept with serenity the things that cannot be changed; Courage to change the things that should be changed; And the wisdom to distinguish the one from the other."
— Reinhold Niebuhr

On my last day two days before New Year 2000, there was a farewell party and a welcome to a New Year - a beginning of a bright new career at a new place far away from Frederick. The room was filled with people who had been there with me throughout my roller coaster ride into the world of politics. I was leaving a staff, the majority of whom I'd hired during my short stint with the city, and I enjoyed working with all of them. I was sad to say goodbye for now to a City Mayor I truly respected and cared about. I was leaving behind a job that would have been my dream job. But would I do something differently if a similar situation happened to me again? Would this story even be worth sharing to the world and what will I gain for doing so?

A Public Servant's Reflections

The opinions I have formed from these incidents reflect upon a bigger problem that is happening day in and day out in our country. My story, though on a smaller scale and certainly nothing compared to what actually happens on a larger scope to other workers in both government and private companies, is a reminder of what power and deception can do in our lives. Arrogance and ego can overtake one's ability to think rationally.

Our own former presidents of the United States have lied to the public, and somehow innocent people's lives and souls were affected without much thought. President Bill Clinton lied about his relationship with Monica Lewinsky. Millions of public dollars were spent in a lengthy investigation. People's lives where affected by it. President Richard Nixon lied about the break in at Watergate, and it caused him his presidency. And only in 2005, did America discover who "Deep Throat" was. He spoke the truth about the Watergate incidents to The Washington Post, but "Deep Throat" hid his identity since the early 70s to protect himself from political prosecution.

We have a war in Iraq going on with lives of soldiers at stake, which started with what a large percentage of the American public view as a lie. In my own native land of the Philippines and all around the world, abuse of power has resulted in poverty, oppression, and worse, war and death.

We have a long list of people in power who claim innocence against charges of abuse by ordinary people. In many cases, it took a long time but in the end, the stinking wrongdoing was hard to keep secret forever.

Justice was served to those who were hurt, and wrongdoing was uncovered. It took a lot of courage for those who stood up and spoke freely about the truth. When they finally did, however late it was, their hurt inside was somehow relieved and past mistakes were somehow corrected. The humiliation inscribed within their souls was finally lifted.

As I reflect about these events, my pain, though not on the same scale, is a reminder of how the people we entrust with power can use this power for their own self-gratification and selfish pleasures. It's a lesson on how some people will mask what they are doing under the guise of benefiting the public, but in reality it's for their own self-vested motives. In the end, the wrong doing of a few affects other elected officials who serve with all their heart for the public good.

There are other examples of vengeful behavior, but the point here is that one's soul can survive many adversities. We must allow the integrity of our soul to guide us to do the right thing even if those around us try to bend us. If you do, in the end, you win!

In retrospect, I am sure there are specific things I could have done differently to help the situation. But more importantly, the lesson to learn is the kind of impact power has on the ethics and dynamics of the workplace, most specifically to our souls as human beings.

Professional ethics should always be higher than any elected position or executive position. Ethics should not be compromised. If one gives in just to please those who are above them, then it is really not serving the best interest of the organization and those who truly entrusted us with this professional responsibility in the first place. While it is true that elected officials are to be representatives of the citizens, it does not mean they have the power to bully or treat people in a destructive way.

People who are successful in their career provide the best and most professional approach to the work assigned to them, regardless of the challenges they face including politics in the workplace. My situation reminds me of how those who are below the ranks are being asked to do something against their professional ethics resulting in many corporate scandals.

Learning to be at peace with someone who does not like you is all that you can do. It is up to each individual person to change. All we can control and change is our own behavior. Therefore, we should not let other's behavior detract from doing the job we are hired to do.

Being exposed negatively through the media is devastating. But in time, the ink fades away and life has a way of correcting the mistakes of the past.

The controversy I was involved in also became a catalyst for change. At a local level, Frederick worked on their policy issues in regards to dealing with public information. The situation is also a good example of why at the federal level the HIPAA Medical Privacy Law was enacted vigorously to protect employees from those who have no business getting personal medical information, no matter how trivial the information may seem.

Despite what seemed to be turbulent times, what really matters is the dignity within our soul and the peace we get after the storm has passed. If you truly believe you did nothing wrong, the newsprint will fade away in time. And for me, it did. What does not go away is the heavy load we carry in our conscience when we harm other people or do a grave injustice against a soul.

View the hurtful times in our lives as fuel for a better life. In my case, it was. It was a blessing in disguise that poured bountiful blessings to my family. So instead of remorse or anger, I give gratitude to the media and to the alderwoman who tested the strength of my inner soul. It gave me a big life lesson on valuing power given to us for the benefit of deserving souls.

A Woman's First Car and House Buying Trip

"Men themselves have wondered what they see in me. They try to so much but they can't touch my inner mystery."
- Maya Angelou's Phenomenal Woman

Frederick gave me a lot of lessons in politics. It also brought other blessings – my first brand new car and our first brand new house.

I would be remiss if I did not share the exciting way that I bought my own car and house in which we currently live in Frederick. Accompanied by Jeff, I went house hunting in Frederick almost every weekend. For several months I looked for a house, but I did not find one I truly liked. "Our house in Baltimore is better," I said to myself. I will admit, however, going to new homes and looking at model homes certainly makes you dream of living in one. The houses we looked at in new communities had lots of extras, bigger rooms and were absolutely stunning. Though there were only three of us – Alberto, Andrea and myself, I envisioned we would be living in a model house. Hey, dreams are free so why not dream big!

But reality kicked in. Spending lots of hours and days checking houses myself and talking to real estate agents dampened my spirit. My income then was not enough to buy a house unless I had a big cash down payment.

Billie Fox, the real estate agent we met in Frederick, confined her home searches within our limited criteria and price tag that my government salary could afford. I had not sold my house in Baltimore and was not really sure how much money I would get for it. Minus commission and all, I felt that I would probably be left without much cash for a new house. The searches were confined to existing old homes. Oh well…there goes my dream of owning a new model house.

But my ingenious spirit told me to go beyond what others normally do. After researching, I learned something new. Sell your house by yourself and save the commission. The housing season was flat, and it was hard to sell a house in those days. The power this information gave me made me think I was dead on right. So, I decided to sell my house by myself with no agent. I started with the goal of selling it by the end of the school year. I was not in a hurry. I had a one-year grace period from my job's start date of January to move to the city as a part of my city residency requirement. I figured I had a lot of time to sell it by myself. I gave myself until September to sell my house by myself and after which I could list it with a real estate. Months went by, and my deadline as my own agent was almost near. Despite my ingenious flyers, Home For Sale by owner sign, complete package of materials and a listing through Multiple Listing Service (MLS) for a flat fee of $295, no one was buying. I was not good at selling houses I told myself.

Then as usual, my angel Jeff who lives in Columbia a few minutes away from my house gave me an unusual tip. "Why don't you engage my saint, Saint Joseph?" He swore he sold his house fast when he did this. Together we went to a Columbia religious store to buy a St. Joseph statue. It included instructions on how to make this ritual effective. So one early morning in July, I started digging in front of my house. Though I believe in God, somehow digging in front of the house to bury a statue of St. Joseph made me a little suspicious. I buried St. Joseph, said a quick prayer and walked quickly back inside the house.

The same week the phone started ringing, and three families wanted to see the house. I was thrilled! "Wow, St. Joseph is really working his miracle. Thank you God!" I said to myself. In less than one month in September 1998 my house was under contract. My plan was to settle in 30 days after the contract signing and pending mortgage approval.

In just about two years of owning this house, the equity was over 20,000 dollars. Though I was told I could not get the full price for the house given the flat market, the real estate agents who looked at my house were wrong. I sold my house at a huge profit!

With the profit I got from the sale of this house gave us extra money to do other things. It was time to give my son Alberto my car. In college at University of Maryland he was the only person that did not have a car. I had to pick him up from the Greyhound bus station every time he came home from a school break. In a country where kids are given a car by their parents at the age of 16, Alberto was 20 when he got the hand-me-down Chevrolet. Andrea and I would share and benefit from a new car I was shopping for.

Jeff was with me as usual, and he was especially interested in my car shopping. He was skeptical about my ability to negotiate and get a good deal. He said, "Car salesmen rip off and take advantage of women all the time. I'll go with you!" And he did, he followed me all around giving his advice, and by the time I knew it, I learned a lot from him. So here I was looking at a mid-end priced Malibu with leather seats, sunroof, CD player, and other recently released extras in top model cars.

"It's too expensive. The car salesman will ask you for a big down payment; the interest on the car will be six to seven percent, and this will mean a big car payment. Not to mention you're buying a house, and this will affect your credit line. Forget it," he said.

But my usual independent mind said, "There's no harm in asking and trying. Let me try! I really like this car."

"Okay, it's your car, and it's your money," and he sat in the waiting lounge overlooking the salesman's office booth. He looked worried; his arms were crossed on his chest, and his shoulders were drooping. I could sense he was upset that I did not follow his advice. Despite this, I went on by myself inside the salesman's booth. By the time Jeff realized it, I had bought a car by myself!

As I walked towards him, he had this look in his face like "Oh no! What did you do?" I approached him with a giggle in my voice as I held the car sales document in my hand, waving it and said, "Guess what? I got the car at three thousand dollars off the sticker price, free destination fee, extended warranty and three percent in interest! My car payment is exactly what I have budgeted for!"

"How did you do that?" he exclaimed. "Three percent interest? That's great! You did better than me!" (He had recently bought a truck with double the interest than mine.) He hugged me with pride! My experience buying my emerald car in Fox Chevrolet in Baltimore was a woman's successful attempt to negotiate without a man by her side for protection.

My Dream House: The Ingenious Mind is Hard to Conquer.

Here I was in my new car with my house sold! On an early Sunday morning trip, we met Billie Fox in her office to see the houses she had searched for us. This time she took us to a somewhat newer neighborhood in the city that still had a rural feel. We discovered the diverse beauty of the city with farms all around and sweeping mountain views. But of course, the houses were still relatively older compared to the seven-year-old house I had lived in Baltimore County. At that time, buying a house worth close to $200,000 thousand was already over $70,000 more than the average house cost. It was almost three o'clock when we finished. After following Billie to several houses in my brand new emerald car, I did not find a single house I liked.

Looking for houses was quite exhausting. I felt it was easier to sell my house than to buy another house. On our way back to West Patrick to the main road of Route 40, we said we would simply go back, but instead of turning back, we went the opposite direction. On the corner, a new development appeared before our eyes – one we had not seen before. The sign said Emerald Farm.

"Hey, Jeff, look there is a model house for sale and it says Emerald Farm." Jeff said, "Forget it. I am sure that is beyond your budget!" But then I said again, "It says Emerald Farm, and my new car is emerald green! This is my lucky day!"

Smiling but feeling somewhat unconvinced he said, "Okay, call your real estate agent." I called Billie to come back and asked her to get us into the house. She asked for the address and said she would pull out the listing description and cost.

We parked our car behind another car while waiting for Billie. Obviously another buyer was inside the house with their real estate agent. My mind swirled with many ideas. My agent Billie was from Fox Realty I said to myself. Just like my emerald car I bought from Fox Chevrolet! The coincidence was overwhelmingly exciting as I dreamed of living in this house. Then Billie arrived. She walked out of the car with a print out about the house and as she walked towards us she said, "Well, I am not sure. This house was originally listed at $267,000, but it was reduced to $232,000. It has a pending contract." Despite this, I insisted to see the house.

As soon as we opened the door, all decorated with beautiful curtains, paintings and nice furniture, my heart jumped with glee and said, "I wish I could buy this house!" Hesitantly, Jeff and I walked inside every room saying "Wow!" Every time we moved from one part of the house to another, we simply couldn't believe our eyes! It was certainly much more upscale than the house we had in Baltimore. It was also the best house we had seen so far, and it even had a mountain view.

Inside the house was the other real estate agent with the couple who had placed the contract offer. The husband and wife were inside the big master bathroom. Seated on the edge of the big sunken bathtub, they were writing some measurements. Jeff and I walked out quickly to give them privacy. They looked at us as if to say, "What are you doing here? We already bought this house."

So down back to the street we were. I was disappointed, but before I left I said to Billie, "I really love this house. It feels like it was built for my children and me."

Billie replied, "Well, there is a pending contract that was done on Friday. But it has not been ratified, and the owner has until Monday to accept it."

My heart jumped and said, "Really? This means I can still make an offer?" "Well, we can try. You need ten percent for a down payment. You said your budget for a down payment was about $20,000," she said. Although Jeff admitted it was a gorgeous house, he gave me a look like he thought I was going beyond my budget.

But my emerald Malibu car buying experience at Fox Chevrolet was a sign of good things to come. I was standing right here at Emerald Farm with an agent from Fox Realty and a lady name Billie Fox. Whether it was coincidence or not, I took my hunch to heart.

Despite some challenges, I said, "Billie, why don't we make an offer and ask to reduce it to $210,000 with a five percent down payment, and ask them to pay for three thousand of my closing costs." Billie had the look in her eyes like, "You are out of your mind." But her job was to extend the offer and not to argue with the buyer. Besides, I learned the other offer had a contingency that the seller needed

to sell their house before they could settle. In my case, I did not have any contingency. I had just sold my house last Friday, and my closings could coincide perfectly. I convinced her to sell my offer to the owner, and she drew up the contract price later that Sunday. If I don't get it, at least I tried.

A reputable company, Regency Builders, had built this house and they were under bankruptcy. It seems everything was in my favor. It was a model house built in this community close to Route 40, Route 210 and Route 70. At the same time, it was secluded with a beautiful mountain view. I couldn't help but pray that night for giving me the courage to at least try to see if my dream of owning a model house would come true.

Monday night, my phone rang. It was Billie. "You won't believe it, but you got the house," she said with a smile in her voice. The owners signed the offer, and it has been officially ratified. Whew! I jumped for joy as I called Jeff on the phone to tell him about this incredible windfall.

That was over six years ago. Our house value has increased almost three times its original contract price. My mortgage payment is like renting a two-room apartment in today's housing market. Our house is a three-level colonial with over 4000 square feet of living space, double the house we had in Baltimore.

My emerald car and my house in Emerald Farm that I bought through Fox Chevrolet and Fox Realty were indeed a testament on what a fox stands for: crafty, clever and ingenious -- ready to outwit man's biggest enemy – assumption and fear of exploring beyond the normal. The ingenious mind is hard to conquer.

This experience is a testament to the blessings given to us, and for my strong belief, "Ask and you shall receive." It was a powerful prayer that indeed materialized for my family.

As for name of the of our street, Hunting Ridge Drive, speaks perfectly about the essence of my dream - to keep hunting for your dreams despite the ridge or the long narrow drive, chain of hills, or mountains that may surround it!

HOME SWEET HOME

Our three-level colonial house in Frederick, a former model house, has been a beautiful witness for many blessings my children and I have received since we moved here in 1998.

First day in our new home in Frederick

My old house in Baltimore

My lucky emerald car I bought from Fox

23 First Regional and National Post

"A strong successful man is not the victim of his environment. He creates favorable conditions."
- Orisen Marden

From the City of Frederick, my career circled back to Washington, DC, exactly 15 years from the time I started there as a maid. On January 5, 2000, I was hired to my first regional post as Director of Office of Human Resources Management of the Metropolitan Washington Council of Governments (COG). It was an alluring position given the responsibilities I would perform for this reputable organization. As I researched this regional organization of local organizations, the Maryland and Virginia legislatures, the U.S. Senate and U.S. Representatives, the thought of working for such a fine nonprofit organization was hard to resist. Its mission "to enhance the quality of life and competitive advantages of the Washington metropolitan region in the global economy" was exciting, but more importantly in the context of my human resources profession, its vision was quite attractive given the role I would play.

"COG is a world class, high performance regional organization recognized for applying best practices and cutting edge technologies to regional issues, making the metropolitan Washington area the best place to live, work, play and learn."

How I got to COG was a story of abiding resilience and belief that when things are not going well, something better will come along. Being a political appointee, it was a practical decision to ensure I had a job, following what I knew would be a controversial election year in the city of Frederick. My instincts were again right! My boss, the Mayor, lost the election several months after I resigned the position. This step was again another career decision that contributed to my overall success that I will forever be thankful for. It was the first job that gave me the opportunity to get involved in regional issues affecting the Washington Metropolitan area.

I remember my interview with COG senior executive staff in October 1999 was very heartwarming and challenging. It was a panel interview comprised of Michael Rogers, then Executive Director, along with his executive staff: Ron Kirby, Director of Transportation; David Robertson, Director of Human Services; Stuart Freudberg, Director of Environmental Programs, the late John Bosley, General Counsel, and Leo Young, Executive Assistant. Together with all these men was Dick Kobayashi, the job hunter who referred my resume to this company. After the interview, Dick accompanied me out of the interview room and said, "You did a fantastic job! You woke up all those guys." It was late in the afternoon, and I was their last person to interview. I must have done a good job reviving their energy after a long day of interviews.

The interview went very well, and I knew in my heart I would get the job. I could see each one, especially Michael Rogers, the Executive Director, agreeing with me as I articulated my responses to very difficult questions. Michael showed full confidence in me and did not hesitate to hire me. Two days after the interview, the job was offered to me.

I consider meeting Michael Rogers, former Executive Director of Metropolitan Washington Council of Governments, as one of the best things that happened in my career. His presence and guidance will forever be in my gratitude book. My success in assuming regional and national roles in my field was also a testament to this man, who perhaps may not know has silently, taught me key leadership skills that will be forever ingrained in my heart and mind.

It is in COG that I experienced the joy of working with professionals and elected officials who are civil and respectful of each other. It was here that I saw the intense dedication of those who are in public service to work towards the common goal of helping the region in various aspects from transportation, housing, environmental issues, planning and public safety issues, and right after September 11, play a major role in homeland security. Regardless of difference in their opinions, together, many regional issues and solutions were brought to the forefront. Political affiliation was never an issue in this nonpartisan organization with its main goal of serving the region and contributing to its quality of life.

It is at COG where I reached the pinnacle of my career in human resources, receiving numerous awards not only in my own agency but also from other regional organizations, including the Jack Foster Executive Award from the Local Government Personnel Association of Washington Baltimore Area. It was in COG where colleagues from the private company of Deloitte and Touché nominated me to the First HR Leadership Award of Greater Washington Area. I was among only 12 honorees receiving such a prestigious recognition in the region and being profiled in the Washington Business Journal.

It is also in COG where I led some of the most interesting projects in my senior management career, including the creation of the

Institute for Regional Excellence, a regional executive development program in partnership with George Washington University and local jurisdictions. It was in COG where my career took me not only to the different local jurisdictions in the region but in different states as a part of my role as the Chair of the National Certified Public Managers Consortium comprised of 28 states, the USDA Graduate Schools and the Virgin Islands.

It is in COG that I stayed longer in one career, longer than any other job I have held in the United States. This rate of stay was a testament to the environment I was in. Together with people who have served this esteemed organization for many years like David Robertson, the Executive Director who replaced Michael Rogers, my other colleagues - Sonny Amores, Carl Kalish, Stuart Freudberg, and Ron Kirby, my position at COG is one of thanksgiving to the region that gave me a chance to work with these regional leaders. It was also here I met new members of the management team, Jeanne Saddler, Lee Ruck, Calvin Smith, and George Rice. Together and as a part of COG executive team, I was fortunate to have the opportunity to make a contribution to the region through my work here.

The work I do has also allowed me to oversee the Personnel Officers Technical Committee comprised of personnel directors in the region and the Health Care Coalition comprised of local jurisdictions and the International City and County Management Association. Together with my staff, senior management team, other staff members of COG and elected officials, I was surrounded with good people who truly cared about their work and the region.

My work at COG allowed me to be involved in many exciting projects. I was privileged to be invited by the International Public Management Association for Human Resources, and be a part of a team to assist in shaping an HR Academy that will prepare human resources professionals to assume leadership positions. I am not sure what other challenging projects I will assume at COG. For now, the eagle has landed in a perfect setting!

Memorable Photos with the Metropolitan Washington Council of Governments (COG) Staff, Senior Management Team and Government Officials

1. Imelda's staff, Janet Ernst and Larissa Williams, receiving awards from Hon. Judith Davis, Mayor, City of Greenbelt and 2005 Chair of COG Board of Directors, and David Robertson, COG Executive Director. (COG Staff Awards Ceremony - 2005)

2. As Program Director of the Institute for Regional Excellence (IRE), Imelda considers it a privilege to work with the region's best visionary public leaders. Left to Right: Michael Rogers, Executive Vice President of MedStar Health, Tony Griffin, Fairfax County Executive, Ron Carlee, Arlington County Manager, and Hon. Phil Mendelson, Council member, District of Columbia. (IRE Visionary Leadership Award Ceremony – 2004)

3. With Calvin Smith, Director, Human Services, Planning and Public Safety. (COG Picnic – 2005)

4. Left to Right: Larissa Williams, HR Analyst II, David Robertson, COG Executive Director, Stuart Freudberg, Director of Environmental Programs, Ron Kirby, Director of Transportation Planning, and Nicole Hange, Legislative Assistant. (COG Holiday Party 2005)

5. With Pat Warren, Executive Assistant, Lee Ruck, General Counsel, and Jeanne Saddler, Director, Office of Public Affairs. (COG Retreat 2005)

6. With Carl Kalish, Director of Purchasing and Facilities and Sonny Amores, Chief Financial Officer during the First Greater Washington HR Leadership Award (2002).

7. Teary-eyed Imelda receiving a surprise Ambassador's Award for "being a source of inspiration and hope beyond the boundary of COG" from Michael Rogers, former COG Executive Director, and Hon. Bruce Williams, Council member, City of Takoma Park. (02/26/02)

8. With Hon. Penny Gross, Fairfax County Supervisor, during the IRE Graduation in 2005. Since 2000, Imelda has the great pleasure of working directly with Hon. Gross and other elected officials in the Washington metropolitan region.

24 Awakening the Barefooted Souls of Corporate America

"We make a living by what we get,
we make a life by what we give."
- Sir Winston Churchill

In the last 20 years, I have had a long, but interesting, journey. I truly appreciate where my journey has taken me. The leadership and decision-making positions I held enabled me to be involved in matters affecting the current and future state of organizations I worked for. With gratitude, I was blessed with a great career with beautiful supervisors, colleagues and friends I met in each of my jobs. Even those who hurt me enriched my life with important lessons.

As I wrap up this chapter, I offer some sensitive reflections that may improve the quality of our workplace. They are a result of my conversations and experiences with thousands of people I have met during over a quarter of century as a professional.

My dear best friend, Farimah, sparked some of the sentiments I have expressed in this article. I met Farimah in 1989 while working in the Human Resources Office of Georgetown University in Washington, DC. Both of us were Employment Officers in charge of recruitment and employment for the University and Medical Center. Farimah will always be my friend, even though we now live far away from each other. Together, we have laughed a lot and always enjoyed each

other's company. When we talked on the phone, it was as if she were right beside me.

We continued our friendship when she moved to San Francisco to work for another university, many years after we left Georgetown. Then, she moved to Colorado with her family. She shared with me her desire to go into interior decorating so she could spend more time with her newborn baby and family. Her new life enabled her to do what she wanted to do and she gladly left the corporate world.

There was one thing Farimah said that I would never forget. She said, "When we do something we don't like to do, we are unhappy with our work, basically dragging ourselves to work each day, in a lot of ways, we are prostitutes." What a powerful image that is! Indeed, what she said isn't far from the truth.

In my lifetime, I've witnessed friends, family members, colleagues, employees and even strangers whose engagement in their work had been lost. I do not need to run a survey to understand why people are less engaged in their work, why they cannot wait to retire, why they line up in stores to buy lottery tickets with the hope of hitting it big and resigning at a moment's notice. In a lot of ways, there is a dark evil seeping into companies and organizations costing millions of dollars in unproductive hours, but we are afraid to confront the root of the problem.

More and more, as I have listened to people, I have come to believe America is a world of overworked, overstressed people. Unlike other countries in Europe and Asia, it seems that Americans pour their heart into their jobs and, in the end, get burned out sooner than their counterparts in other countries. As a result, we have a plethora of medical problems reported to be associated with stress including heart attacks, obesity, depression, fatigue syndrome, and others. Even best selling books like the "Chicken Soup Series" made it big for offering stories that heal the soul mainly because of one key word that millions of Americans are experiencing – STRESS!

In addition to stress, I have also observed the dynamics of why employees are becoming less engaged in their work and, as such, there is a feeling of emptiness eating away at their talents and their enthusiasm for the work they do. I call it corporate depression.

With over two decades of experience in America, I have talked to many people desperately seeking other positions, who can't wait for retirement, or simply want to quit their work due to a variety of reasons including feelings of alienation, feeling of being used and abused, or even simple frustration. America is facing a huge challenge. I call these challenging issues the barefooted souls of corporate America.

I offer the following honest reflections as catalysts for authentic conversation concerning the issues affecting employees' soulful engagement at work, isolation, depression and what Farimah called, "prostitutes" of America:

Though employees are not expected to bring work into their homes, the blurring of the workplace and personal life is quite clear. With the advent of technology, emails and other 24-hour communication systems like blackberries, palm pilots, and laptops, it is no wonder why more hours are being spent on work-related activities. Though technology has helped us do our work more efficiently, in a lot of ways, technology has also become a barrier to people's connections. Just imagine two people working in one unit, simply divided by a wall. These co-workers use email in communicating with each other, and, at the end of the day, the only connection these employees have with one another is through their computer. When they go home and check their emails, before they know it, it's time to sleep. What kind of dynamics does such a life bring into one's inner soul?

"Don't mix business with pleasure," appears to be a common mantra in the corporate world. There are too many pressures to make sure social connections and personal matters are not brought into the foray of corporate world. Of course there are some boundaries in these social connections and personal matters that should not be brought into the workplace, but the extreme, in which employees work in isolation, completely independent from one other, contributes to interpersonal problems, alienation, and conflicts we now see in many organizations. We require employees to work in a team, and never understand why they can't work like a team. What is wrong with this picture?

Corporate America screams and heralds the value of diversity in the workplace. But let's take the example of women. A number of experts said that in order to succeed, we expect women to act like men, business-like and no tears allowed. No wonder we have a lot of confused women stressing themselves to act like men. One hesitates to talk about religion with the fear that someone may be offended. We have to walk on eggshells to discuss anything that is even remotely race-related with the fear our words might be taken out of context. We impose fear instead of opening a dialogue where we can better understand one another's cultures, religions and other protected issues. Where will this lead us?

Most of our working time is spent at work. Yet, activities related to nourishment of the soul such as funny stories, friendly encounters, and other creative exchanges that nurture our hearts are subtly restricted through barriers in typical business practices. Private companies and government agencies alike would prefer not to hear anything that comes from our heart or inner soul, especially our religious or spiritual experiences. We send mixed signals and, in some cases, ban employees' own spirituality.

Employees who are regarded as police, gatekeepers, paper pushers, and anything in between who have more abilities than what their jobs allow them to exhibit. In the end, their creative souls are trapped by their own gates and their own police work.

The litigious nature of the American society has weakened people's desire to have open, authentic discussions about race, ethnicity, religion, sexual orientation and other protected issues. To be safe and thorough, business processes are created by professionals like myself where employees are asked to focus solely on objective, mind-driven discussions within the rule of law, essentially avoiding any potentially offensive topics. Doing so avoids potential lawsuits or complaints. After all, current legislation has made it easier to file a grievance than ever before. In the end, don't we then lose the chance to learn from each other's culture, religion and experiences that would only make us better people?

Organizations hire and promote people into management positions without the leadership skills and experience necessary to perform the job effectively. These employees lack the skills that aren't gained by degrees but by experience and interaction with people. Most employee relation cases I have heard arise out of this very specific issue, a supervisor-employee conflict that eats away millions of dollars or productive time. Doesn't management feel responsible for placing people into a position of power who eventually contributed to the low morale among the employees they are supposed to mentor, guide and lead?

The same under qualified people who were placed into positions of power are the same people who abuse this power. In my generation, we have a lot of corporate scandals from the infamous Enron collapse to WorldComm. The ethical dilemma these corporate scandals that scared our generation has been widespread news, overwhelming our country, especially many of those people who lost their jobs as a result. As if the above is not enough, we have bullies, difficult people, politics in the workplace, and other forces that contribute to the painful realities of the corporate world. Where are the souls and consciences of our organizations?

More and more American companies rule the world through their overzealous passion to be profit-oriented. In the process of doing so, how many get burned along the way?

In the end, many people are just working for the money they receive and nothing else. They are devoting their talent to a cause unworthy to them. Some people are being used and abused against their will and stay in their jobs because of the fear of losing them. Aren't these problems akin to corporate prostitution?

Please don't get me wrong, I believe in a professional business environment that is free of personal matters that would hamper the effectiveness and productivity of the organization, but not to a point where the organization is too serious and restrained, too profit-oriented, too worried about the board they report to, that, in the end, the office atmosphere can be suffocating to one's soul.

Organizations are made of people, human beings, not computers, not robots. In the end, as we slowly take away their engagement, spirit, and everything that nourishes their heart and soul, the result is a devastating emptiness and corporate depression.

My career in the human resources field has allowed me to help people. I have accomplished numerous projects that were heralded as cutting-edge in my field. I truly believe I have contributed to the well being of my employees and my organization, but I am troubled to hear friends, relatives, colleagues, and others share tales of workplace woes. Corporate depression is a sad reality happening not just to thousands but perhaps millions of Americans.

The profession I held in human resources since 1977 had become more complicated since I began. I personally believe our work has become more complicated, not necessarily because the nature and basic principles of people have changed, but rather, I believe we have imposed too many restrictions, legislations and other barriers that do not allow people to truly enjoy the freedom of expression, freedom to be creative, freedom to say who they are as individuals and as people, and freedom to even speak about their spirituality. We have imposed fear on our own selves by guarding the actions of our employees. In a lot of ways, we can't blame employers; current legislation has made it easy for people to take us to court. The rule of the law has overpowered the guidance of a higher power that advised us to work in harmony with one another.

In most recent times, our century was plagued by a war on terrorism, natural disasters, and ethical corporate scandals that have shaken our spirits but also drawn us closer together. The September 11 attacks; the Tsunami, and Hurricane Katrina are just a few events that have made us see each other like one people. These events that shook the world are devastating enough, but when coupled with our own daily stresses and isolation, it is no wonder we see a lot of lonely people walking mindlessly, with sadness in their faces, and barefooted soul feelings within them.

Do we need another cold war to remember why America's motto: In God We Trust was adopted by the 84th Congress of America in 1957? Can we not have more compassionate organizations to provide avenues for employees to express their souls and well being? The answers may not be easy, but they are not impossible if all of us, employees and employers, come together.

I am sure some of you may find my reflections challenging and provocative. Others may find my insight questionable, and perhaps even subjective. However, regardless of any feelings you may have

about them, I only hope it will result in honest and free exchange. Only when we truly open our hearts to these types of discussions can we start addressing issues affecting the soul of corporate America.

Regardless of our religious beliefs, we cannot escape our hearts and souls. They a part of who we are as people. Let's recognize this before we all become heartless robots and PC machines.

A Dozen Soulful Leadership Nuggets

"Integrity is one of several paths. It distinguishes itself from the others because it is the right path and the only one upon which you will never get lost."
- M.H. McKee

In my career in America, I have worked for executives who I highly respect. I have had the tremendous opportunity to work with people I consider close friends, colleagues, and leaders and they have honored me with their teachings of leadership that have engaged my spirit as a professional. Below are a dozen leadership nuggets I have learned throughout my career.

1. Treat staff well and surround yourself with good people. Take care of your management staff and employees. Allow them to do the jobs they were hired to do and provide them with guidance as needed. Give them the chance to do their jobs and grow in their jobs. When you surround yourself with good people and treat them well, positive energy radiates back to you. As a leader, you will not only look good yourself; you will feel good as well.

2. Have an even-tempered voice and keep a calm composure. Be calm and collected, even in the most difficult, frustrating situations. Never give away any bit of arrogance in your tone of voice. An even-tempered, calm voice allows you to share your ideas in a way that eases those critical moments, allowing you to communicate your words and ideas most effectively. This is what separates a true leader from those whose power has gone to their head and whose voices tend to crush the spirits of others instead of lifting them up.

3. Be a respectable communicator. Though we may not all have all the answers to certain questions, and though we may each have a different point of view, leaders must show their ability to communicate ideas without offending or putting down the other sides. True leaders show a non-confrontational, respectful, suave style that makes employees feel more like one of your colleague instead of an insignificant subordinate.

4. Show sincere interest in the development of your people. Say what you mean and walk your talk. Find the time from your busy schedule to promote this idea personally, throughout your work environment.

5. Be a big thinker with strategic approach and enthusiasm for big ideas. This is a leader's role. Why would a true leader worry about every nitty-gritty detail of every problem when he/she doesn't need to? That's what technical experts, other professionals and managers where hired to take care of. You can have your pulse in the heart of the matter, but you do not need to have a hand in each step of the solution. Give other professionals space and allow responsible employees to apply their own knowledge and style to the work they do. In the end, you will engage your staff and they will derive a true sense of ownership and pride in the work they do.

6. Be secure and confident in yourself. Leaders do not need to receive all the credit for work done by his or her staff. When you share glory with your employees and exalt them for a job well done, you will be exalted as a true leader. Give employees a forum to be a part of the organization, including making presentations to important people, as much as possible. When you do, you will allow your staff to become engaged in the essential processes of the organization, making them feel good about themselves by contributing to the organization. When people feel good about themselves, amazing creative energy arises and productivity increases.

7. ***Challenge your staff to get out of their comfort zones and test big ideas.*** Allow your staff to look beyond one avenue and explore other creative ways of dealing with issues. Allow employees to find their own solutions to the issue at hand. Don't dictate. Instead, provide a forum for independent thinking and see big ideas become realities.

8. ***Be a rational, prudent risk-taker.*** Nothing great was ever achieved without risk-taking. Don't be afraid to take a bold step into areas you have never ventured before. Risk-taking opens numerous opportunities you may have never imagined. Share this value with the people around you and let their courage shine through responsible risk-taking.

9. ***Be a forward-thinking leader.*** Use historical data to give perspective to your decisions, but don't dwell on the things of the past. Take one or two steps ahead of your competition. Your ability to anticipate and project beyond today without losing perspective of history and the present needs of your organization will allow you to move forward in a decisive way.

10. ***Be a leader in heart and mind.*** One who believes that being a good leader means simply using your head and not your heart would be losing the real essence of what makes a good leader. The social and emotional connection a leader makes with his/her employees in an organization has a far more extensive impact on the organization than simply ruling with one's intellect.

11. ***Harness the power of networking.*** Draw from those people you meet along the way. The power of networking can be a powerful strategy, giving strength to great ideas and opportunities. Harness the power of networking to the advantage of your organization and your cause.

12. ***Lead with the spirit of goodness and faith in people.*** The center of a true leader's core success is the belief in the goodness of those around you. Believe in those people you entrusted with the responsibilities their jobs entail, and, in the end, they will believe in you.

I have been blessed to have worked with many leaders and bosses who have touched my career in a profound way. The integrity each one has brought to his or her position is a testament to the innate goodness in each one of them. It was this standard, the highest level of ethical values that has guided my career through the years.

In her role as the Chair of the Executive Board for the National Certified Public Manager® Consortium (CPM), Imelda works closely with CPM program directors in 28 states, the USDA Graduate Schools and Virgin Islands. Left to Right: Jim Robinson, Executive Director, The George Washington University, Center for Excellence in Public Leadership (CEPL), Errol Arthur, Program Manager, District of Columbia Government, Natalie Haughty-Haddon, GWU-CEPL, and Jack Lemons, Administrator, National Certified Public Manager® Consortium. Taken during the District of Columbia CPM Leadership Day, 2005.

Optimism is an onward bound positive energy that lifts the spirit and where one sees and finds opportunity in the midst of difficulties. It is the light despite darkness, it is the smile within sadness, it is the laughter within our soul, and the wide wings that make us fly and soar against the wind.

Optimism. In New Latin, the word optimism comes from the word, optimum, which means, "the greatest good." Gottfried Wilhelm Leibnitz, a philosopher well known for his philosophy on optimism, introduced the doctrine "that this world is the best of all possible worlds." From this thought, comes the most known view of life when given a glass of water: "half full or as half empty?"

The power of the mind and positive energies cannot be underestimated. It is this mindset that helped me throughout my life. The optimism within my heart and soul enabled me to rise above the most difficult journeys I faced in both my personal or professional life.

Liebnitz doctrine that "the belief in the universe is improving and the good will ultimately triumph over evil" is manifested in our lives. Indeed, this lesson crosses my life and the rest of humanity, including historical tragedies engulfing our present world.

A Gift of Light and Songs

Overcoming Adversity

Overcome adversity in life. Whether it is a tragedy, poverty of the heart, the mind, the spirit, or poverty itself, nothing is greater than the beauty of life itself. The tenacity of human spirit cannot be underestimated. It is in difficult times when our spirit and courage do rise and shine.

September 11, 2001 was a day America and the world will always remember. It marked a tragic event that will forever define the way we live, the way we work, even the way we travel. But, despite the tragedy, it also brought out the best in people. American people of all races, ethnic backgrounds, and religions came together in unity.

I am not a sculptor, nor an architect, nor a songwriter, but this tragedy has sparked a creative side of me I never knew existed, in the same way it touched many Americans in an extraordinary way.

On my birthday, October 3, 2001, at age 44, with no songwriting or product design experience, I found myself writing songs and designing a light modeled after the twin towers light, though I had never done anything like it in my lifetime. With this experience, my volunteer project, A Gift of Light and Songs was born!

A letter written to me by President George W. Bush about this simple act of giving:

THE WHITE HOUSE

Thank you for writing about the acts of war committed against the United States on September 11 and for sending your thoughtful remembrance. In the face of this evil, our country remains strong and united, a beacon of freedom and opportunity to the rest of the world.

Our government continues to function without interruption. Our intelligence, military, and law enforcement communities are working non-stop to find those responsible for these attacks. We will make no distinction between the terrorists who committed these acts and those who help or harbor them.

We must remember that our Arab and Muslim American citizens love our Nation and must be treated with dignity and respect. Americans of every creed, ethnicity, and national origin must unite against our common enemies.

Since these terrible tragedies occurred, our citizens have been generous, kind, resourceful, and brave. I encourage all Americans to find a way to help. Web sites like LibertyUnites.org can serve as a resource for those wanting to participate in the relief efforts.

God bless you and your family, and God bless America.

Indeed, my family, friends and I heeded the President's words and found a way to help, culminating in a number of volunteer projects honoring and remembering the victims and heroes of September 11. This experience inspired a number of heartwarming volunteer projects my family and I welcomed with humbling joy.

I truly saw the best in America despite this tragedy and this inspiring experience gave way to my CD-Album, We Saw The Best In You, a collection of musical stories drawn from my life's experiences and September 11th events.

This amazing journey started with this question, "What can I do to help heal the pain, and share my love and hope?" The tragic events reached the deepest core of my heart. With a strong desire to help overcome such a devastating tragedy and to express my feelings to victims, families and heroes of September 11th, for the first time in my life, I discovered I have music in me. With this, a divinely inspired gift was unleashed from my soul. The Gift of Songs Story was written right within my heart!

The Gift of Songs Story

This moment in our lifetime,
A day I will remember
When you and I felt the fear
When you and I felt the pain
You and I were one and the same
We stood with one voice
We stood with one mind

Refrain
Our nation was wounded
The world was astounded
A defining moment
A true emotional event
What can I do, what can I say
To help heal the pain
You and I feeling one and the same
You and I feeling one and the same!

What can I do, what can I say
To help heal the pain
Many things are beyond my hands
I like to share my deep thoughts
And wished that I could sing
For the world to hear and feel
What I feel
For the world to hear and feel
What I feel

I never felt this way before
Never wrote a song in my life
But touching true stories
Moved my very soul.
What can I do, what can I say
To share my hope and love
I like to share my thoughts
Through this gift of songs!

Repeat Refrain

What can I do, what can I say
To share my hope and love
I give this gift of songs to you!
I give this gift of songs to you!

26 A Gift of Light and Songs, a Musical Tribute

For the Victims and Heroes of September 11

The musical tribute demonstrated the generosity, love and unity, that has emerged from this horrible tragedy."

Ron Carlee, County Manager
Arlington County Government
Arlington, Virginia - Cable 3

The tragic events of September 11 touched all Americans, including my family and me. As all of us watched the terror live on television on that fall day in 2001, our lives changed forever. It was a time when all Americans who value peace and freedom stood together, in one voice, echoing the pain of the victims and their families. From New York, to the Pentagon, to the field of Pennsylvania, every opportunity to show our love to victims and heroes was profound and heartfelt.

This day was also a day when Jeff and I had a car accident in the midst of traffic on that chaotic day. With the Metro being rerouted and stops being limited, Jeff picked me up at the last station in Greenbelt, Maryland. In his truck, we were hit from the rear by a speeding State Trooper. Before we knew it, our crushed truck landed several feet away from where we were at the time of impact. Though we were not seriously hurt, the tragic events and this accident all on the same day made us realize what it would be if it had truly been our last day on earth. What would we leave behind? We had escaped death and a new appreciation of life had begun.

In the following weeks, despite our busy schedules at work and our store in Columbia Mall, something very powerful came into my being. I began drawing the Twin Towers Light and writing poems first. Then, between the Dorsey train station to Union station, by the time I knew it, I had written several verses with a melody I can hear in my head.

Having worked for Arlington County Government and spending many happy moments with my colleagues in this great county, I was profoundly touched by the tragic events of that historical day. I was moved to do something to show the victims I was with them in their pain and to honor them for their heroism during these tragic times. What started as a simple idea to perform a tribute in Arlington County would forever stay in my heart and soul. How this idea emerged was truly a divine inspiration.

One solid light and one united voice can lead thousands of spirits out of the dark!

In no time, I was able to complete six songs, entitled *A Gift of Song, Victory for Liberty, Pennsylvannia, Heroes of Pentagon, We are the Children of the World, and, Every Light, In Every Candle.* Together with the Twin Towers Light, we presented a program entitled, "A Gift of Light and Songs" in honor of the victims and heroes of September 11. Several volunteers helped me make this musical tribute a reality. Without them, this tribute, held on December 28, 2001, would not have been a reality. Following the event, our tribute was commemorated in several local newspapers, magazines, radio, and cable television shows.

What would we leave behind?

The Gift of Light and Songs Project was unveiled as creative works and a part of the Eleventh National Make a Difference Day, the largest national day for helping others, sponsored by the USA Today Weekend and its 500 newspaper carriers, in partnership with Points of Light Foundation. This was a unique and personal project I created with the help of other volunteers to honor and memorialize the heroes and victims of the September 11 tragedy.

The following materials, descriptions and photos captured the events of this day.

TWIN TOWERS LIGHT:

The Twin Towers Light is a miniature model (24 x 24 x 36 cm) of the World Trade Center Twin Towers, surrounded by other World Trade Center Buildings 3, 4, 5 and 6. The lights in the Twin Towers symbolize the gift of light and leadership guidance provided by those who helped in this tragedy. It is made of silver- and gold-plated metal to symbolize the strength of our conviction and our resilience as a Nation. A miniature flag flies proudly in front of The Twin Towers. A small trapezium behind the plaza is marked with the following words:

The Twin Towers Light

World Trade Center,
New York, USA
September 11, 2001

Memorable Photos of Historic September 11th Musical Tribute

Navy Commander Yvette Brownwhaller, representing families of 189 victims in Pentagon, and Firefighter Scott Forbes of Montgomery County Government, lighting candles in memory of September 11 fallen heroes.

Ruth Jones and Jennifer Lori Soto, singers from Maryland and Washington, DC performing Imelda's songs with Duwain Dillon piano accompaniment.

Citizens viewing the Twin Towers Light designed by Imelda.

Arlington County Government

HEROES AT PENTAGON, SEPTEMBER 11, 2001
ARLINGTON COUNTY BOARD ROOM
One Courthouse Plaza, 2100 Clarendon Blvd, Arlington, VA
December 28, 2001, 1:00 P.M.

In a heartfelt appreciation and a special tribute to heroes and victims of September 11th, their children and families, please share the spirit of the Season of Giving with citizen-volunteers from Washington, DC, Maryland and Virginia through a Gift of Light and Songs Musical Tribute!

2001 Memorable Photos of Historic September 11th Musical Tribute

"Grassroots heroes, whether trained emergency response personnel, amateur songwriters like Imelda Roberts (whose day job is Director of Human Resources at the Metropolitan Washington Council of Governments) or teen-aged volunteers who help out at Bailey's Community Shelter, set an example for others to follow and give everyone hope for the future."

Hon. Penny Gross, Fairfax County Supervisor, Falls Church News

1. *Jeff Snively and Imelda Roberts present to Arlington County Officials a Twin Towers Light with a pentagon base during a special musical tribute held in Arlington County, Virginia. Seen left to right: Fire Chief Edward Plaugher, Police Chief Edward Flynn, and Ron Carlee, County Manager.*
2. *Presentation of Colors by Arlington County Honor Guards.*
3. *Lighting of the candles by citizen representatives.*
4. *Arlington County Board Room packed with citizens and employees of Arlington County sharing this heartwarming event.*
5. *Michael Rogers, former Executive Director of the Metropolitan Washington Council of Governments greeting and introducing Imelda Roberts.*

CD Music Album: We Saw The Best In You

"Imelda Roberts had never written a song in her life before September 11. But the Frederick, Md., resident says she was so moved by the tragedy and suffering of that day, the words just began to flow. She wrote songs about the World Trade Center twin towers, about the Pentagon, about the firefighters and police officers who worked to save lives, and about the children on whom, she said, the future now rests."
Washington Times

"We Saw The Best In You," is a collection of original compositions inspired by profound feelings in the aftermath of the September 11 tragedy. It is my way of sharing my hope, love, and deepest thoughts about America, the victims, the heroes, our children, and you!

This recording, however humble, is extraordinary and special in its own way. The production was a collaborative effort from talented men, women and children who had never met before, yet unselfishly shared their best. All artists approached the effort as if it were their own, imparting it with immense dedication and creativity. Collectively, we feel the album is a true remembrance of our ability to work together and achieve something extraordinary, despite difficult times in our lives and in our country. I am blessed to be a part of this project.

My first attempt at songwriting, these compositions were transformed into music with the help of several outstanding artists who included Jennifer Soto, Juli Hood, William Ray, Cindy Shelton, Roxanne Barcelo and Scott Forbes. I was also heartened by the work of great producers – Doug Benson, Gerry Peters, George McClure, Butch Albarracin and Tony Barcelo.

Together, our team created what I think is a collection of "musical stories," reflecting upon America's spirit, diversity, heartfelt sentiments and inspiring experiences.

This recording is a part of the "A Gift of Light and Songs" project, originally initiated as a family project in September 2001. Since then, the project has taken on a life of its own with other artists and volunteers taking part in this meaningful project.

The following are the official materials used as inserts for this CD-Album. I feel, these are a part of history and were distributed at a number of events in Washington, D.C., Maryland, New Jersey, New York, Pensylavannia, and other places throughout the country and in the Philippines. Through this book, I give them to you, from me!

About the CD Album...

We Saw The Best In You CD-Album is not an ordinary album. It is a heartfelt, musical testimonial of America's spirit captured in songs and music! A part of the "Gift of Light and Songs" project, it is a musical story about America's patriotism, strength and enduring love for freedom and liberty. It is a story of hope and giving— a musical tribute to victims, heroes, children of the world, and you!

How this CD Project Began...

Imelda Roberts watched with co-workers in horror from her Washington, D.C. office as the September 11 events unfolded on television. Touched by the profound emotions of these tragic events, she began writing to express her deep feelings of love, hope and praise for all Americans. Having no musical background, she composed songs for this project using a microphone in her computer, and then had them transposed for orchestration. What began as audio files in her computer and scribbled poetry inspired by events and news she read on her way to the train station, this album reflects an ordinary citizen's view of the extraordinary historical events that have allowed America's enduring spirit to show. Whether it was a divine inspiration or a simple act by an ordinary American about an extraordinary time, "We Saw The Best In You!" CD-Album is a magical transformation, involving numerous performers who had never met before! Together, they shared their best talents to give tribute to America and you!

Imelda also designed a Twin Towers Light with a Pentagon base and a map of Pennsylvania to memorialize the areas directly affected by the event. The stunning memorial lamp provides a lasting symbol of the Twin Towers, the Pentagon, Pennsylvania, and our hope for the future.

On December 28, 2001, Imelda and many volunteers presented her first six songs together with the Twin Towers Light to government officials, heroes, and victims of the Pentagon attack, in a ceremony held in Arlington County, Virginia.

Together, the memorial light and the "We Saw The Best In You" CD-Album grew as "A Gift of Light and Songs Project" with numerous people and government officials from Washington, D.C., Virginia, Maryland, New York, California, North Carolina, Nashville, Minneapolis, Italy, China and the Philippines supporting and helping in this project.

Through the dedicated work of a team of talented artists, the album, containing 17 original songs, was completed in less than four months. One of the songs dedicated to the children entitled,

"We are the Children of the World" was also translated into several languages within the same period by native speakers from around the world through the assistance of Clark Translations. The English, Filipino and Spanish versions are included in this CD album.

About the Songwriter:

Imelda Roberts does not have a music background but what she offers in her first CD-Album is real, touching depictions of how she felt as an American, an immigrant and an ordinary citizen during these turbulent times. Touched by the profound emotions of the tragic events of September 11, she began writing to express her deep feelings of love, hope and praise for Americans. Having no musical background, she composed songs with beautiful melodies she vividly heard in her head. Using a microphone in her home computer, she then had them transposed for orchestration.

What began as scribbled poetry originally written while on a MARC train on her way to work as Director of Human Resources for the Metropolitan Washington Council of Governments, her songs were inspired by powerful human interest stories she read in the news or personally witnessed following September 11. The original songs were truly heartfelt reflections of America's spirit, extraordinary historical events, and profound feelings shared by millions of Americans! Whether it was a divine inspiration or simply an ordinary act about an extraordinary time, this project took a magical transformation with Imelda composing most songs in only a few hours. Through the Internet, Imelda crossed borders, meeting talented artists from here and abroad who were quick to help her with the project.

From this special and extraordinary collaborative effort, "***We Saw the Best in You!***" was born!

This is the cover of the "We Saw The Best In You" CD, with the Twin Towers as the imposing backdrop to memorialize the significance of this the event.

List of 15 Songs composed by Imelda Roberts plus three special tracks on the Filipino and Spanish translation of her children's song, and the Star Spangled Banner, performed by Scott Forbes, a firefighter from Montogomery County, Maryland.

1. The Gift of Songs Story
2. Thank You New York
3. Heroes of Pentagon
4. Pennsylvania Field of Independence
5. Victory for Liberty
6. You Are Our Hero
7. Forever
8. Every Light in Every Candle
9. Divine Inspiration
10. We Saw The Best In You
11. A Gift of Songs
12. We are the Children of the World
13. America, Land of Liberty
14. Fly Away, Soar Like An Eagle
15. Make Our World A Better Place
16. Kami'y Anak Ng Mundo
17. Somos Los Ninos Del Mundo
18. Star Spangled Banner

Special Letters From Officials of Directly Affected States...

THE GOVERNOR OF PENNSYLVANIA

Dear Ms. Roberts:

Thank you for sending me a "We Saw The Best In You" CD and a beautiful twin towers light lamp. Your kindness is very much appreciated.

You can be certain that I will enjoy listening to the CD in my leisure hours and will find a special place for the lamp in my office.

With warm regards,

Mark Schweiker

Mark Schweiker

GEORGE ALLEN
VIRGINIA

United States Senate
WASHINGTON, D. C.

September 6, 2002

Ms. Imelda Roberts
Project Director
A Gift of Light and Songs Project
8775 Cloudleap Court, Suite P52
Columbia, Maryland 21045

Dear Imelda:

Thank you so much for wonderful CD, *We Saw the Best In You!*. It's great to hear from you and I appreciate your taking the time to extend this kind gesture.

As we strive to protect our nation's cherished freedoms while embracing new opportunities for all Americans, please know that I consider it a high honor and privilege to serve in the United States Senate. Please do not hesitate to contact me on issues important to you.

With warm regards, I remain

Sincerely,

George Allen

George Allen

Special Letters From Officials of Directly Affected States...

HILLARY RODHAM CLINTON
NEW YORK
SENATOR

RUSSELL SENATE OFFICE BUILDING
SUITE 476
WASHINGTON, DC 20510-3204
202-224-4451

United States Senate
WASHINGTON, DC 20510-3204

August 1, 2002

Ms. Imelda Roberts
Suite P52
8775 Cloudleap Court
Columbia, Maryland 21045

Dear Ms. Roberts:

Thank you for sending me a copy of your CD, We Saw the Best in You!. The good wishes that your thoughtful gift represents are very meaningful to me. At this challenging time for our nation, I am especially grateful that you have so graciously shown your support for me and for the United States Senate.

With appreciation, I am

Sincerely yours,

Hillary Rodham Clinton

Hillary Rodham Clinton

LEGISLATIVE AFFAIRS

OFFICE OF THE ASSISTANT SECRETARY OF DEFENSE
WASHINGTON, DC 20301-1300

September 12, 2002

Ms. Imelda Roberts
605 Hunting Ridge Drive
Frederick, Maryland 21703

Dear Ms. Roberts:

Thank you very much for the CD album featuring the songs you wrote. The CD arrived this morning. I look forward to listening to it and I will share it with as many as I can in the Pentagon.

Sincerely,

Richard L. McGraw
Principal Deputy Assistant Secretary
of Defense
(Legislative Affairs)

Overcome adversity in life. Whether it is a tragedy, poverty of the heart, the mind, the spirit, or poverty itself, nothing is greater than the beauty of life itself. The tenacity of human spirit cannot be underestimated. It is in difficult times when our spirit and courage do rise and shine.

Overcome Adversity. When faced with the cataclysms of terrorism, industrial negligence of the environment, and other man-made catastrophe, it is not sorrow, but anger that is evoked. Selfish and senseless wars continue to claim lives by the millions, and yet there is sometimes a call to arms when death is an honor and not a tragedy. At what cost will our nation continue to subject its people to bloodshed and overlook the industrial wastelands that pollute our lives? Who will be the ones that write the history of tomorrow? When unavoidable disturbances from nature unearth the greatest sorrow, with earthquakes that rumble everyday beneath the tumultuous skies and seas, where do we go from here?

To just glance through the news today we are overwhelmed by catastrophe and violence – many are man's own making. Indeed, our world is full of challenges including tragic events like September 11th and natural disasters that are not within our control. When these tragic events and everyday adversities collide into our lives, we cannot allow them to hold us hostage.

Though conflict between nations still bloodies the battlefield of life, we must find peace. We must also learn from the past, with better disaster preparedness that can avoid the human toll from disasters.

Despite all these adversities in our lives, we learn one thing. The human soul has the tenacity and the courage to bounce back. It can overcome whatever adversity it faces. In so doing life moves on!

VIII What On Earth Would I Leave Behind?

Tolerance & Trust

Tolerance is opening our hearts and minds to those who may be different from us, less fortunate than us, or who may believe differently from us. Tolerance of the heart means greater trust and understanding of the human being inside each one of us. Trust that there is innate goodness in people and that hope resides in each one of us. We learn these traits first through our families and those around us. Live and pass them on for others to inherit and for the earth to live in peace.

For almost half a century my life was consumed with daily challenges, search for a better life, material wealth, and the glory of my career. The tragic events of September 11, the ongoing war in our world, and my epiphany in 50th year here on earth have collided like one strong force to awaken my soul to finally unleash my inner gifts and respond to one inevitable question – What on earth would I leave behind?

Following September 11, 2001, and moving forward my life stories reflect upon this provocative question through heart songs and stories of a Filipino-American baby boomer like I am.

What On Earth Would I Leave Behind?

I

Every step I take, every move I make
Did I step on you? Did I make you blue?
Oh, what on earth did I really do?

II

Now I come to think of the life I've lived
Would I be ashamed, would I be to blame
Oh, what on earth would I leave behind?

Chorus:
Oh, what on earth would I leave behind?
Would I be proud of myself?
Wherever I'd be, would my legacy
Make my world truly free
Ooh, ooh!

III

Barefooted, I came on this earth
Barefooted I would go to my grave
Would my family be so proud me
And the footprints I would leave behind.

IV

Oh, baby boomer, it's never too late
To make this world a better place to live
Wherever we'd be, would our children see
Our footprints of a better world

Repeat Chorus...

Oh, What On Earth Would I Leave Behind?

28 My Family is My Ministry

"Go home and love your family."
- Mother Teresa

From 1984 to 1999, I never turned back to visit my family in the Philippines. For 15 years after leaving my native country, I focused my life on my career and my two growing children, Alberto and Andrea. My busy work and other career-oriented goals sharpened what we refer to in my field as KSA – Knowledge, Skills and Abilities. My life was focused on my own.

My Mother, Ana Roque

I was in the process of sharpening my saw, as Stephen Covey, a famous leadership guru puts it in his bestselling book, "The 7 Habits of Highly Effective People." I was in the mindset of taking a vacation to cleanse myself of any burnout and I expected my trip would be a welcome period of relaxation. I had planned my vacation just as I was getting ready to take my career to the next level and begin another leadership position in Washington, D.C.

My heart was pounding with excitement as I prepared my suitcase and two big boxes of "pasalubong" or gifts for my mother, one elder sister, and four younger sisters and brothers. Though I wouldn't see my two other elder sisters who were both living in Italy, I was ready to have a fun time and reunite with the majority of my family who

still live in the Philippines.

Little did I know that this journey would become my personal ministry. The state of my family shocked me when I arrived; they were ailing due to the deep poverty my country was experiencing. The once clean street where I had grown up and found solace was now packed with people. The traffic was far worse than I ever imagined and a trip that had once taken 20 minutes or less now took two long hours. The number of cars had flooded the narrow roads and the construction of a railway system was desperately needed in this country of 87 million people.

There were so many beautiful, amazing sights and open land in the provinces I visited, yet everyone seemed to flock to the central financial district of Metro Manila, the hub of employment. Of course this was natural - people need to work and so everybody congregated in one city too small to hold the millions of people who made it home.

The patience I learned as a child growing up in the Philippines had been dulled by 15 years of comfort living in America. The traffic in Washington, D.C. – third in the United States in terms of traffic congestion, was no match for the traffic in my own beloved, native land.

My heart cried when I saw my family's deplorable living conditions. My sister's house was the size of my garage in Maryland and my mother, now 76, was moving from one house to another, with no place of her own.

My mother was given the choice of staying with me in America, but she decided not to. Every time she was in the US, she was heart-broken and, finally, after her third try in America, she decided to go home and not return.

How could my mother endure going back and forth to her children's houses and be content with such living conditions when she could be living in comfort in America? How could poor families really be happy when their water was still being rationed, shanty houses were made from aluminum roofs, and windows were made of corrugated boards? How did children grow and receive nourishment when the daily food served was barely enough to feed not one or two children in a family, but had to serve an average of six children in a single family.

No one from a rich country, or those who have lived a life of comfort could fathom the answer to these questions. But I did. It reminded me of where I came from and the most important lesson I had learned early in life: poverty is not a degradation of the soul. In fact, it brings richness and pure joy to my being.

My family reunion was refreshing and heartwarming despite the poor conditions that surrounded us. The laughter was crisp. The smiles were sweet. The hugs were warm, and the embraces from my sisters, brothers, nieces, nephews, and especially my mother, were like a warm sun soothing my cold heart frozen by the time I'd spent in the comforts of my newfound land far away. It was a reunion of the souls.

Just as my family has been my ministry, I was their ministry. Just as I became living proof of how education, hard work, and belief in your dreams can change your life for the better, my family reminded me that poor people of this world can administer the most important ministry God has given us: the ministry of love, pure joy and family.

Memorable Photos of My Mother While in the United States (1992-1993)

My mother's first trip to America.

With friends during my Mom's 69th birthday.

Enjoying cherry blossoms in Washington, DC with my Mom.

In Honor of Ana

"Honour thy father and thy mother:
That thy days may be long upon the land
which the Lord thy God giveth thee."
- Exodus 20:12 KJV

Since the first time I returned to the Philippines after 15 years of concentrated life in America, it has been my personal devotion to go home to the Philippines at least once a year. My desire to go home and help my family became more profound after September 11 tragic events in 2001. Somehow this tragedy made me realized that our life on earth is temporary and that we need to make the best use of our lives here on earth to touch others most especially those we love and care about.

With this personal commitment my trip to my native land was certainly not a rest and recreation, but a personal mission. December was a good time. It was a holiday month with lots of opportunities for a break from my busy work and my current job allowed enough vacation to fulfill this commitment I had made within myself.

In many ways, the two worlds in which I live are extremes. December feels like warm, summer weather in the Philippines while it is wintertime in America. Christmas is celebrated in both countries but the celebrations are two extreme opposites in terms of extravagance and depth of celebration.

The Philippines is a Catholic country representing two-thirds of Asia's Catholics. Christmas in my native land is a season for honoring Jesus Christ, even if it means borrowing money, working night and day to buy gifts, and celebrating with all their heart and soul. In contrast, America's celebration is comparatively quiet and simple. While every nook and cranny of the Philippines is filled with the joyous announcement of Christ the King, in America, offices and government buildings are not allowed to use anything that refers to Christ as it may offend others who are not of the same religion. One must use the word "holiday" instead of "Christmas." Likewise, Christmas celebration in America is muted compared to the festivities in my native country.

December in the Philippines is the time for Christ. For a moment, in December, this part of the world is richest in its glory to its Creator. It is a time when every family gathers in celebration of the blessings God has provided even the poorest of the poor. December is thought to contain all the miracles that could happen in one night as children wait for Santa Claus.

December 2003 was somewhat different, however. My mother, sisters and brothers were sad to hear I wouldn't be able to go home this time. I had told them it was a busy time at work and I wasn't sure if I could go. I spoke to my sisters in Italy and told them my plan as well.

I have always dreamt of buying a house for my mother so she wouldn't have to continue moving from one place to another. Her tired, old body deserves a comfortable house wherein she can rest and be happy. With limited funds in my bank account and all my savings entrusted in my retirement, I was really crazy to dream of buying a house in a matter of days, let alone, bring my mother home so she could have a permanent place to live before Christmas.

My dream continued as I thought about my friend, Myrna, who was willing to accommodate me in her house and help me look around for houses for my mother. It seems both Myrna and my other friend, Abot, would play a part in my dream.

As usual, I envisioned, focused and researched all possible properties I could afford to make this dream come true. I was thousands of miles away and I thought there was no way I could make this wish a reality. But, the Internet is a click of a mouse away, and sure enough;

it proved an invaluable tool for this type of research. I did house hunting on the Internet, dreaming that one day I could buy one of those houses for my mom.

It was the first week of December and I had found several houses in my research on the Internet. Some were as far away as provinces I had never been before and some were near where my sisters lived. However, Myrna suggested I look for something in Quezon City. This location would be convenient for my mother because it is near public transportation and her children could easily visit her.

Contrary to what my mother and family thought, I was actually not in America while I was doing this. I was already in the Philippines, planning a surprise for my mom. For two weeks, I had spent my time looking for a house. With only few thousand dollars with me, it seemed an almost impossible task and I knew I would need a lot of time to arrange all the financial issues. My heart was convinced, however, that something will happen before Christmas and before I went back to America on December 23 to be with my children and Jeff.

From the time I arrived on November 25 and after almost two weeks, I had no house and no hope of surprising my mother. Every house I found on the Internet, including the new ones I saw on the ads, bore no hope now that I was actually in the Philippines.

The only joy I had was the great time I spent with Abot and Myrna as we traveled all the way to Laguna and Cavite. While looking at a model house in Laguna, we met a real estate agent named Esmeralda, a name that, in English, means emerald. There goes my sign again. My conversation with her clarified what I needed to do.

I commented that even in Laguna there was already too much traffic. I was hoping for a more peaceful, serene place. Esmeralda responded, "Mom, traffic is a sign of progress." Myrna, Abot and I chuckled. But this remark reminded me there would be traffic everywhere, so why go far away to a place my mother might not like? I remembered my mother being unhappy in suburban America where I lived, but she was happy when she was around lots of people. I reminded myself this house was for her and not for me so I told Abot and Myrna, "Okay, let's go home and look for a house in Quezon City."

I had been staying in Myrna's house in Quezon City, the capital of the Philippines, while planning this surprise, and it became my secret home. Myrna had been extremely welcoming, but I was beginning to worry I wouldn't make my deadline. I told her I'd be there for about two more weeks and she assured me she was happy to have me.

Way into my second week, I finally found a house in Quezon City, 20 minutes away from Myrna. From the sound of it, Eric Roxas, the owner was willing to negotiate for a small down payment. My plan was to buy a small house with a small down payment and arrange other payments after I returned to the U.S. But who would be willing to deal with me? As an American, I could not even buy a single-family house; the country's laws restricted foreign nationals like me to a condominium, but I was not deterred. The house was for my mother, so, in essence, that was really not an issue. I could name the property under her.

Myrna accompanied me to check out the house. It was a huge home, but with signs of neglect and the gutter on the side of the roof was about to fall. Other than some cosmetic work and some renovation, the house had a very strong foundation. As you go inside, you are greeted by a soaring entrance and light shining through the overhead sunroof. It was a total of over 6000 square feet of house with three units of property. Each unit had four bedrooms, three bathrooms, and a wrap-around veranda in front. I was overwhelmed with the thought of buying this house so my mother could live in

one unit, the second middle unit for rent to cover her expenses and keep the third unit for me to stay in when my family comes to visit. I had it all figured out, even before I made an offer. I checked my finances in my bank and other sources of cash to make this happen. I knew exactly how much I wanted to offer, and if it didn't work, I would be left with no surprise house.

It was Friday when I looked at the house. I made an offer on Saturday. Sunday was the celebration of the Immaculate Conception, a perfect celebration for the mother of Christ. Incidentally, the Immaculate Conception from Spain was in Quezon City that week so I went to church that Monday evening. The next day, my miracle happened. My offer was accepted and my dream of buying my mother a house came true.

On December 10, following signing of the sale documents, I returned to the house with my friends and other workers Myrna had hired for me. We went to work to clean the unit that was vacant for my mother so she could transfer before Christmas. I knew she would be happy to finally settle into a place of her own. We had two days to paint and clean the house, put in some furnishings, curtains and anything else we could find to make the house look welcoming. Even my closest friend from San Miguel, Susan, was there to help in cleaning the house. I even bought a statue of the Holy Family and arranged for the house to be blessed by a priest on the same day of the surprise. It was an overwhelming plan, but with the help of my sisters in Italy, friends like Abot, Myrna and Judy, the real estate agent, I accomplished my mission.

On Saturday morning, my friends told my mother that a package from the Philippines was waiting for her at Myrna's house and gave her directions to the house I had just bought. Abot met my family at my family's house in a big van and transported my large family as well as the two boxes I had brought from the United States with goods for the house and gifts for my entire family.

My mother came with my nieces, nephews and four sisters and brothers into the unit I had prepared for all of them. I was upstairs waiting for a signal to come down. I had called her earlier and promised to call her on this day and promised to buy her a cell phone. Myrna gave her the cell phone and said, "Oh, yes, Imee promised she would call today and she told me about this cell phone." Myrna also gave her some framed photographs of me. My mom thought they were all gifts from me, not realizing they were all now fixtures of her new home. Everybody was laughing and telling stories, while I secretly descended the stairs. With a quick step down, I shouted, "Surprise!" My mom was surprised with all her heart started jumping and hugged me until I finally looked at her face. We were both teary-eyed with the warmth of our love for each other. My sister, Ate Juliet, brothers, Junior and Carding where there, as well as my niece, Oneck, and my nephew, Antonio. All my friends who had helped me, including Dan, Aisser, and Ludy, the real estate agent, were there with their families as were the children of the owner of the house who were occupying the two other units.

It was a reunion I will never forget. That night, the priest came into the house and gave an impromptu blessing to my mother's new home. Eric Roxas, the person from whom I bought the house was also there to witness this heartwarming event.

My friends were impressed with how quickly I had transformed this one neglected unit into a beautiful home in just two days. Perhaps watching home renovation television shows in America had given me all the ideas I needed. My stay felt too short, but it was just enough to be together with my family for a week. On December 23, I went back to the United States to spend Christmas with my children and Jeff. Having family in the Philippines and in America is sometimes a balancing act, but I seem to be able to do it well.

In April, right after the sellers vacated the two units, we started the renovation. I sought the help of my brother-in-law, Kuya Dording, and he hired all the carpenters and other workers we needed to do the job. Back in the U.S., the process of renovating the house was a labor of persistence, but no distance proved to be a barrier. I sent and emailed drawings, color guides and other things I wanted for my mother's house and, in less than three months, just in time for my mother's 80th birthday, the house was starting to transform beautifully.

In December 2004, I returned to a completely renovated house. The blessings were unbelievable. Located in a nice, secured subdivision, within the employment center in the country's capital, this house was truly a great investment and a true blessing.

The transformation was captured on camera and proved that once you envision and believe, nothing is impossible. In honor of Mother Mary, a grotto was built to forever inscribe what I think is a miracle of the Immaculate Conception for making my dream come true to surprise and honor my mother, Ana, with the gift of a home sweet home!

Grotto of the Immaculate Conception

Reflections: Before and After Photos of My Mom's House

It is hard to put into words the transformation that came to my mother's house a few months after I bought it. With the use of drawings I made and sent to the construction worker through the Internet, my vision of how I imagined my mother's house became a dream come true when I finally saw it completed. It was a dream for my family as well, as they had been living in a state of poverty before finally moving in. I know in my heart that my angel and the spirit of my late father was guiding me as I worked on this project to provide decent housing for my mother, brothers and sisters in the Philippines.

The renovation was done in three months as depicted in the photos below. Following the renovation the property assessment value doubled in price. This fully paid house with a rental property is a true blessing for my family.

Before

After

Before *After*

The side unit was spruced beautifully with new plants welcoming our renters.

The dirty garage was transformed into a welcoming and beautiful receiving room with plants hanging from the second floor veranda.

Other Parts of the House

He's My Brother & Roma in My Mind

"Dear children and young people, we cannot forget all those of your own age who are suffering hunger or violence, and those who are victims of hideous forms of exploitation. Let us give children a future of peace"
- Pope John Paul II

I have two brothers, Miguel, named after my father, and Ricardo, whose nickname is Carding. But my younger brother Carding is sometimes called "Palit" which in English means, "exchange." How he got this silly nickname was quite a drama.

My mother gave birth to Carding in a hospital in Sampaloc, Manila, when she was already over 40 years old. I was very young and in elementary school, but I remember very well this happy time. Every one was happy because our new brother was coming home. We were still living in Sampaloc, and my father's business was still doing very well. In fact, giving birth in a hospital was a sign of progress. With previous children, my mother had given birth through a midwife that came to our house at the time. Ate Pining, Ate Baby, Ate Julie, Cora, Miguel and I were all born through a midwife. Carding is the second to the youngest child. Next to him was my youngest sister, Lisa. They were the lucky two who were born in the hospital or so I thought.

Carding was the first one born in a hospital. My father was proud and excited to visit my mother in the hospital and after two days in the hospital, my mother and father were headed home. My father went to the nursery to check out my brother.

A short time later, my parents arrived home with Carding. My brother was in my father's arms coming out of a taxicab, while also trying to help my mother who was walking slowly as if she was still sick, but had a smile on her face. Everyone was so happy to see our little brother.

We were all still in a state of joy and happiness when all of a sudden another car stopped in a hurry in front of our house. Who could it be? Everyone was already inside the house and we were not expecting anyone. Of course, in the Philippines, neighbors came to visit when they knew there was a new baby. It was a community where we knew almost everyone, even those who lived two or three blocks away from us. Since we had a factory and business, my father and mother were quite popular.

But then, all the excitement disappeared. I remember everyone seemed confused as the nurse and an administrator from the hospital came in with another baby in just few minutes after my parents had arrived home. What had happened?

In a hurry, the nurse and hospital administrator discovered and rushed to correct it. Well, the nurse said, "Mr. Roque gave me a wrong room number. He said room 32 instead of room 23. So, I am sorry I did not pay attention, but here look at the tag on this child's wrist, the boy you have is Serrano. Your son's name is Ricardo Roque. Here look..." By this time, the nurse was teary-eyed and very embarrassed because of her mistake.

"Oh my goodness! Yes, you are right. This is my son," my father said. For awhile, I was wondering why he looked somewhat different than the first two days I had visited him in the hospital! My mother was still dizzy and almost asleep. Awakened by the commotion, she took the baby from the nurse, and she knew right away that it was my brother. But then, who was the baby beside her? Then, my father repeated to her what was going on. She had this look of confusion and said, "Yes, this is my baby, Ricardo, not this one on the bed!" Speaking in Tagalog she said, "Bakit mo pinagpalit ang anak mo sa iba?" (Why did you allow them to exchange your son with someone else?)

Though it was a somewhat confusing event, everybody in the family was just thankful the hospital caught their mistake in few minutes and rushed to our house to correct it. Since then every now and then, my brother has been teased with the name "Palit" which he took with a grain of salt.

But yes, he is my brother! Carding was a very young man when I left the Philippines. When I went back after 15 years, the poverty in our family's life had taken a toll on his young unguided life. With no father and just my mother plus other children my mother had to worry about, he did not escape the harsh reality of the streets. He had some problems with his own child, named Roma, a baby he had with a girl he had met. They separated and did not get married since the girlfriend had vices. My brother took Roma away from her so they'd both be safe.

Carding appeared to be somehow of a lost soul when I first saw him back in 1999. Since I trusted him and gave him the full responsibility to our new house in Quezon City somehow life has dramatically changed for him and other members of my family. Today, Carding is in charge of our rental property and maintenance of my mother's house, collection of rental fees, and other special needs of the family.

What was once a lost soul has transformed into a young man who is very responsible and very caring to his child. I was touched how Carding and his daughter would wake up early. Carding would take his daughter personally to school every day and pick her up religiously. He did everything a loving parent would do for a child including bathing her, feeding her and teaching her. In no time,

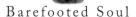

Roma has blossomed and is becoming quite a young lady -- far different than when I first saw her.

Yes, he is my brother, and I am very proud of him! I am sure Roma is proud of her Dad, too.

Roma in My Mind…

The first time I saw my niece Roma was a heartbreaking day for me. I broke into tears thinking about what her mother had done to her child. "Her vice may have gone to this child's body," I said to myself since Roma is disabled. She cannot speak even one word, and her tiny little body including her eyes shows signs of physical problems. She is a beautiful girl, but a victim of poverty and vices of her mother's womb.

She was very shy, would curl her hand and body and would not even look up to me the first time I saw her. She was unable to say a single word other than a screeching sound coming from her throat when she tried to. Every year I go home, I am getting closer to her, and she is now beginning to touch me and then would run away.

Since the day I saw Roma, she has always been in my mind that I wanted to adopt her. I was told that it would be difficult, so instead, I purchased a house four years after I had first saw her for my brother, Roma and my mother. This move was a great move. Roma needed a mother and a secure loving home most especially given her circumstances.

The year I bought the house for my family changed their lives for the better. Now that we have a house, and Roma lives with my mother and her father, this condition has helped tremendously. I also enrolled her in a special education program. This little help I've given her has given way to much progress.

One day, she came into my room, and I started talking to her. Out of nowhere she started hugging me like this was the first time she had ever hugged someone. She looked at me in my eyes and kissed

me like I was the best thing that had ever happened to her. Though she was six at this time, she still could not speak. I started asking her some questions, and she would respond with her hand. She understood every word I said, and she would even signal in a very enthusiastic way. "She can actually hear," I said to myself. I started telling her to say, "Tita" (Aunt), I love you." Every word I said she repeated and though it was hard to understand at first, she repeated exactly what I said and she would jump up and down, clapping her hands and hugging me.

When I realized that Roma was not totally deaf and that she could hear, I instructed my brother to teach her words every morning and throughout the day. My heart jumps with joy every time Roma repeats the words I say. It was a heartening moment to hear a child try her best to speak even a word or two.

Before I departed for America in December 2003, Roma was teary-eyed, crying as if she was saying, "When are you coming back?" She signaled the airplane and pointed at herself as if to say, "Please take me."

Though I was unable to take Roma with me, I knew she was in good hands with my brother, and my other family members in a new home that has sheltered their hurt bodies. I departed for the US with some peace but with Roma still in my mind.

Back in the US, I would call my mother regularly and would speak to Roma even though she could not talk. She would murmur some sounds, but when I'd tell her to say, "Tita, I love you!" she could easily follow me.

The following December, I was back to visit my family and right before my eyes was a child quite different from the one I had left a year ago. Her school and special education class had made such an incredible difference in this child's life. A confident, young girl blossomed in just one year that I had not seen her.

No longer does she curl up her body and hand. She had a straight body, a walk and a demeanor exuding confidence with her hands ready to hug me instead of shying away. No longer did she bend her head down. She now looked straight, pointed her finger into my nose, and though still difficult for her to speak she said, "Tita" without me telling her to. My heart cried, and I hugged her.

I was blessed to have been given the chance to keep the powerful image of Roma in my mind and to be touched by a child who despite her disability can make me smile and happy. Just like me, she would have been a victim of circumstances not within her control.

Roma is a vibrant young girl now; posing in photos with beautiful smiles and wearing a uniform she was proud to show me. She gets her school bag, wakes up early, and knocks on my bedroom to give me a kiss and a hug. When she comes back from school she puts down her bag, and the first thing she does is run straight to me and give me a kiss and a hug. When I would sing Karaoke, she, along with my other nieces and nephews, would be my biggest audience. They would pose for pictures and have fun watching themselves on a video camera I plugged into the TV. Seeing themselves gives them a big kick and a tickled spirit.

Roma is not alone in this world. There are millions of disabled children that need help. Her photos speak of the transformation of her life right before my very eyes. It did not take a lot of money to help this child, but the transformation was more than money can buy.

I thank God for giving Roma the blessings of a happy life.

30 My Long Lost Sisters: OFWs Story

"Mobility always implies an uprooting from the original environment, often translated into an experience of marked solitude accompanied by the risk of fading into anonymity..."
- Pope John Paul II

Since leaving the Philippines in 1984, it had been 20 years since I've seen my sisters, Pining and Baby, until my most recent return to the Philippines in January 2005. It was our reunion, at last!

My older sisters or "Ate" have also followed my footsteps, joining about 7.5 million Overseas Filipino Workers (OFWs) who migrated to Europe, America and other foreign countries with the hope of getting a better job and a better future. Ate Pining and Ate Baby both hoped for the same thing so when an opportunity to join our relatives in Italy arrived in 1987, they both went.

Though we regularly spoke on the phone while they were in Italy, the reunion in January 2005 gave me a lot of insights into the lives they have lived in Italy as they, too, did some manual jobs like I had. The only difference was, they worked for almost 20 years doing domestic jobs. Day in and day out, they have put in their hard labor to send money to their families to ensure a better future for their children. Ate Baby was even able to send and save enough money, not only for her family, but was also able to buy farms which became the source of her family's future income. She was also able to build a brand new, beautiful house in Pampanga, and, before I returned to

America after our reunion, she was proud to build another house for her daughter. With three children, she was able to ensure each one of them had his/her own decent housing, a far cry from the nipa hut, a house made of bamboo, they used to reside in. The life of isolation and alienation in a foreign country, the loneliness and the homesick heart were endured for the sake of her children's future!

My Ate Pining's life was somewhat a different story. Unfortunately, she had a stroke over four years ago while in Italy. However, through the wonders of medicine, unlike my Dad, Ate Pining was doing well. But, her last years in Italy were mostly spent taking care of her medical problems. She was thankful the Italian government has a generous medical system that paid for her surgery and other medical bills. Just like Ate Baby, she joined other OFWs who pour their heart into working hard and lonely in a far away place for the love of their family. Just like my generous Dad, Ate Pining helped other friends in Italy even though she, herself, needed help. Unfortunately, the people to whom she had lent money did not pay her back. She even helped me buy the house for my mother and now resides there with the rest of my family in Quezon City.

Ate Baby was quick to say that both of them were luckier than those who were working in the office doing administrative or clerical jobs. They were given free lodging, Italian food or whatever they wished to cook with and they were treated like family where they worked. According to her, Italy also has a work permit system for people like her. Unlike America, where there is an obvious labor shortage in specific positions, it seems European countries appear to have handled these types of migrant worker issues very differently. In America, the media, private citizen groups and even politicians are prosecuting undocumented immigrants, even those who occupy the oddest of jobs that Americans would not care to do. I wonder what would happen to America if they were not here to do these jobs? I wish a better immigration system was set up to address this important issue. I believe a balanced system addressing complex issues of immigration enforcement, and at the same time compassion for those who have truly served America is the right thing to do.

Ate Pining and Ate Baby had shown resilience, patience, and love for their families for many years. Though Ate Pining, the oldest of the family, still has medical issues, she decided to return to the Philippines a year ahead of Ate Baby. In January 2005, Ate Baby also returned, having secured her own beautiful place in the province of Pampanga. Her return coincided with my visit, so it was a great, exciting reunion in our house in Quezon City. Though the opportunities abound in Italy, the call of love, family, and homesickness was hard for my two long lost sisters. They are also much older than I, so retirement was about time. Finally, both had decided to stay for good in the Philippines. Though the money in Italy was much better than their previous lives selling food in Divisoria, the happiness of living with your own loved ones never fails to tell the story of a homecoming – the joy of hugging and kissing your own family who longs to be with you is a unique and unrivaled experience. Money is not everything as the old saying goes. And, to my sisters, this was indeed true.

Reflections on OFWs

In 2005, there are an estimated 175 Million OFWs with about 7.5 million Filipinos overseas around the world, filling jobs whose pool of applicants in the host country are quite scarce including nurses, domestic help, and, in most cases, jobs the natives of the host countries do not want to take. Professionals require H1-B Visas and need to go through an extensive immigration process, so the chances of them getting into professional positions are very small. In fact, even if you are an immigrant and have a resident status, landing a professional job is difficult, as one competes with those who already have the required experience in the host country.

In the Philippines, OFWs are such a big thing our government has even created a highly organized deployment and assistance office to serve them. And why not? OFWs are one of the biggest sources of revenue. With several billion dollars of remittances each year, the earnings from abroad make a positive impact not only for the families of the workers, but for the whole country as well. OFWs contribute to the overall economy of the Philippines, bringing billions of dollars in stable and consistent remittances that even the Asian Development Bank has conducted the first study of its kind on the subject. Remittances have been studied for the past 10 years and it has been called, "a new mantra for development." Being the "second migrant sending country" and the "third largest remittance country" in the world, the Philippines, stands to have one of the most highly organized OFW deployment systems in the world.

Of course, the issue of migrant workers is a worldwide one. In America, it is a constant debate, not only for those who are in charge of crafting government policies, but other private groups and the media have cast their thoughts on the negative and positive effects of immigration. After all, immigration in America is what made it the great country that it is today, but the pressing issues of illegal immigration, border security, day labor, crimes, and gangs have become the focus of the debate. Rarely do I see news on what truly happens out there, and the great contributions migrant workers have made to this country.

Perhaps, soon, America will finally find a system of saying "Thank You" to the poorest migrant workers who are simply here to fill jobs rejected by our own Americans. While there are social issues that come with immigration, particularly with the homeland security issue America faces following the September 11 tragedy, the positive economic impact, not only in this country, but for the Third World countries the workers come from, is tremendous, not to mention the spirit of humanity it gives to those who need it most. To me, this

issue is as important an opportunity to help the truly needy people of the world as is sending troops to war-stricken countries. I hope the immigration issues we face in America will take into consideration the plight of the poor and its impact to the world we live!

I can't help but share the words of Pope John Paul II spoken during the 87th World Day of Migration in 2001 calling for a profound analysis of changes and addressing urgent problems affecting migrant workers.

"Although in varying forms and degrees, mobility has thus become a general characteristic of mankind. It directly involves many persons and reaches others indirectly. The vastness and complexity of the phenomenon calls for a profound analysis of the structural changes that have taken place, namely the globalization of economics and of social life. The convergence of races, civilizations and cultures within one and the same juridical and social order, poses an urgent problem of cohabitation. Frontiers tend to disappear, distances are shortened, the repercussion of events is felt up to the farthest areas."

- Pope John Paul II
The Vatican, 2 February 2001

Reunion with my sisters from Italy I have not seen for over 20 years.

With my mom and sister Pining from Italy.

With my sister Baby.

My sisters Pining, Juliet, and Baby together with my nieces, and nephews.

Christmas with My Love and Four-Legged, Barefoot Friends

"To sit with a dog on a hillside on a glorious afternoon is to be back in Eden, where doing nothing was not boring, it was peace."
- Milan Kundera

I am one of 77 million baby boomers born between 1946 and 1964. I am also part of a busy generation of overworked and overstressed America. My children, Alberto and Andrea, were born in 1978 and 1979, and they have their own generation of computers, high-speed Internet and all sorts of complicated high-tech gadgets. My children and I have lived two separate generations -- two separate times. But they are the ones who remind me of life's simple pleasures with my four-legged, barefoot friends and the joy they bring to our daily lives. These barefoot creatures have taught us what going back to basics really means.

Growing up, my daughter, Andrea, had all kinds of little pets. In fact, I never paid much attention to them so I asked her the names of her pets while writing this book. At age 26, she remembered her childhood pets like a rhyme in a song –

"Nippy the turtle, Binkey the hamster, Squeaky the guinea pig, and Hucky the rabbit – and now my lovely Lucky," she said.

Her instantaneous reply reminded me of myself in days gone by. What happened to the days when all the creatures I played with as a child were ingrained in my head and in my heart? The stress of my living in this time of technology had stripped my once spirited senses. I was heartless like a PC machine.

Mostly, I remember how my kids' pets invaded our house and added work to my already busy schedule. My son Alberto would simply smile and try to distract me as the rabbit dirtied the garage on a daily basis. These tiny pets were in my house for a few days, and they were out soon after. At the time, I did not appreciate the joy these little creatures gave to my children. I was more concerned with the work they required – the filthy carpet, the smell, the dirt, and the stains they left in our otherwise spotless house. However, a child's joy is hard to resist. After all, the last pet, Hucky the rabbit, was no longer with us. I severely restricted dogs and cats; worrying about the damage they would do to my beautiful house.

So when my daughter Andrea begged to get a dog, my answer was "Absolutely no pets allowed!"

Just like I had been when I was a child, my children had their own rebellious streak. Despite my stern and ruthless disagreement over a dog and over a month of nagging and saying "No animals," Andrea continued to negotiate in hopes of buying a newly born puppy. She begged, holding her two tiny hands in prayer in front of me, "Mom, please, please, please! Look at the picture of this beautiful Pomeranian! Isn't he adorable?"

"Raising a dog is like raising a child," I explained. "You must have time to train them, feed them and bathe them..." I discouraged her with so many on and ons that I broke her spirit. (At least I though I did!)

"But I want this puppy," she said as she pointed at the photo, crinkled her tiny lips, pouted and gave me a teary-eyed look that went straight into my being. She kissed me quickly and hugged me firmly when I said, "Okay." She had won and melted my heart over my firmly stubborn head.

Our Lucky Dog

The day this Pomeranian came into our lives in one hot summer August made me feel like I was having another child. I was 44 years old, a single mother, and my children were already 20 and 21. They could barely afford to buy anything for the dog since both were new in their jobs. Alberto worked in computers for a medical billing company, and Andrea worked for Citibank. (She has recently moved to a much higher paying job with a large corporation in Rockville, Maryland.)

Andrea called our first dog Lucky. "Lucky you! You have a house and a beautiful place to live," I thought. He bathed in clean, running water and had his hair trimmed, nails cut and teeth brushed for 40 bucks. He was checked by a veterinarian and immunized for all sorts of germs and rabies for another 40 bucks. He even got his own bed, own nametag, and registration with the city's animal control for another 40 bucks! "Did you know 40 bucks can buy food for several children and a family in the Philippines for a week or even a month?" I jokingly exclaimed to my kids as my already small, almond eyes got smaller in disbelief of all the expenses of raising a dog.

Despite all this, dogs like Lucky have a way of getting into our hearts once we allow them to come into our life. Most days, they have beautiful souls, but they have their bad days, too! I used to chuckle when Lucky did his crude tricks. I melted like butter when he jumped into my lap and looked at me like I was the most beautiful person in his life.

Lucky has a dual, schizophrenic personality. I learned this term in college, having graduated with a bachelor's degree in psychology. I never got to use this term with people at work so at least I could use it fondly with our Lucky. One day he was sweet, almost teary-eyed as he begged for our attention and love while the next minute he growled with his teeth seemingly ready to bite as his round eyes turned red and he barked as loudly as he could. Andrea reminded me that since he had been bred, he must have gotten his split personality from his two roots. "You and Lucky have something in common since much of your life has been torn between the Philippines and America," she said.

Raleigh, Our Australian Cattle Dog

Jeff, my boyfriend, also had a dog, named Raleigh. "My three-level colonial house is more than 4,000 square feet, and it has more than enough room for all of us, but what used to be a model house in this new subdivision of Frederick, would no longer be a model house with all these dogs," I said to myself. But Raleigh was a special dog. He was a gift to Jeff from his children, Brian and Stacie. They thought Raleigh would make great company for Jeff since he lived alone in Columbia, Maryland. Though Jeff was not thrilled at the idea of raising a new pup, how could he say no?

Raleigh grew up with both Jeff and me as parents as I visited both of them frequently. At the time, we both owned a retail store in the Columbia Mall as we ventured into other business opportunities in addition to our day jobs. An Australian cattle dog, Raleigh is much bigger than Lucky. In fact, standing up on his behind legs, Raleigh is almost as tall as I am! His face and body look ferocious and his hair resembles his master's - a salt and pepper blend. Come to think of it, Lucky's color resembles the golden wheat that shines in his master's colored hair as well. Andrea's hair, along with the golden tone in her petite Filipina brown-skin features, were a perfect match for this tiny Pomeranian.

Raleigh and Lucky love to run and play like crazy. They sniff each other and then curl up like a giant and a tiny mouse beside one another. Despite his size, Lucky is the dominant dog, having lived in our house longer than Raleigh. Though he's small, just about the size of Raleigh's head, he scares Raleigh into giving up his bones and toys in a hurry. Jeff shouts, "Lucky, you are a thief!" as the tiny Pomeranian runs away with his bounty.

Raleigh may be big, but he has the soul of a teddy bear. He barks a lot to the outside world to protect our house from intruders including the garbage collector, the postman, and everyone in between. However, he is a loving dog, jumping into bed, cuddling and whining for attention just as a child does.

Having Raleigh and his master, Jeff, visit our house is amusing and interesting. Raleigh barks when Jeff and I start kissing. There have been many times when we've teased Raleigh. Jeff and I pretend to be kissing each other and as soon as we do, Raleigh would get on Jeff's side of the bed and start whining. Only when his master rubs his hand on his smooth, silky hair would he stop whining and begin wagging his tail in satisfaction, as if he was saying to me, "Jeff is mine!"

God's Little Creatures: A Reminder of Love and Life's Simple Pleasures

As if the dogs were not enough, Alberto went out and bought an aquarium filled with a myriad of fish. He placed the aquarium in his room, which is now cramped due to all his clothes lying on the floor. His hobby is a combination of fishing and golf and our garage is now filled with his golf balls, clubs, putter, bait hooks and fishing rods. Between my children's animals and Jeff's animal, our house is like a zoo in a fun, messy way.

As if two dogs with strong personalities weren't enough, Stacie, Jeff's daughter, came to visit with her dog, Cal, last Christmas. This was an absolute riot!

But Cal, as his name implies, is a calm, cool and very loving dog. He is a dachshund with a black brown coat, drooping ears and tiny, short legs. You can't help but fall in love with Cal – he is a sweet apple pie with gentle eyes; an angelic soul who follows you everywhere you go. He cuddles like you are the most important person in his life. His personality is almost akin to his master's who is almost always very sweet and loving - but can also snap a loud comment from her petite, flat belly once in awhile.

Christmas with the three dogs was simple but very memorable. Joyous laughter erupted while we opened our gifts and the three dogs made their way to the boxes under the Christmas tree. All of a sudden, the dogs started sniffing like little kids, amusing Alberto, Andrea, Stacie, Jeff and me. All of us were in our pajamas and enjoyed every minute of this time together. The spirit of Christmas was alive with kisses, hugs, beautiful Christmas notes, and, of course, four-legged barefoot friends that sparked our morning laughter. It was a crazy, fun time all wrapped into one – pets, family and love!

You may think what does this story have to do with the barefooted soul? There is something about being happy with the creatures of God and being happy with loved ones and family that makes our lives profoundly meaningful. This time of my life helped me to relish the happy days of my childhood and remember the animals that had given me joy. It's important to get back to the simple things in life that make us happy versus the big toys, extravagance, and high rolling days of my once stressful life.

This Christmas, there were no frills, no huge parties, no fancy clothes, no high-heeled shoes. All of us were barefoot in socks, right along with our four-legged barefoot dogs! Humans can learn the path to happiness by watching and learning from animals in nature. God's creatures can't talk, but they can demonstrate love and faithfulness.

As I reminisce about life's simple pleasures while looking through a family photo album, I find a photo taken back in 1984 when Alberto and Andrea were just by themselves. Immediately, I contrast this photo with pictures of us all together during Christmas 2004, and I sit in awe of all of the changes in our lives and lessons our once barefooted souls have learned.

The photos below speak a thousand words. We have found peace. We have found each other. We have found and truly comprehend love and the simple pleasures that make us happy.

Christmas morning with my loved ones - Jeff, Stacie, Andrea, Alberto, Lucky, Raleigh and Cal

32 Citizens' Voices

"Never doubt that a small group of thoughtful, committed citizens can change the world. Indeed, it is the only thing that ever has."
- Margaret Mead

Two weeks before Memorial Day of 2005, a headhunter summoned me to go to San Francisco and Napa Valley with its beautiful mountains and bay views. Headhunters have a way of finding people, even those who are not looking for a job, providing them with a completely free trip, including flight and lodging, in order to get them to consider a position. During this same period, I had also been planning to write a book to capture some of the most interesting chapters of my life.

But something was happening in my City, it had overtaken the importance of my book writing and the allure of the San Francisco Bay Area-- something I found so incredible I wouldn't exchange it for anything.

One morning that same week, I read my horoscope, which said, "Something happened that you did not initiate but will overtake your other plans and ideas but it will be for your benefit and good." Wow, what a revelation! By now, you must think I am really superstitious, but, I believe it is simply being reflective of silent hunches in the wind. I didn't put the horoscope together with my life until the following incredible story!

It dawned on me that the one thing not within my control was the layoffs initiated by the Mayor of City of Frederick, with whom I had never worked or even seen personally before. The layoff and budget had become one of the most controversial news stories in the city.

From March to May, the layoff issue facing several people I used to work with, including the HR Director and Compensation Analyst I hired when I was still in the City of Frederick as a cabinet official touched me. Their jobs, including ten others, were slated for layoffs. The first thing I did was composed a letter to elected officials and simply sent emails, as many others did, to my former staff to provide them moral support.

Knowing the city's human resource policies upside-down since I had been involved in creating them while I was there, it was clear to me that something unfair was going on. I could smell that no matter how far I was from them. I researched the situation and a burst of renewed energy pushed me to do a lot more work than I had originally planned. I wrote to the Frederick News Post and, on April 30, 2005, despite the 200-word limit, my editorial expressing my views and opinion was published in its entirety...

> I have seen too many negative incidents and lawsuits against the City and the Mayor, and it's about time citizens demand accountability and transparency. To me, the lawsuits, budget issues and layoffs are symptomatic of bigger issues affecting the City – balance of power, management issues, and accountability for unnecessary expenses destroying the City's coffers.
>
> The Mayor seems to use "fiscal constraint" and "doing the right thing" mantra on her budget proposals. But is it fiscal constraint when the Mayor herself is spending large sums of money for legal expenses at a time of dwindling resources? Is she doing the right thing when she is asking the Aldermen to take personnel actions

contrary to the spirit of the City Charter and its merit system? You be the judge!

When the Aldermen passed an amendment changing the City Charter on Mayoral residency requirement, the Mayor vetoed it. She declared, "the Aldermen chose to ignore the will of the public and so her veto would rectify that." As we know now, she's in a couple of lawsuits - all at the taxpayers' expense. One would respect the Mayor's conviction to stand by the City Charter until her recent actions. Her layoff proposals are riddled with potential violations of the City Charter. The very same Charter she vowed to protect and faithfully execute is the same Charter she has now compromised. It appears the Mayor forgot her own words.

Without going to the Aldermen, the Mayor has the luxury to spend thousands of City taxpayers' money and hire her own private lawyer bypassing five City Attorneys. Despite a large number of legal team for such a small City, the City is in a loosing ground. Recently, the City lost in a blight abatement case and a wrongful termination filed by Stewart Seal. Each case has its own unique set of embarrassment for the City. What's more embarrassing, the Mayor had to issue a press release twice for violating the settlement agreement calling for a public apology to Stewart and his family. A public apology is in order for those who were hurt and humiliated by her personnel indiscretion, including the citizens she serves. Since the Mayor is using the taxpayers' money, Alderman Joe Baldi was right to demand public disclosure.

Despite a costly settlement paid for by taxpayers for the Mayor's personnel mistakes, the Mayor has not learned from this lesson. Stewart is not the first Director let go by the Mayor. In her tenure, we have heard much bad news and personnel lawsuits. Now, she's under fire again for presumptuous layoffs she announced even prior to the Aldermen ruling on the budget. Unless the City performs due diligence and ensures these personnel actions are in accordance with the City's layoff procedure, Stewart's and other pending cases will not be the end of the City's legal battles.

The budget process the Mayor said was for the citizens, but I have yet to receive even an automatic reply to my four-page letter sent in March, on why the Aldermen are being asked to take several actions that will essentially change the Charter, including layoffs for positions mandated by the Charter and classified positions that require adherence to the City's merit system? Under what part of the Charter does it say that the Mayor has the power to do so without going through the Charter amendment process? Allowing the Mayor to not faithfully execute the terms of the Charter and interpret it the way she likes essentially makes the power of citizen's input, the Board of Aldermen, and the legislative side of the City null and void.

But I still have faith that the City still has the opportunity to provide citizens the best decisions and governance they deserve. Recently, I heard of Alderman Baldi and other officials taking positive actions. While the City Mayor finds fault on Alderman Baldi's proposals, the Mayor can learn from him. Collaborative efforts, inclusiveness, fairness, and working with officials and staff in finding creative solutions to the City's problems are signs of good leadership. In contrast, who can blame the media for characterizing the Mayor's tenure as unpleasant, divisive, and full of negative publicity and lawsuits. While it's been said that Alderman Baldi's saving employees' jobs is smart politics, it is also the right thing to do. He presents solutions to costly personnel issues damaging the City's reputation. He knows that treating employees fairly is the heart of good governance. Without good people, we won't have

good public service. At a minimum, employees deserve fairness and due process without which we will see more lawsuits. In the meantime, it's about time the Aldermen as a body put the Mayor on check on her legal expenses and costly personnel mistakes! The citizens you represent deserve transparency and accountability.

- Imelda Roberts

In addition to my letter, I created a website I called FrederickVoices.com during the Memorial weekend instead of a barbecue, or a family trip. I had a little sleep and I even asked myself, "What am I doing?" But the response was clear in my head - there were people I personally knew whose lives were about to change, and their livelihoods were at stake. It is also about my community and my city being tarnished by politics. Every morning, I opened my email and the local newspapers in Frederick, and read yet another story so painful I knew I had to do something. Though it was hard to go back to the city, the same place that was witness to the pain and bullying an alderwoman had inflicted upon me while working there, I gathered my courage and returned one more time.

On Thursday night, June 2, 2005, after being away from the Frederick City Hall for almost six years, I returned. I attended a heated board meeting to testify and make a presentation to the Mayor and the Board of Aldermen. I also presented them with a petition, complete with 125 signatures I had gathered in my neighborhood with the goal of saving employees' jobs. Our efforts were headlined in both the Frederick News Post on June 3, and on the Gazette on June 1.

But despite the efforts, the Thursday night Board meeting I attended, ended with a 3-2 vote in favor of saving jobs, but this was not enough. The City Mayor, who had proposed the layoff in the first place, could still veto this resolution. No one wanted to budge on either side of the decision; two alderwomen and the City Mayor wanted the layoffs, while three men on the opposite party were opposed to it. The women seemed not to listen to citizens' testimonies and unpleasant remarks were exchanged among elected officials and other citizens. The City Mayor asked for citizens' comments on the matter and I was the first to speak.

As I began to speak, my strong emotions caused my voice to crack as members of the audience who had been laid off, watched me, teary-eyed. I was the only one who spoke during the budget discussion.

The night was almost over, when it was announced that final public comments would be allowed before the meeting adjourned. Then, something happened - those who had not spoken a word, including citizens who were there for other business matters, began to rise. One by one, people stood up, including one particular employee who seemed afraid to talk. She repeated twice she was speaking that night as a private citizen; she echoed my name and repeated what I had said in an impassioned plea, "I am full of emotion as I see loyal employees with swollen, teary eyes listening at the back while their lives are being yo-yoed in public!" Another resident said, "You all looked like you weren't listening to what Imelda was saying. I don't have the background that she had. When she was here in the City as HR Director, there were times we did not see eye to eye, but I happen to agree with what she said tonight."

I gave my final comments, challenging elected officials, especially the City Mayor, to consider the signed petition I submitted to them from 125 citizens. I asked firm questions inquiring about the merits of their decision and repeated why they should not proceed with the layoffs. With specific questions that challenged their decisions, the Mayor interrupted me and said, "Ms. Roberts, this is a comment

period and not time for questions."

I continued and told her respectfully that I understood, but I emphasized that I would still like them to think about the decision they were about to make and made a final plea for the employees' jobs.

Following my impassioned plea, a well-respected lawyer stood up and said, "Yes, for the life of me, I can't fathom how a city of this size would do this to these good employees. I have a service business and the first thing I do is budget their salaries because I want to keep good people!" Another citizen, running for alderman, also stood and spoke.

Despite the drama that unfolded that night, cold hearts beat the compassioned voices. The night ended with a big question as to whether the Mayor would veto the decision made by the vote. People's lives were again in the balance, and would remain there for another fourteen days, the period during which the Mayor can veto a decision. It had been six months since the Mayor had announced layoff in October and the back and forth. Afterwards, the disagreements between elected officials since the budget hearings began in March had become exhausting to watch.

After the meeting, I went out to say hello to former colleagues and board members. I was greeted with warm handshakes and hugs from employees I had not seen for almost six years. I proceeded to greet and reach to this alderwoman who, almost six years ago, made my life miserable. My life had changed for the better since then and I decided it was time to heal, hopefully turning the negative into a positive relationship. I went to see her and offered a handshake, but instead of shaking hands, she refused and started mumbling words, scolding me in an angry voice and treated me like I did not belong. In a calm voice I said, "I was simply saying hello; why are you mad?" With an indignant voice, she murmured words I couldn't make out.

Finally, fuming at me, she said, "No, don't touch me!"

My boyfriend, Jeff, couldn't help but notice her uncivil behavior and got involved. He said to her that what she had done was uncalled for and asked if that was the way she treated her citizens. Surprised that someone else had observed her behavior against a resident when the camera was not on, she was unable to answer any of our questions and left the room completely flustered. Aldermen, Joe Baldi, Bill Hall and David Lenhart also witnessed the event and said in chorus, "That's the type of things we deal with every day!" Another citizen whispered, almost afraid to speak, and said, "That's the kind of place we have here. Employees can't speak for fear they will lose their jobs."

As tired as I was from this meeting, the work we had done to influence the board's decision, in addition to the added drama of speaking with the unfriendly alderwoman, I thought, "Who am I to change the course of the City's history?" Despite inspiring my own family to join me in this journey, voices of citizens through 125 signatures on my petition, and our best efforts, some elected officials were still unmoved! Their egos and hatred of each other were so ingrained in their souls they had forgotten why they were there to begin with – to serve the citizens of the city.

I was still feeling bad for employees who were being laid off but I told myself there was nothing more I could do, so I simply prayed. Then, a "miracle" happened - I got a personal call from the Budget Director of City Hall - the City Mayor had reversed her decision! All positions had been returned in the new budget and they planned to hold a special meeting on Wednesday to act on a balanced budget. I asked if this was official and he said, "The Mayor just finished a press conference at 3:30 and announced she was saving all jobs. It will be in the news tomorrow!" What an incredible turn of events in just a few hours!

The event was overwhelming. Immediately following this call, I received a flood of emails and phone calls. I had an email from Alderman Joe Baldi that simply said, "We did it!" He was the alderman who had been very supportive of my petition and had been instrumental in forwarding a revised budget to save the employees' jobs. Several friends and employees called and sent emails that night asking me to run for Alderman, saying they would love to vote for me. A columnist in the local newspaper contacted me and asked if I was running for office and I responded that I didn't have any intention of running for public office. His editorial in the local newspaper confirmed that fact.

I was on the radio the next Saturday morning with Blaine Young, radio host and former alderman, and other elected officials. I was given public accolades by Alderman Bill Hall for being instrumental in turning the layoff problem around and saving employees' jobs. The former City Mayor, Jim Grimes, who used to be my boss, called in to the radio and the event became a radio reunion. He said wonderful words that sparked my spirit.

One employee called to tell me I was so instrumental in the dramatic change in City Hall during the last 24 hours that she cried on the phone. She said it was like the whole country was praying for them and, somehow, because of my knowledge of the city and human resources, I was asked to come back after almost six years.

The drama that surrounded this layoff had involved my family, neighbors and the strangers who had signed the petition, and it was worth all the time I had devoted to it. I was most grateful for the lives that had been touched. Behind these lives were the most touching stories, including the mother and grandmother who had cancer and cried when she saw people they personally knew being hurt by this event.

The event had been close to the hearts of many city residents. As

I looked out my window one rainy night, I saw a senior citizen who had driven to my house, hardly able to open the door of his car, to leave a signed petition in my mailbox. I saw a reflection of a young boy with MS who, unable to write properly, had to scribble, then type his name in Teletype, but despite the difficulty, he was proud to do his part to help prevent the layoff. I had even met a man on the MARC train who couldn't talk, but signaled he wanted to sign. Together, there were 125 signatures, each with a unique story.

It was my belief that as a citizen of the city I have the responsibility to speak out on matters that are important to me. In the end, I hope my actions made a difference in the lives of twelve employees and their families, including a cancer-stricken 85-year-old grandmother in chemotherapy who had cried on my shoulder. She was the first person I called. In her weak voice, she said, "My dear, I am awfully tired today, but hearing your voice lifted me up. Thank you for helping those who were being laid off. All of us are jumping with joy today as we watched the Mayor in the press conference announced there would be no layoffs." Her voice faded as I said goodbye on the phone and said, "Honey, you did a tremendous job. May God bless you!"

I had been truly blessed as I took this journey with an energy and spirit I had previously thought unimaginable, but so many people who believed in what I had to say inspired me. I had goose bumps all over thinking about how citizens can really make a difference.

In the 2005 City of Frederick elections, it was no wonder the theme of the campaign was "Civility in the City." It had been a controversial year, filled with lots of negative words back and forth from City Hall. On November 2005, the incumbent Mayor lost her reelection bid. The people of the City of Frederick had spoken, and only time will tell when they will decide who else needs to be out of that office, in order to give back full civility to the beautiful city of Frederick.

Tolerance is opening our hearts and minds to those who may be different from us, less fortunate than us, or who may believe differently from us. Trust there is innate goodness in people and that hope resides in each one of us. Tolerance of the heart means greater understanding of the human being inside each one of us.

Tolerance and Trust. From our family to the community we live, our lives and who we are as individuals are in many ways unique and different.

We start understanding our world and acquiring diverse perspectives through our own lenses, through our families, the people around, and the communities we live. We breed what we teach our children and can therefore, make a big difference by teaching the innate goodness in people starting from our own home. When we do, we give our children the gift of human understanding that ultimately benefit the communities we live.

We also enrich our lives by experiencing other cultures and listening to other voices around us. Our elders, parents, and community leaders also play a big role. We cannot expect to teach respect and tolerance to our children when we don't respect others opinion and opposing views.

Ultimately, when we leave this earth we will be most remembered not by the wealth we acquire, but on how we touched the people around us, including those whose circumstances are different from us.

Priceless Memories

Material things you can buy,
but you can't bring them with you when you leave this earth…
A warm spirit, a smile, a hug, a kiss and a sweet "I love you," don't cost a dime
But they are gifts you leave behind to your loved ones' hearts and mind
Priceless joy and happiness that last beyond our lifetime!

Vacation and fun times with Jeff and kids.

With All My Heart and Soul

Excellence is symmetry of perfection as grand as the mountain, as wide as the ocean, and as sparkling as any gem. It is an ideal state we view within our mind and we continuously aspire for.

Finding what love was all about has been a long journey and a story of faith and dreams. My busy work and my obligations as a single parent were all I thought about until I met Jeff Snively.

Jeff lived in Columbia, Maryland and I lived in Woodbridge, Virginia when we first met. Life has a way of bringing people together, regardless of distance, time and space. This chapter of my life was filled with honest friendship, love and personal transformation. We used our love for one another to strengthen our own dreams and enjoy our life together.

Our love story has many happy times, some silly, and others incredibly risk-taking including business ventures that truly tested our trust and love for one another. The stories within this chapter also speaks of seeking higher ground towards excellence the way Jeff and I view it, be it in our everyday life, relationship and endeavors we undertake together.

"With All My Heart and Soul" is song I wrote to share my deep love to blue-eyed Jeff. May the heartwarming stories Jeff and I shared together rekindle the love in your heart.

With All My Heart and Soul

(Woman)
I love you, oh, oh
I love you,
I love you baby, with all my heart and soul, oh, oh
Feel the love I have within me, oh baby
I love you, with all my heart and soul, oh, oh

Here is my heart
Here is my soul
Feel the love I have for you
It is so deep, it is so true
Feel the love I have for you
I really do love you, oh, oh
With all my heart and soul.

(Man)
My dear love, I waited for so long
To share with you my heart song
To show I really care about you
But many things consumed me
Oh baby I can't live without you,
Oh baby, I really do love you, oh, oh
With all my heart and soul.

Here is my heart
Here is my soul
Feel the love I have for you
It is so deep
It is so true
Feel the love I have for you
I really do love you, oh, oh
With all my heart and soul.

DUET
Let's take the time
Let's hear each other's heart and mind
And show we really care about each other
As we live our lives,
Oh, oh, Together,
Forever
And show our love forever, oh, oh.
Don't let a day gone by
Without showing we really care
Cause we really care
We really love each other

Oh, oh
We really love each other
Oh, oh
With all our hearts and souls.

DUET
Here is my heart
Here is my soul
Feel the love I have for you
It is so deep
It is so true
Feel the love we have for each other
We really love one another
With all our hearts and souls. *(8 x fading)*

Jeff and Imelda

Blue-Eyed Jeff

"Faith is the strength by which a shattered world shall emerge into the light."
- Helen Keller

It was the week of Valentine's Day when Jeff invited me to lunch. Though I had not seen him after the seminar when we'd first met and we had only spoken on the phone during evenings, something inside me told me he was a special man. He had a very warm, soothing voice and I just couldn't resist his invitation to meet him again for lunch on Friday.

I was so excited about our date, I took the day off from work just to prepare for it. I was nervous like I had never dated in my life. From the time I saw him walking towards me, I was overcome with excitement but, at the same time, my legs where like bumping each other and my hands felt clammy for the first time in years. As he walked towards me in a dark, moss green suit, my heart was beating fast. He shook my hand in a gentlemanly way and his warm hands soothed my cold hands in this cold, winter month. We walked inside the restaurant with his hand resting gently on my back as he showed me through the door.

While we ate lunch, I was still nervous. I crumbled the sandwich into several pieces and only managed to eat a few bites. I was afraid that every time I took a bite of the sandwich, he would see my hand shaking, so I decided to just hold both my hands under the table until we finished eating. After lunch, I excused myself to go to the bathroom. I was perspiring despite the cold, winter air of February and I experienced a feeling I couldn't explain.

He waited for me and when we were ready to go our separate ways, he shook my hand again. His grip was tight and warm, and he asked, "Can we see each other again tomorrow?" His warm, firm, hand seemed to reach through my whole being as his blue eyes looked straight into mine. They were hard to resist and as my beating heart filled with excitement, I said, "Okay, do you want to come over to my house?" He cancelled his trip to his daughter in North Carolina to visit me. I learned he was divorced from his wife of 19 years with two children a little older than mine. He was just like me, a single parent with one son and one daughter.

The next day, with roses in his hands, he knocked on my door and entered into my life. That was over twelve years ago. Our attraction and feelings for each other were mutual, and the love and friendship Jeff and I shared grew and remain strong to this day.

As I reflect upon the many things we did together, I found myself reliving my youth when I did not have a boyfriend as a young, ugly duck. Times had changed, however, and so had I. It seemed America exposed me to a world where a woman can freely express her thoughts and feelings in the same way a man can. Don't think we have a wild streak. Oh, a few… but, sorry, those will remain in our private memoir!

I should say though, every time, hour after hour, Jeff has been the most fabulous, passionate lover any woman could ever dream of. I can also share a few silly, funny things we did together that always make me smile as I remember them.

Jeff was the first man who showered my mother with flowers on Easter Day. It was my mother's second visit in the United States and she had finally gotten to meet Jeff. With a lily in his hand, my funny

mom would say, "I am still alive. Lilies are for dead people!" In the Philippines, lilies are generally used in funerals while, here in America; they are common flowers on Easter. Despite the seemingly sarcastic remarks, that was the first time my mother had such fun with a man who courted me. She was just joking.

Next time my mom and Jeff met, it was my mother's 70th birthday. Jeff gave my mother a lady's wallet. When she received it, she jokingly shrugged her hand while stomping her foot, and said, in Filipino, "Ay! Anong gagawin ko dito?" (Ay! What will I do with this?) She opened the wallet and looked inside for money, and said, "Naku, ni kusing walang laman!") (There is nothing inside; not even a cent!) In our country, when someone gives a gift like a wallet, they usually include some money inside. With a smile on my face, I explained to Jeff what my mother was saying. My mother hardly spoke English so I acted as interpreter between the two of them. I was glad Jeff took my mom's remarks as jokes and I was truly glad my mother met the man of my life.

Jeff and I are generally not affectionate in public. To me, our first public show of affection was under the 14th Bridge Street, in a picnic area overlooking the water. Like teenagers, we parked the car under the bridge, like we were the only souls in this deserted picnic area. As the Metro train passed by, I felt as if the Metro train of full of passengers had stopped for a moment to watch the lovebirds under the bridge and we pulled ourselves together until the train completely disappeared from sight.

Jeff and I would have a picnic every now and then at the park near his office. One day, we were seated in the blanket eating the food I had cooked for this special day, having fun just talking and enjoying the day. As we were about to embrace, a familiar car drove by. Oh, oh… It was Jeff's boss. We quickly packed our blanket and left the park.

Our first live show was at the Kennedy Center were we watched "Shear Madness," followed by "Miss Saigon." As if the fun of watching the show was not enough, we spent the late night at the Key Bridge Marriott for a late evening dinner. Despite the late night, I was full of energy as I returned to work the next day, radiantly smiling from the intoxicating late night out.

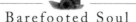

During this time when we began dating seriously, the HIV AIDS was big news and an epidemic that startled the whole world. Clinics were everywhere. I was reading an article in the newspaper about AIDS when we parked near a clinic in Arlington. I said, "Hey Jeff, there is a free HIV-AIDS clinic and counseling. Look, they have lots of information. Let's get some." We went inside and by the time we know it, my curiosity had gotten us into an uncompromising situation. We were convinced to get HIV testing and counseling. He was given a male counselor, and I was given a female counselor. Of course we both passed with flying colors and it was a healthy way of knowing we were safe for each other. At the time, Jeff was 40 and I was 38 years old, we were counseled on how to have safe sex. We were chuckling as we left the clinic because by the time we got out of the rooms, both of us were holding brown bags filled with free "goodies" from the clinic; he had condoms and I had birth control pills.

Jeff and I also did things together with our children. Our first trip to a beach was in Ocean City and it was a family trip with Alberto, Andrea and Brian. Stacie, his daughter, was in North Carolina so I didn't get a chance to see her as often as I would have liked to. We spent time together wading in the beach, playing miniature golf with the kids, walking on the boardwalk, and doing fun things people in love do together. I displayed my beginner's luck as we bet on a horse together at a nearby racetrack, and Jeff was amazed at how good I was at choosing numbers.

Our first roller coaster ride was in Kings Dominion. Well, correction, please. I actually did not ride with him. I was afraid of the big roller coaster, so I went on the Scooby Doo ride instead, while he was down below waiting for me. He was too embarrassed to ride Scooby Doo with me, so I rode with my friend, Tess. Anyone would think this small ride would be perfectly tame, but, at the top of my lungs, I shouted and cursed in Filipino language so no one would say, "What in the world is wrong with this woman?" Other than Tess, no one else could understand me. Jeff and I, together with our friends and children, went on a bunch of other rides that day and I had more fun that I'd had in a long time.

The first book we read together was, "Men Are From Mars and Women Are From Venus." I guessed, aside from our cultural differences, the man and woman thing was another issue we would have to overcome and understand so our relationship would last. Both of us had failed relationships in the past, and we were sensitive about how long we would hold each other's hand. We exchanged articles to read. He even volunteered to take the Myers Briggs Personality Indicators test, hoping we could both determine our inclinations and temperament and learn about each other on a more intellectual level. I was happy to comply and gave him a booklet. He lived too far away to give it to me in person, so he mailed the booklet with a short note tucked inside that read: "I wish I was looking in your eyes right now!"

Of course, not everything was perfect. There was one thing Jeff didn't allow me to do: wash his clothes. In my desire to help and straighten out his house when I visited him in Columbia, I washed his clothes. I felt as if it was what I had done to get fired in my first job in America, I almost got fired. He was upset I had ruined his clothes and I was upset that he was upset with me so I told him just to take me home. But, finally, I said to myself, "This is really good. I have a good excuse not to do the laundry.

But we weren't also always that serious. Like kids, we had our first irresponsible, silly act together while at the movies. We even watched two movies for the price of one. After watching "True Lies," we acted like kids, holding hands as we quickly snuck across to the other movie theater and took a peak at the other movie. We snuck in and watched "Forest Gump" without paying. It was the movie theater beside a county jail and, though I was nervous we would be caught due to the silliness of love, there was something about sneaking as we giggled our way out of the movie theater that connected our souls. God may not have been happy with us at that moment and would not recommend this to any other kids. Jeff was an altar boy growing up and I was a catholic child; we just hoped that our first time to be bad would be forgiven.

All joking aside, what I really would like to share is how two different people from two different cultures stood the test of time and have enjoyed several memorable years. We had not thought about marriage, and I believe it was our circumstances that made us at peace with not getting married. We compromised and talked about issues openly, just like special friends would. We understood that both of us had careers and family, and we had to be selfless and at the same time selfish for our relationship to flourish.

Our respect for one another transcends beyond the two of us. Each of us has two grown children. I have Alberto, now 27, and Andrea, now 26. His daughter, Stacie and his son Brian are older than my kids. Together, everyone gets along and we have a warm relationship.

Several years of being boyfriend and girlfriend, confidants, true best friends, lovers, travel buddies, business partners, and especially soul mates are all that matter to us. We have a caring, respectful, and honest relationship - what else could we ask for? For now the song we wrote together entitled "Forever," speaks of our deep love for each other.

34 Blue Dreams: Imena Azul

"In our own names... In our own styles
We dare to be different. At Imena Azul
we capture your dreams."
- Imelda Roberts and Jeff Snively

Imena Azul, which means Blue Dreams, is a business venture Jeff and I put together. It was our way of building our dreams together. Though we only agreed to a temporary lease at Columbia Mall while it waited for a bigger store to take over our small one, Jeff and I took advantage of the lease and considered it an opportunity to expand our horizons. We signed a lease for the holidays, beginning in August, 2001 and ending in March, 2002. My daughter, Andrea, became our store manager and Abot, my friend and classmate in college, also helped us in the store.

Jeff and I had a wonderful time doing this project together. We turned an ugly space into a store that appeared to have been designed by a professional. We designed the floor layout, the furniture, the fixtures and we even stayed overnight there while painting the store together. We were forced to work at night since the high-end mall did not allow painting during the day, and we slept on the floor after an exhausting night of painting. Everything from the signs, to paint color, to fixtures, including products we sold went through the mall's approval process. When we were finished, even the mall representative who inspected our store was impressed by what we had done with it, given this was our very first store. It was like our first baby and we named it after the meaning of my name – Imena. Since Jeff has blue eyes and he likes blue, we added Azul, a Spanish word for blue. We even wrote a poem together that captured the essence of not only our business, but also of what we were about.

Imena Azul
-Blue Dreams

Imena reflects our faith and dreams
While Azul touches our hopes and strengths.

It's our "Blue Dream" that brings out
Our essence as men and women –

To reach out for something simple yet beautiful,
Something bold yet sophisticated.

To seek out life's blue sky in elegant fashion
And a diverse sense of style.

To travel the world for fine things
That captivate our rich minds and spirits.

We seek our own sense of identity.
Our individual style reflects our own faith and desires –
To be casual, bold, provocative, confident, sophisticated.
In our own names… In our own styles
We dare to be different.

At Imena Azul we capture your dreams.

It was through Imena Azul that we learned every detail of running a business. From incorporating our company, designing our own collections and sending our designs to Asia for production to compete with other retailers. From jewelry and handbags to men's

silk ties and briefcases, our collections bore both our names, Imelda for ladies, and J Snively for men's items. This was where we learned from the custom office that most ties in the world are made in China. But not just silk ties. We imported most of our products from China and some from Bangkok, Thailand and the Philippines.

This project gave us a lasting experience we could not have received anywhere else. Through this venture, I also discovered that Jeff and I have a very strong bond no amount of financial failure would break; we never had any conflicts on financial issues relating to our store. This was one thing some friends cautioned against; they warned us never to do business with a boyfriend or girlfriend because it could break apart the relationship. But this was not the case with Jeff and me. Both of us were secure enough within ourselves and with each other to make it work. We trusted the decision we made from the very first time we signed the contract and believed no matter where it led us, it was a learning opportunity. Though we did pick on each other every now and then, for the most part, there was no real blaming game involved.

The only time I can recall where we had some conflicts was with the schedule of whose turn it was to be in the store. Given our existing jobs, we realized we could not be in two places and give your best shot to your business. Our day jobs took priority over our temporary business venture. We also had a few differences on the prices we would charge. I tended to be more generous with the prices while Jeff was a cut and dry businessman.

Just like in everything, timing is very important. Unfortunately, a month after we opened Imena Azul, our dreams were shattered. America was in a state of chaos. Businesses were affected. People were scared and devastated. The terrorists had hit our country's business center, New York, followed by the Pentagon and then Pennsylvania on September 11, 2001, less than three weeks after we

opened our store.

The War on Terrorism began and at Imena Azul – many dreams, including our blue dreams where temporarily suspended as chaos, fear and devastation ravaged America for weeks and months to come.

But, just as all other Americans, we stood up and continued our business as usual. The thoughts of September 11 victims and heroes were so strong in both our minds and hearts that Jeff and I decided to get involved in the cause despite our busy schedules. Together, we formed a group of volunteers and put together a "Gift of Songs and Light" program in Arlington County, a musical tribute honoring the victims and heroes of September 11. It was another journey and discovery of who we are as people. Since this volunteer effort, our lives have never been the same.

Imena Azul Designer Collections at high-end Columbia Mall, Maryland. Abot Mendoza, my friend, helped us to set up the store.

Blue Ocean Princess Getaway

"Instead of two footprints, there were four, like a musical quartet pumping rhythm and harmony from the soles of our feet all the way into our hearts. Walking lovingly with Jeff at this moment was a perfect melody."
- Imelda Roberts

Jeff and I enjoy doing many things together, especially vacation travel. Each year, we have had great vacations together to places like New York, North Carolina, San Francisco, San Diego, Arizona, Las Vegas, Ocean City, New Jersey, Florida and other places within the United States. Despite the drastic change in the hassle of traveling due to enhanced security checks and other homeland security procedures since the September 11 tragedy, we move on with our lives. Jeff and I have not been deterred from traveling and enjoying our leisure time away from our daily routine. It is always good for our hearts and souls.

Our vacation during Memorial week of May 2004 was especially exciting, totally cool and different. This time, we took a seven-day cruise on the Princess Cruise Caribbean Getaway via Puerto Rico! Just the sound of it made me feel like dancing salsa! We would spend a week in the eastern Caribbean islands of St. Thomas, St. Kitts, Grenada, Isla Margarita, Venezuela, and Aruba plus a stopover in Puerto Rico; I knew it would be a memorable get away. It proved to be a dream vacation, and it felt as if the big love boat were just for the two of us.

Oops... did I say just the two of us? Not really. This time, Jeff was taking me on vacation with his children, Brian and Stacie. Jill, Brian's

girlfriend, also joined us along with other friends. It was a family and friendly get away across the blue oceans and into foreign places we had never visited before. There were lots of things to prepare – from passports to shopping for swimsuits and tropical clothes.

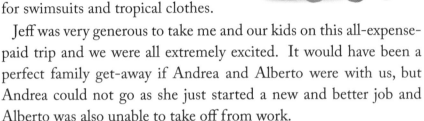

Jeff was very generous to take me and our kids on this all-expense-paid trip and we were all extremely excited. It would have been a perfect family get-away if Andrea and Alberto were with us, but Andrea could not go as she just started a new and better job and Alberto was also unable to take off from work.

Jeff got a balcony room for us, which overlooked the ocean, and he joked to the kids they were in the regular cabin far away from us. While we looked out onto the ocean from the balcony, they would look out from a window. His silly jokes were his way of connecting with the kids. The kids didn't care, though. "We won't be in the room most of the time, anyway," they said. "No big deal, Dad! And thanks for the free cruise." Young and old alike, we were excited about the trip. Just the thought of the blue waters of the Caribbean prompted a sigh of refreshing relief from our city life and busy eight-hour days our careers entailed.

We arrived in Puerto Rico a day before the ship left from its port. It was raining on and off while we were there, but this didn't dampen our spirits. We walked with our yellow raincoats and umbrellas purchased hurriedly from a nearby CVS Store and explored the city. We had lunch and walked down a steep alley in the city that connects to the water. It proved to be a fun start to the trip, despite the rainy weather.

Going through the lines to enter this big ship was overwhelming. With almost 2,000 people lined up, the falling rain added to the excitement of waiting in line as a couple thousand eager vacationers checked into the Blue Ocean Getaway Adventure, eager to totally escape the busy world we were leaving behind.

Once inside, I understood why this kind of ship is called a love boat. The luxury cruise line was just like a five-star hotel with a huge, very impressive lounge and a large, crystal chandelier connoting opulence and rich elegance.

From the balcony of our room, Jeff and I looked beyond the horizon as if our future were as wide as the ocean. It was a different kind of blue water. It was calm and peaceful, making a rippling sound that vibrated into our hearts as we held our palms firmly together and our heartbeats sung a happy, soulful melody. In that moment, we were in unison. The pure, white seagulls flew perfectly… lightly… in unison with the waves and, in our presence, became our witness for this solitude and pure joy we felt in our hearts.

Walking along the beach with Jeff barefooted reminded me of my childhood days when my free spirit transformed into whatever creature I dreamt myself to be. This day, I was a barefooted princess being held firmly by the hand of this handsome, blue-eyed man. At that moment, my child-like being emerged with sweet smiles and a sparkle in my eyes. Gone were the lonely tears that painted my heart with bitterness and loneliness. The love within my heart for the man I was walking beside was a tremendous thanksgiving for seeing the beauty of love. Instead of two footprints, there were four, like a musical quartet pumping rhythm and harmony from the soles of our feet all the way into our hearts. Walking lovingly with Jeff at this moment was a perfect melody. There were two lounge chairs overlooking the blue water that seemed to have been reserved for Jeff and me, with a perfect view of beautiful fishes on the clear, blue water. It was a stark contrast to the canvas lounge chairs I used to sleep and sit on during my younger years in Divisoria, back in

Manila, Philippines, in front of a pile of mud and fishes ready to be hauled off for vendors to sell the next day.

Renewing our spirits from the tired stress of working and other obligations back home, in an instant, we were laughing and joking, with no thoughts of emails, voicemails, snail mails.... It was a total escape from our sedentary routines that ruled our days back at work. We pampered ourselves in the spa. Jeff even got a body wrap and, for the princess lady, a face treatment, haircut, and a massage. The lavish gym overlooking the blue water was a perfect set-up for physical exercise to complete the mind and body experience. For seven straight nights and eight days, it was our own perfect getaway.

Our adventure, a selfish love for one another balanced by selfless act of giving to our kids, friends and others on the cruise made Jeff and me who we are today: a modern-day couple. We had dinner with friends, Tess and Duwain, Jeff's children - Brian and Stacie - along with Jill, Brian's girlfriend. With us at the dinner table were Barbara, Jeff's ex-wife and mother of his children, and Barbara's boyfriend, Gordon. Though others may find this an odd group, to me it was a perfect group.

My unconditional love for Jeff was secure and trusting. Having met Barbara and Gordon before, I was happy to see them again. The happiness I see in both Gordon and Barbara radiated in their smiles and gazes at each other. They were a wonderful couple, wishing to share happy times with their children. Our friendly and respectful relationship towards each other made our time together extra special; there was no worldly jealousy in our hearts. No "Desperate Housewives" drama.

Despite the pain that may come from divorce, it was all in the past. The present moment and the reality of the two beautiful children before us were more important. In fact, I actually admired the way Barbara and Jeff treated their divorce. It was far different from the way I was treated by the father of my children. Though divorce is unfortunately common in America, it is not everyday that you come across divorced couples who are at peace with each other and share an amicable relationship, not only for the sake of their children, but also for their own sake. If bitterness were allowed a seat in their hearts, I am sure I would not enjoy being with them.

We scheduled our dinners together as a group in specialty restaurants except on special nights when couples parted ways to have a romantic dinner alone. We became a loud, giggling fixture in Sabatini's Restaurant. Stacie was constantly being followed by the wine guy as he convinced her to drink wine from a shot glass and this funny looking man made all of us laugh.

We had lunch in the buffet restaurants along with hundreds of others, scooping the endless amounts of food lining the buffet table. The array contained all sorts of food from salad, dessert, drinks and a variety of main dishes.

We enjoyed watching Duwain join the karaoke bid for the Princess Idol and the team of Brian, Jill, Jeff, Barbara and Stacie joined the Family Feud. Though our team did not win, we proudly cheered for them as they made it to top finalists. I enjoyed watching them on stage and limelight, and had a great time seeing my friends and especially Jeff transform into different, spirited, happy human beings.

Into the night, we went dancing and watched shows and musical extravaganzas. We played bingo and went to the casino together. One thing I was proud of that no one else had on that trip was my lucky streak. I won over one thousand dollars in roulette. Though I had been in casinos before, I had only played slot machines. It was on this cruise that I was introduced to the roulette table. I recommend setting aside a specific amount of money and stopping when it runs out. I set aside 20 dollars worth of starting money

and came out more than 50 times more. Everyone was just amazed at how good I was at choosing winning numbers just like I had on our first horse race experience in Ocean City with Jeff and my kids! With Jeff beside me, he was like my lucky charm.

We had a glimpse of each other's bodies as we wore our swimsuits into the swimming pool and on the beach. My, my, the days of sexy swimwear, at least for me, were gone. I had to buy a swimsuit designed to hide my belly doubled up by sitting in front of the computer most of my waking time back home. I even put a blouse on top of it like "Maria Clara," a conservative reflection of a Filipino lady known for being demure and shy.

At any rate, I enjoyed Jill, Stacie, Brian, and Jeff's company at the beach. While the children snorkeled, I enjoyed wading into the cool water near the shore. My childhood trauma of swimming and almost getting swallowed by a river at a young age was a traumatic experience I have yet to overcome. With Jeff's help, I tried to overcome my fear during one of our swimming escapades, but swallowing water most of the time was not good. I went back under the tree with a blanket and read while watching them enjoy the blue water. We also got a chance to renew our friendship with Tess and Duwain. It was very rare we got this chance, so, there on the beach of St. Thomas, we had a great time while being serenaded with guitars and Caribbean songs by the natives. The beach vendors and children selling their crafts reminded me of the other world I used to live in, selling mangoes to sustain my living. Yet, on this Caribbean island, I was a princess being serenaded.

Some days, we split up on our activities. Depending on what we wanted to do each day, we checked with each other to see what we are doing and where we were going. There were lots of activities… snorkeling, whale watching, scuba diving, train rides, horseback riding, the list went on and on. We also went shopping, finding rare ethnic crafts not available in the U.S. We went swimming, toured scenic spots, and many other activities and programs to choose from in each island we visited.

The final night was marked by what seemed like a New Year's celebration atmosphere. All the men and women were in formal wear, partying the night away. Camera shots glittered with smiles as couples and families took a special moment to have a souvenir photo taken of their time together. With dancing and music everywhere, the lounge was filled with total excitement as the crowded room and balcony overlooking the lounge area was filled with vacationers watching the ship's crews perform its final showcase.

Champagne was literally overflowing as the crew poured it into hundreds of crystal glasses arranged on top of each other to form what looked like a crystal Christmas tree. Each crewmember and passenger took a turn pouring the champagne with the guided hand of the ship's captain. It was thrilling to watch and not one crystal glass fell while pounding music played and the champagne pouring was successfully completed when the last crystal glass was filled and marked with an olive to signify the completion of the spectacle. It was an awesome night.

The seven nights and eight days onboard the cruise and island hopping experience went by quickly. It seemed so short. As we walked down the long walkway to the end of this big, Princess Cruise trip, heading back to reality of our own world, we brought with us the tan in our skin, the renewed sparkle in our eyes, photos depicting many smiles, giggles and lots of laughter, a little pound here and there from the food we ate, but most of all, the joy in this

trip had given us special moments of friendships, happiness, caring and sharing.

The blessing of our Blue Ocean Getaway was a renewal of our love. The 676 sparkling crystal symbolizing the height of a successful beginning and a New Year in May 2004 inside this love boat was heartwarming to our souls. It was like reaching the top of a mountain to find a reward on the top for those who patiently wait.

While waiting for our numbers to be called to disembark the Princess ship, my cell phone rang! A new market to explore and a blue horizon await our creative, patient souls.

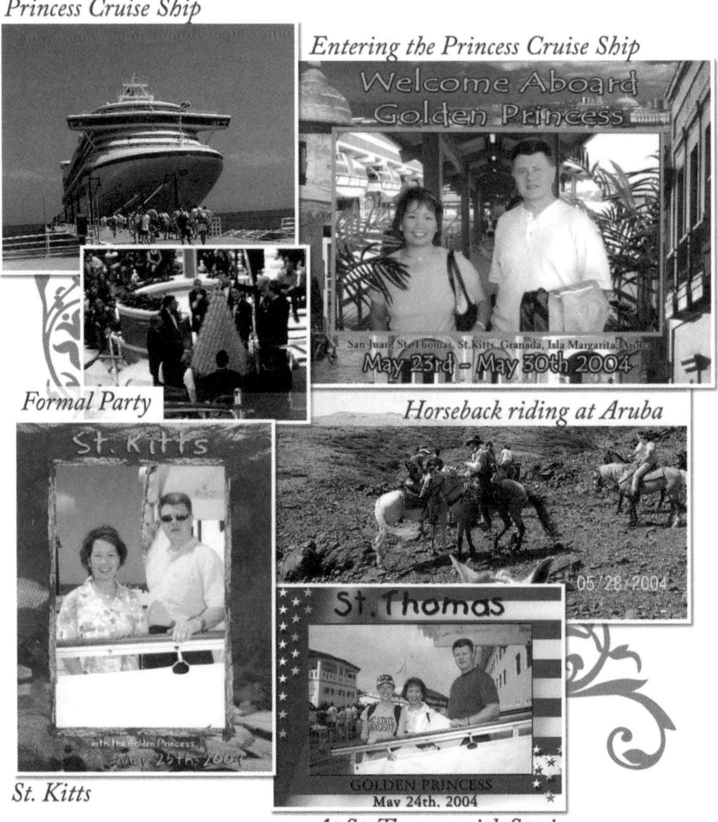

Princess Cruise Ship

Entering the Princess Cruise Ship

Formal Party

Horseback riding at Aruba

St. Kitts

At St. Thomas with Stacie

Blue Horizon

"If the sight of the blue skies fills you with joy, if the simple things of nature have a message that you understand, rejoice, for your soul is alive."
- Eleonora Duse

My life has been full of great abundance from the graces I have received from the good Lord. My life with my children and Jeff was transforming before my eyes like a cocoon of the past, turning into a beautiful butterfly of the future. I became surrounded by roses of love, blue oceans, and mountains with a perfect view of the blue horizon. They were no longer metaphors of my life, but a reality of the beautiful world in which I live. The before and after life experiences I had became more profound during recent years when I found love with Jeff.

Ours was a love filled with trust and faith. We had hopes and dreams and together we pursued them. It was a blue horizon, wide and open where we could paint our own future with boundless imagination. And we did.

Before we left on our trip to the Caribbean, we were waiting for the results of Jeff's offer on a 25-acre piece of land in New Market, Maryland. This dream started with another twist of fate.

Together, we spent many days going in and out of houses and properties, trying to figure out what we wanted. We shared our most intimate wishes of a dream house together. With practical Jeff and risk–taker Imelda, we managed to find a balance between what we could safely afford and what we could push. However, my life, as you know by now, has a lot of blessings guised in unexpected turns of events. This was also the case with our house hunting.

Jeff and I were planning to buy another house. One day, my usual, creative mind explored beyond the boundaries of what Jeff and I discussed. In the newspaper was an ad for a 25-acre piece of property in New Market. I said to Jeff, "Look, here's a 25-acre piece of land in New Market, for sale by owner. That's just 15 minutes away from here." We certainly did not know what we were doing. It was one of those things that simply caught my eye, and in an instant, I had envisioned it to have a beautiful home with an orchard in the backyard.

Jeff got excited and we called the owner. We went to see the lot and, right before our eyes, was the property we had dreamed about. It had a sweeping, mountain view with trees, spring water, and wide-open spaces. It was close to the main highways and other important roads, but the scenic view made it appear to be in a different peaceful world altogether. We knew from the very moment we saw the property that it would be the perfect piece of land on which to build our dream home.

The cost of the land was higher than what Jeff had budgeted for, so I did a lot of research on prices of similar properties and, sure enough, we learned this one had been well priced. I also called in a couple of mortgage bankers I knew personally and, bingo, we had Bank of America and Sandy Springs Bank more than willing to help us out. Before we knew it, a contract was written. Days passed and everything was going on, but then the assessment of the property could not be established because there had been no similar piece of land sold recently. We got stuck for several days with the owner not

willing to come down on the price, and the banks weren't willing to budge. But, as blessings were on our side, the day we exited the Princess Cruise, Jeff's cell phone rang and the news, "You got the land!"

After much back and forth discussion, the owners, Liz and Joe, agreed to sell the land for $50,000 less than the original price and simply agreed with the bank's assessments. Jeff settled the land with both our names in the title.

It was another blessing filled with lots of opportunities. A year later, after a sharp increase in real estate, the land was valued much higher than what we had paid for it. With the plan of building our dream house together, Jeff and I went back and forth to see the property on weekends. It became our great getaway as we parked the truck on the highest point of the land, or what we called the crest, overlooking the sweeping mountain view. We were transformed as the blue sky witnessed our dreams for a beautiful home and a vineyard.

Though our past consisted of two different worlds, our futures looked beyond onto the same path surrounded by a blue horizon and dreams lifting our souls. Jeff started going to vineyard and wine making seminars. After all, as a child growing up in Pennsylvania, his father had grown grapes and made his own wine. This was a time to fulfill his innermost dream. It was also my time to help him the best I can and in whatever capacity he wishes me to be involved.

It had been 20 years since I left the Philippines in 1984, and I now stood in America, the land that stood witness to the prosperity of my life with Jeff. I took a deep breath as I dreamed of my future on this land with its breathtaking mountain view of the blue horizon, clear sky, fresh air, and green foliage. The poignant memory of my Smoky Mountain of trash in a landfill that stood as a metaphor to my childhood poverty is now gone.

Like the land in New Market, our life is an open farm and a new market full of potential opportunities. It is up to us to plant whatever seeds we want to see growing in this beautiful, wide land. Not too many people can see the bountiful beauty such a property can provide. The fertile soil provides clean land, just waiting for us to plant. Whatever dreams come into our minds and hearts, the land will be there for us to till its soil and grow to our hearts' desires. In no time, the fruits of our labor would show as the spring greets us hello and as we reap whatever our imagination has generously planted in the rich soil beneath our feet. As the bible says, "We reap what we sow."

Jeff's plan was to have a vineyard, a house that would be a home to both of us with a tropical pool and grotto in the back of the house to continuously give our gratitude to our Lord through Our Lady where we frequently visited on Mount Saint Mary. Together, our future was a wide, blue horizon and it was up to us to seize it.

The 25-acre land in New Market overlooks a wide horizon and a road just off the main highway.

Jeff and Imelda at Napa Valley, California (July 2005). They visited several vineyards to see for themselves what the New Market property may look like.

Our Lady in White and Blue

"To one who has faith, no explanation is necessary. To one without faith, no explanation is possible."
- St. Thomas Aquinas, 1225-1274

I believe it is not only our emotional and physical attraction that has made my relationship with Jeff last for over a dozen years. After all, the law of gravity can pull down our physical body, and when the dust has settled and everything is done on earth, what is left are the spiritual connections we have made with the people we truly cared about. We come on earth barefooted, and we live this earth barefooted one more time. Our hearts and souls will speak of the richness of our legacy on earth as individuals and as partners, wives, husbands, friends or parents of those we truly love.

Spiritually, Jeff and I are truly connected with each other. We love going together to St. Mary's Grotto. It is a place we frequent to pray for our special intentions and give thanks for the blessings we receive. Together, this is our special church and special place to make our wishes for each other and for our family, but most importantly, to express our gratitude.

The National Shrine Grotto of Lourdes is located in Emmitsburg, Maryland, about 20 minutes away from the City of Frederick. The holy Grotto is in a sacred spot and a romantic part of the mountain.

The Shrine attracts thousands of pilgrims each year from all over the world. Built in the early 1800's, it is the oldest grotto that marked the beginning of the Catholic Church in the United States. A 25 ft. great gold leaf statue of Our Lady sits on top of a 95-ft tower called the Pangborn Memorial Campanile, welcoming everyone into the solitude of this peaceful place. The pathways leading to the Grotto and St. Mary's Chapel are lined with trees and the station of the cross. Directly behind and several steps up the highest point is a statue of Jesus Christ. In front of the holy Grotto are candles and a marble stone that says:

For those who believe in God, no explanation is necessary.
For those who do not believe in God, no explanation is possible.

For several years, the shrine has been witness to the many blessings Jeff and I have received. It is our spiritual retreat and a place we go to for thanksgiving and special prayers. Sometimes, we bring bottles to get holy spring water from the faucet located across from a replica of Saint Lourdes, which entails standing high in the man-made pond. Before and after each interview I have had in my career, I visited this grotto to give thanksgiving and ask for guidance from our Lord. When someone in our family or one of our friends is not well, we say our prayers and intentions.

My faith has never failed me, and I truly believe that, because even when I did not receive what I wished for, sure enough, something better was waiting for me around the corner. Throughout my life's journey, especially during the past twelve years since meeting Jeff, my life has been filled with many opportunities that have enriched the lives of my children, my family and myself.

Though I frankly cannot claim I have been a consistently faithful person in attending church on Sundays, I can honestly say every day

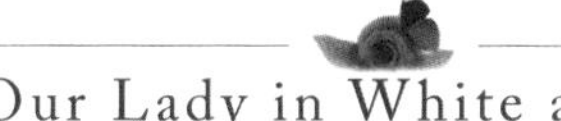

of my life is filled with thanksgiving and prayers for all the good things that have come my way. My actions and behavior towards others reflect upon my strong faith.

We are thankful to be near this historic grotto. Our Lady has witnessed our love and ardent praises as we pray to God and Blessed Mother Mary. In return, we have been showered with what Our Lady in blue and white represents… peace and love.

A 25 ft. great gold leaf statue of Our Lady sits on top of a 95-ft tower called the Pangborn

Memorial Campanile, welcoming everyone into the solitude of this peaceful place.

Entrance to the pathway leading to the Shrine.

Millions of people come to the grotto to get spring water for their loved ones and for those who are sick.

The 25 ft. great gold leaf statue of Our Lady overlooks the Mount Saint Mary University and Seminary.

A colorful door graces the St. Mary's Chapel.

The Grotto of Our Lady

Bronze statue of Jesus Christ located at the highest point and behind the Grotto.

Excellence is symmetry of perfection as grand as the mountain, as wide as the ocean, and as sparkling as any gem. It is an ideal state we view within our mind and we continuously aspire for.

E***xcellence***. Life is full of opportunities to find the very best both in our personal and professional lives. How we view the world depends on our past and current circumstances. How we define excellence will also be largely based upon our expectations, as well as our internal and external environments. Having delicious food the next day will be excellent for those who are constantly struggling for their daily basic necessity, while for others it may mean far beyond eating and drinking. Whatever it is, excellence is something in our mind that we continuously aspire for.

To me, excellence is measured not only by what I gained in life but also by what I feel from my heart and soul. It also means love, happiness, and living my life to its fullest, and sharing these beautiful things with those I care about.

Forever: In My Own Way

Destiny is your life's journey. Where you were may reflect upon your future, but you have the power to change the course of your journey and reach where you vividly envisioned you want to be.

For over a dozen years, Jeff and I have ventured in many places we have never been before. Together, we accomplished a lot as best friends, business partners, and most important as soul mates. The song entitled *Forever* is a song we wrote together to describe the impact of our lives to one another. It is our own way of sharing our feelings for one another, but in a deeper sense, it also speaks about our faith that has blessed us with rich life's journey. Time will tell what our destiny would finally be. But in our heart song, we call it, "*Forever.*"

FOREVER

By Jeff Snively and Imelda Roberts

Forever, you will always be in my life
And forever,
You will always be here with me
For you are my light in times of dark night
Forever, you will always be my light!

Forever,
you will always be in my heart
And forever,
You will always be here with me
For you are my life, my everything.
Forever,
you will always be in my heart!
You inspire me…
You give me strength
You hold my hand …
When I need a helping hand

You make me feel so very special
You are my love
You are my life.

For you light my night
In my own way, you will always be in my life!

For you light my night
In my own way,
You will always be in my life!

In my own way,
You will always be in my heart!

38 Unlocking My Pain in San Francisco

San Francisco's Golden Gate Bridge stood as a witness and a metaphor to my life. My port of entry in 1984 was no longer a metaphor; it is a reality. I have traveled a long journey and have had a long climb. I weathered rainy and cold winter days, but I am now enjoying real and glorious times in America. I have passed the chilling test with the bursting of chilled champagne, mellowed just in time to celebrate a Fourth of July.

In July, 2005, a few months before my 50th birthday, Jeff and I visited San Francisco one more time. It is Jeff's favorite place. It is an absolutely beautiful city that immediately captured our hearts. Since my last visit to the park, where I stood over 20 years ago, overlooking the water and the Golden Gate Bridge, I noticed the fog was still there. The incredible view that had given me hope when I first arrived in America was still there. The long, but beautiful, vibrant, red bridge that had been a witness to the lonely journey I had made way back in 1984 was still there. Nothing had changed physically. But, amazingly, time and love had done a lot to change the loneliness that used to dominate my life. Certain pieces of my pain were now finally opened, lifted, and healed.

Holding hands with Jeff in San Francisco on a summer day in July, 2005, was a stark contrast to the chilly day of April, 1984, when I had been all by myself, braving the chilling test of coming to a country I had never imagined, but would welcome me with abundance, love, and the greatness of people who now surround my life. Even those who tested my being were a part of my victory. To all of them, I raise my head up high to look at the bridge one more time and say, "Thank you from the bottom of my heart!"

I certainly don't know what the future holds for Jeff and me, but one thing is sure. The San Francisco Golden Gate Bridge will forever be a witness to our life together and to the transformation of my life from poverty to personal prosperity… from loneliness to a loving life of selflessness.

We will sing our heart song that bonded my once barefooted soul with my soul mate. In our own way, the song Jeff and I wrote together, speaks of our love for our Creator, for our family, and for each other and our future!

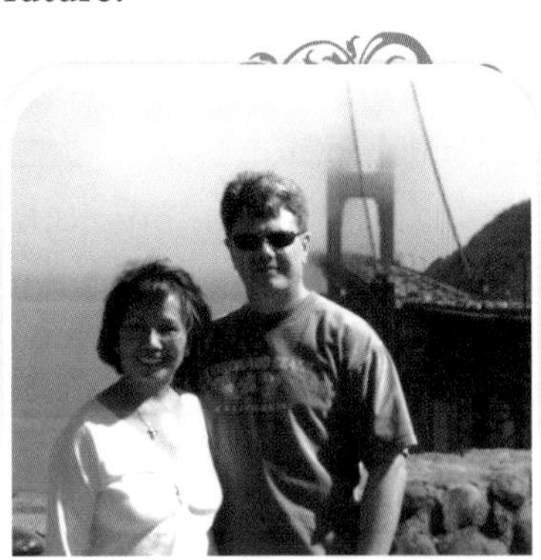

San Francisco is our favorite city. Jeff and I find this place extra special in many ways. The Golden Gate Bridge shown on the background was a witness to my humble beginnings in America. Revisiting this place with Jeff, during our 4th of July vacation speaks of the personal transformation of my life.

39 Washington, DC: Back to Where I Began

On November 21, 2005, I received an invitation to speak in December, before 300 public leaders and employees in the District of Columbia. I was invited to speak about leadership in this one-day leadership conference seminar including special qualities that make effective leaders including sharing perspectives, experiences, solutions, and strategies to participants.

Coinciding with this invitation was my self-imposed deadline to finish this book within 40 nights. This invitation sparked the question, "What will I talk about at this Leadership Conference?" I was having a feeling of déjà vu going back to Washington, D.C. The event was a stark contrast to my past in our country's capital, for it was also in December, 21 years ago that I began my first government job in December 1984, as domestic help at the Embassy of Australia.

Thinking of this December event, I envisioned myself sharing the power of the human soul as a moving force toward leadership excellence...

Leadership and the Power of the Human Soul

Today is a special celebration on leadership and sharing special attributes of a successful leader. With so many great public leaders present today, I am sure this event has given you diverse insights you can apply and take back to work.

But, as graduates of the public management leadership program you already know leadership concepts. I also believe that knowledge and skills are things that you can easily acquire from others. So what I want to share is a more profound insight that only you can provide - your own personal courage and spirit through the power of the human soul. I believe that if these personal attributes resonate in your heart, you can fly like an eagle, high in the sky and take your journey anywhere you wish to go.

You are here because you do have the knowledge needed for you to assume the roles as public leaders. You have the attributes of the human mind that guide you in making leadership decisions affecting your community and your organizations. Given this, instead of sharing strategies that you can easily learn by yourself, let me share with you personal experiences that may show you the highest point a human soul can possibly achieve. For I believe that if I do this, I would finally share with each one of you my biggest secrets of success and my heartfelt gratitude in coming and living here, twenty one years ago, in the most powerful city in the world, Washington, DC.

You and I live in the same region. Washington, DC was my home when I arrived here 21 years ago as an immigrant. I lived in places like Dupont Circle, Foxhall Road, Chevy Chase Circle and Cleveland Avenue. Yes, folks, these are rich neighborhoods in DC I called my home at that time. The only difference - you are the master of your homes, and I was a maid in these homes.

Yes, my dear friends, I started in America right here in Washington, DC as a domestic helper. Despite my management experience in San Miguel Corporation, the Philippines' largest multinational corporation with 30,000 employees, and Southeast Asia's number one publicly traded company, this stature did not deter me from starting all over again in my new country.

This experience takes me to one important lesson of leadership, the humility of spirit. The power we gain in any leadership position is temporary, one day you may have a job, the next day you may not have one. One day you win an election, the next day you may lose. But the humility of spirit is a strength you can use to stand up every time you fall. Humility in spirit can also balance the mind and the soul. It can protect you from egoism, greed, and arrogance – three fatal evils that can lead to leadership death such as the fallen executives involved in the $3.8 billion dollar case of fraud by communications giant WorldCom. In the same way, the collapse of energy powerhouse Enron was attributed to leaders of this company lying about profits and exalting themselves higher than they truly were. In the end, the Security and Exchange Commission, as you all know, started a wave of investigations that shocked our country with many innocent lives affected because of greed. In all these cases, it was a small group of clever executives we call leaders who manipulated the hard work of thousands of unknowing employees into their own greedy ambitions.

We can't call these executives - leaders. True leaders take a higher road that would exalt the human spirit instead of toppling it down. Indeed, to be an effective leader, we must not let humility fly out of our heart. Otherwise, we may end up in a place we don't want to be, lose the people that made us who you we are today, and worst, lose our own soul.

Next, I want to share another trait that I think separates great leaders from those who are not – those who use their abilities to benefit the needy and to overcome adversity. These, I believe are among the most powerful secrets of a successful leader.

In my lifetime, I have used adversity, as my driving force to find prosperity in my life, be it in my profession or in my personal life.

I have learned and have been inspired by world known leaders not at the time they were doing well, but when they were in a state of adversity, or when they are serving their community. For the best leaders in the world in the likes of former President Jimmy Carter, Nelson Mandela, Mother Theresa, and even the first female President of the Philippines, the former President Corazon Aquino, and many other great leaders of the world became known not when they were doing well, but when they served the homeless and the poor, and led themselves and their community in times of adversity. Given the state of our country and the world, overcoming adversity and thinking of more than a billion poor children in the world who truly need us, are what I think will define the next greatest leaders of our generation.

Adversity is not new to me. I felt it and lived it from the time I was young.

Through a government scholarship I attained in the City of Manila, I completed my college education paying only fifty pesos or an equivalent of one dollar per semester.

If not for the government scholarship and for the people in government who believe that even the poorest people in our community deserve a place in this earth, I would not have a stake in the land I now call my own land. Believing in what you and other people can become is another lesson in leadership.

It is for this very reason why since I arrived in Washington, I dreamt of working for the government and educational system. This brings me to other important leadership lessons. You must have a purpose. You must be passionate, and you must be committed to what you want to do in life, otherwise you will be unhappy. If you are not happy, you cannot expect to radiate enthusiasm for your employees to emulate you. If you are in public service, you must put yourself in

the heart of the public. These to me are important attributes of great public leaders. You cannot serve government if you want to make big money and take care of yourself alone.

From my roles in Georgetown University, Arlington County government, Enoch Pratt Free Library in Baltimore City, to cabinet official in the City of Frederick, to serving 19 member jurisdictions in this region, and leading a consortium of 28 states in the entire country, I have seen time and time again people who are changing the course of history, and touching the life of one poor child, one abused woman, one homeless family and one financially needy student. They made a difference and all of us could do that too!

Just like the people who gave me their compassion, as a homeless scholar in the Philippines, I would not be speaking to you today if not for the public leaders who had the great vision to see that even the poorest of the poor have a place in our community. We can repay the government institution that trusted and believed that we too can make a difference in government by not just leading this region and this nation through our mind but also leading with a vision, leading through our hearts, and leading through our souls.

All of you work here in DC serving the government officials and the general public. I also worked and started my official government job 21 years ago here in DC. Perhaps the difference was I was a domestic help to the Ambassador of the Embassy of Australia.

As an immigrant of this country way back then, I was invisible. I bet none of those dignitaries and prominent officials I served with food remember me. But, I took this experience with enthusiasm and gratitude. After all I ate the same food as dignitaries, why would I complain for this was my choice. But more important, I accepted the job knowing it is just a part of my life's journey. I also had a powerful vision in my heart and in my spirit, that one day, I would join other government officials and public leaders just like you are -- not serving food for the stomach but serving food for the human spirit and for serving one recipe of success – gratitude and enthusiasm in whatever you choose to do in life.

Though dignitaries and public leaders would not remember I served them food for their stomach, while I was employed in my first government job in the embassy, I hope you will remember me for serving you with the greatest food any human being can have – the food of the human SOUL – an acronym which stands for S, for selflessness, O for obedience, U for unity and L for love.

Though each one of us is different from each other, we have one thing in common. This one thing can take your dreams to unimaginable places. This one thing can give you strength to overcome adversity. This one thing can bring you to the height of leadership. This one thing is the power of the human soul.

For when you believe and practice the power of the human soul, you have achieved a leadership place higher than any leadership position you could ever assume.

Before and After – Coming Full Circle

The speech I prepared sparked many memories of my humble beginnings in the Washington, DC area. It was also a full realization that over two decades after I first arrived in this city, there are indeed many things I need to be grateful for. Like the before and after photos of my life captured in this book, my life stories are testaments to the power of the human spirit and when we unleash the power within us anything is possible!

Over Two Decades After...
Before and After Memorable Photos

Revisited in 2005, this rented room was a witness to my young days as a student. It was located near the poorest neighborhood in the Philippines with bars and cardboards to cover our room from the outside. Overcoming poverty is a testament to those who gave me a chance for a good education, and more important my faith and beliefs growing up in a God-loving country of the Philippines.

Our house in Frederick, Maryland is a far cry from my humble beginning. My family and I have been blessed. Our life has been a testament to leaving the American dream.

Our house in Maryland is almost 4000 sqm. It's garage is almost the same size as the rented room where I used to live in my college days in the Philippines.

Taken in 1985 when Alberto (7) and Andrea (6) lived in my sister's house in the Philippines while I was a starting a new life in America for their future.

After almost two decades, Andrea and Alberto blossomed to be beautiful adults. Taken during their school prom nights.

In 1984, I started working here in America as a babysitter and a maid. I did all the household chores, took care of the baby, including the family's dog.

In December 1984, I worked with the Embassy of Australia as a maid at the Ambassador's residence at Cleveland Avenue, Washington, DC. Taken with George, my favorite butler, in the Embassy's dining room. During those days, I lived in the Ambassadors residence and used to work even on holidays.

After 20 years, we now have our own dogs. As a single parent, I took care of my own kids instead of other people's kids.

Alberto and Andrea are now both professionals living their own life's journey.

I now work as Director of Human Resources serving local governments in the Washington, DC area. I can now enjoy my holidays with my friends and loved ones. With Carmen Canda, my cousin who has been a witness to my colorful life in America. (December 2005)

In 1984 to 1985, I worked as a domestic help at the Embassy of Australia. Part of my job was serving food for dignitaries during special events hosted by Ambassador Sir Robert Cotton (second, back row) and his wife Mrs. Eve Cotton (with glasses).

Speaking in front of graduates of the Institute for Regional Excellence (2005).

From serving food for the stomachs, I am now involved in regional and national leadership roles with opportunities to serve food for the human spirit and my recipe for success. Taken with colleagues during the District of Columbia's Leadership Day. (2005)

My mom in a rented house with her grandchildren.
Taken in 1984.

My mom, with my sisters and brothers. Taken in her own house in the Philippines. (2004)

Before I bought a house for my mother, she was moving from one house to another, including this nipa hut in the province of Arayat, Pampanga I revisited in 2003.

In 2003, I bought a house and a rental property for my mother. Now fully paid, this house has also been a home to Roma, my sister and my brother.

Roma was a thin shy girl when I first saw her back in 1999. In December 2003, I took her in to our new house in Quezon City, Philippines to live with my mother.

Now in special education classes, Roma has blossomed to be a beautiful confident girl. Whereas before she would shy away from people and could not speak a word, so many great things had happened to Roma. This speaks of the power of the human spirit. We just need to give a child like Roma a chance to live her life to the fullest. Taken in January 2005 when I last went to the Philippines.

Winning Moments and Other Memorable Career Events

Imelda with Marci Shimoff, one of the best selling authors of the Chicken Soup for the Women's Soul. Imelda draws inspiration from Marci during the writing of her book. (Women's Conference in Frederick, Maryland, October 2005)

Receiving the Jack Foster Executive of the Year Award, June 2001, Local Government Personnel Association of Washington-Baltimore Region

With her former staff at the City of Frederick during the "Best and Brightest Annual Local Government Personnel Association Awards Ceremony" held in May 1999.

With Tony Gardner, former Arlington County Manager, receiving a Countywide Exceptional Employee Award. Arlington County Government. (1993)

Imelda with Hon. William M. Gardner, New Hampshire Secretary of State, author and New Hampshire Primary Expert. Imelda considers it a great honor to meet Hon. Gardner during a conference she attended in New Hampshire. (2005)

Receiving Ambassador's Award for "being a source of inspiration and hope beyond the boundary of COG" from Michael Rogers, former COG Executive Director, and Hon. Bruce Williams, Council member, City of Takoma Park. (February 26, 2002)

With former Maryland Governor Parris Glendening and members of the Maryland Information Technology Board. Imelda was a recipient of the "Vision and Dedication in Technology in Maryland" for three consecutive years, 1995-1997 for her volunteer efforts in technology.

Imelda was one of only 12 honorees during the First HR Leadership Award of Greater Washington Baltimore. Also shown is Maureen Bunyan, primary anchor for WJLA-TV, as Emcee for this event. (June 2002)

Imelda receiving an Outstanding New Employee Award from the former Mayor Jim Grimes in her capacity as the Director of Human Resources for the City of Frederick. (1998)

2005-2006 Executive Council Officers

With officers of the Executive Council, National Certified Public Manager® (CPM) Consortium. As the Chair of the entire CPM Consortium, Imelda considers it a privilege to lead a national organization dedicated to positively impacting public management in the country through accredited training and leadership development programs. The Consortium is comprised of members from 28 states, the USDA Graduate School, and the Virgin Islands.

OVER TWO DECADES AFTER:
Lasting Friendships and Gratitude to My Angels

In many ways you touched my soul with your kindness, confidence and belief in what I can do and share with this world. With gratitude, I pass on to others the image of you and the gem of friendship you engraved in my heart for others to see the beauty in YOU!

Thank you for touching my life!

My Family

My family in America – my kids, Andrea, Alberto; my love, Jeff Snively, and his children Brian and Stacie

My family in the Philippines

My Close Relatives

With my close relatives in America – Asuncion, Canda, Paterno, Gironella, Buan and Kerstetter Families.

Seated and beside me is my aunt Rita Paterno, my mother's only sister.

My Career Angels

Pat Connelly, Georgetown University, (1989-1991)

Ray Vanneman, Arlington County Government (1991-1994)

Carla Hayden and Gordon Krabbe, Enoch Pratt Free Library (1994-1998)

Former Mayor Jim Grimes, The City of Frederick (1998-2000)

Michael Rogers, Former Executive Director, Metropolitan Washington Council of Governments (2000-2003)

David Robertson, Metropolitan Washington Council of Governments (2003 - Present) Also in photo are Imelda's staff, Larissa Williams and Janet Ernst.

Not in photos are Haydee Albayda, David Santos, and Ricky Bunuan, former bosses in San Miguel Corporation, Philippines - (1977- 1984)

My Friends and Former Officemates at San Miguel Corporation Who Helped Me in the Production of the Barefooted Soul

Susan Vidal, my friend from Makati, Philippines

Soc Tiongson, my friend from California

Johnny Pecayo, my friend from California, Tony Barcelo, my friend from Quezon City, Philippines

Best Friends

Tess Dillon, my friend from Virginia.

Eleanor Alfonso, my friend from Virginia.

Myrna Juat and Abot Mendoza, my best friends since college, Manila, Philippines.

Mary Din, my Cambodian friend from Arlington, Virginia.

Farimah DesRosiers, my Iranian friend at Georgetown University who now lives in Colorado.

Josie Collins, best friend from college. What a small world! Photo taken when I unexpectedly saw Josie and her family at Universal Studios, Florida while I was on vacation with Jeff and my kids. Josie lives in New York.

Thank you for touching my life. I appreciate your presence in my journey as I pursue my life's destiny!

Destiny is your life's journey. Where you were may reflect upon your future, but you have the power to change the course of your journey and reach where you vividly envisioned you want to be.

D***estiny***. Do you believe in fate or something that you never planned or beyond human control? Despite your best efforts, did you end up somewhere, or you are doing something that you did not even thought about before? Indeed, our life on earth is complex and has a lot of surprises. Our overall circumstances or condition in life may sometimes puzzle us. At the same time, the choices and how we handle our everyday life will also dictate who we are, what we become, and our totality as one individual. And when things are not going the way we want them to be, we still have the power to change the course of our journey.

Our Creator has given us the mind, the heart, the body to live a full life. It is up to us to discover our full potentials, envision where we want to be, and live a life in harmony with what is truly our purpose on earth.

XI My Soul-Defining Moments

SOUL

***S**elflessness as you share the innate abilities you have in you to touch those around you, most especially the poor, the sick and the hungry.*

***O**bedience in the rule of law, the ethics of your profession, all those you respect, and whatever Higher Power that you believe and that moves the human soul.*

***U**nity for peace and for the sake of family, region, nation and the world.*

***L**ove for yourself, love for your family, love for your community, and love for your country.*

A New Day ... A New Life's Meaning

Whatever you have gleaned from this book, I hope you will remember most these last chapters of this book. Where I was before and where I am after all these life experiences are molded first and foremost by my inner faith in God and the parts He played in my life.

As I begin a new day and a new chapter in my life, I am filled with hopes for a better life for my family and the rest of the world. The Barefooted Soul inspires a new meaning and a sense of purpose that I will aspire to live by.

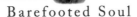

Our Creator gave us the ability to live the life He has entrusted to us, regardless of our circumstances. The poverty of our life, our hearts and our minds, are states of life we can overcome. We were given free will to do something with these most important elements of our lives no one else can take away from us. Our hearts can feel, our minds can think and our bodies can take action to overcome whatever poverty we face in our lives – be it financially, emotionally or mentally.

Our success is proportionate to the belief we have within us, the aspiration, enthusiasm, energy and passion we put into our dreams. Envisioning destiny, resolving and overcoming obstacles with optimism and doing so with a sense of excellence have proven to be a powerful strategy that has molded who I am today. Whatever it is you believe in your heart and soul, I hope you would pursue it, in the end, you achieve.

I also believe there is no such thing as a perfect world, only a perfect state of mind. It is up to us to shape how we view the world we live. If we think it, we become it. But, most important, it is the state of our own mind and inner soul that will dictate the kind of world we will live in.

The Barefooted Soul challenges each one of us to unleash our innate abilities and the power within us. It also reminds us that we have the power to change the course of our lives and our world.

I hope you have now seen what I meant when I say in the beginning of this book that the Barefooted Soul transforms my once dark secrets into a source of reflection, fuels strength from within me to break away from being a maid to life's daily syndrome of pain, stress, and misery, to finding the ONE higher purpose that will fill my inner soul.

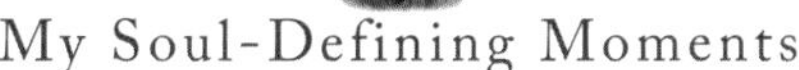

I have used this opportunity to turn my own barefooted soul inside of me as an opportunity to define who I am and what I want to be as a person.

I now know, one cannot expect to fully live within the SOUL's attributes until the pain of the barefooted soul can truly fly away and lift our spirit from the burdens of our own making. I believe we need to set ourselves free from whatever heavy load we carry within ourselves in order to achieve authentic selflessness, obedience, unity and harmony with the people and the world around us, and in order to truly love.

Indeed, I strongly believe the barefooted soul can move our spirit to unimaginable places where we can finally see the highest points in our lives and hopefully leave our own footprints for a better world.

40 The Barefooted Soul Forty Nights Journey

"The Bible is clear that God considers 40 days a spiritually significant time period. Whenever God wanted to prepare for his purposes, he took 40 days... The next 40 days will transform your life."
- Rick Warren, The Purpose Driven® Life

November 28, 2005

"Today is a jubilee," as my dear friend, Susan, who inspired me to write, said with glee. Today, I write the last chapter of my story – My Soul-Defining Moments.

It is hard for me to say how one may view my life, my angels, and my barefooted soul's defining moments. The way you view it, I am sure, will be through your own lenses, your own fabric of imagination, feelings and experiences. The stories you have read were all true, not a fiction, not a fantasy. My reflections are my sense of perspective I can honestly say I actually lived, smelled, touched and felt.

I hope when you think of the Barefooted Soul, you will think more about how a barefooted soul becomes the moving force that takes us to the goodness in our hearts as we mature in our spiritual journeys. It is the courageous soul that brings victory in the midst of poverty. It is for those who seek a purposeful life where destiny is eternity.

A Summary of Special Gifts: From a Maid to a Life Made in Heaven

"Now that my life experiences have transcended every dream or expectation I ever imagined, I know for sure that we have to keep transforming ourselves to become who we ought to be."

- Oprah Winfrey

What began as a book about my life, my angel and my soul defining moment became bigger than I thought. After 40 nights of reflections, the Barefooted Soul is not just a book about me – it is a story of the human soul and finding the special gifts within us. In itself, the 40 nights became a journey in isolation to honest reflection. It is a trip that took me from my childhood to my adulthood and a rediscovery of beautiful characters along the way. The characters are real with new players joining me in this new journey. Most important, I clearly saw the most prominent faces that became the main characters of my life's drama.

Being able to complete 40 stories, reflections and songs about the human soul in 40 nights is a revelation of the power of the human spirit. If you think it, you can achieve it. It is a discovery of who I really am – a writer and a musical storyteller to uplift the human soul.

It is also reliving my childhood dreams at last! Each one us has a dream that someday we want to be something or somebody. The Barefooted Soul is a testament to listening intently to the wind, feeling the rhythm within our soul, opening our eyes to the signs of the future, and reaching to the ONE purpose that GOD gave us. This is a powerful mandate not from anyone, but from our Creator. But how many of us listen to the wind and to the voice within us?

At age 50, I now know that my restlessness was caused by not paying attention to what He has entrusted me to do. I was busy

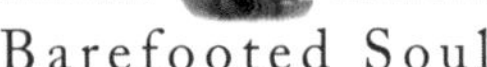

living and acquiring all the glory in my own profession, taking care of others in my work as HR Director, taking care of my family as a single parent, and my own family back home besieged by poverty. I consumed my own spirit with many things, enslaved myself to daily living, and forgot about the inherent things that were made for my heart. It took my own children and loved ones to remind me for what purpose I am on this earth.

Susan Vidal was sent as a messenger to tell me it is about time to write again to inspire others as I inspired her. My soul mate Jeff Snively was there to whisper, "Now, you can tell your other great stories." Even a friend, Johnny Pecayo, from Manila US Times, a true publicist, was there to publicize to the world what I was here for. Despite his busy schedule, he saw there was something in me that my own self has failed to see.

Other friends affirm the happiness they see in me since I've started this journey. New friends emerged while others touched my heart as they shared how I inspired them even with just limited information initially released in my website. The power of words can bind and inspire people.

But touching the core of a mother's heart is very powerful, for it was my own children who truly awakened the deepest part in my inner soul. In my hurried life, I had forgotten the child in me. Just like when I was a child, children's intuition and the power of the soul come from within us. It is up to us to seize it and accept what God has given us.

As I summarized God's gifts to me, indeed, these gifts were the ones that made me truly happy. He also tested me along the way to refine these gifts for when I am finally free, they will be in perfect harmony with what He has planned for me.

As a child, I was a creative soul. No one taught me how to write poems, but at seven, I was writing rhymes in the sand as a barefooted child in Apalit, Pampanga. In Legarda Elementary School, I was awarded the Most Prolific Writer of the Year. In Ramon Magsaysay High School, I was an award winning feature editor and writer. As a college scholar at Pamantasan ng Lungsod ng Maynila, I was sent to conferences for my ability to speak my heart and mind in public. These were my happy times I set aside to pursue other things to survive the circumstances of my life.

Poverty can take away a tremendous burden and toll on children, adults and anyone, but most especially our souls. The earth is filled with over a billion poor souls whose dreams were set aside to take care of day-to-day physical needs. Now that my worldly needs are taken care of, including basic needs of my family in the Philippines, I do not have an excuse. This new decade in my life is a time to seize lost times… lost dreams…and a lost soul.

As a child, I liked to sing and write poems. It took pain, adversity and 50 years later for me to be reminded I have music within my heart. As a child, I remember joining an amateur singing contest. With the Beatles' song, "Yesterday" and lyrics more appropriate for a man, I sang in front of hundreds of watchers in an open stage in Manila, Philippines. I hit the high note, but the giggles within the audience gave my voice a snag. I did not hit the next high note, and I was told to take a hike. I did.

For many years, I stowed away my musical notes in a box. Man's cruelty, weird looks and condescending attitude to creative souls was like a devil snatching my inner child. The chuckles and hurtful words made me keep my talents in me, until finally they kept jumping out of the hard dark box while I was in the shower, while on the MARC train, while asleep in the middle of the night, and into the computer. It took the adversity of the world and the tragic events of September 11, to bring them back to life.

But then, my spirit took another slumber. It was my epiphany

on my 50th year here on earth that woke them up again for the world and you to hear. The praises to the Lord within the Barefooted Soul came naturally like the beat of my heart. It is a lesson on the importance of nurturing our child's innate abilities to come out as naturally as the wind.

For one person who had never professionally written a song in her entire life, the songs you will hear that anchored the chapters in my book are a testament to God's Divine inspiration and intervention to sing praises to remind the world that we are children of God. The songs I completed in a few minutes, and as naturally as breathing, are all a testament to the innate gifts waiting to be shared to the world.

As a young lady, I joined the Balagtasan, a form of public speaking and debate. I was an undefeated contender for several consecutive weeks. I lost the contest. I was sad and forgot the happy times this experience had given my young life. Depression and sadness in our young life sometimes takes away the luster within us. Reclaiming the stage after 50 years is not too late.

As a new immigrant in America, I experienced being typecast as "compliant and soft spoken" Filipino. I was denied an opportunity for which I was highly qualified as a result of such prejudice. I resigned without a job replacement but used this adversity to prove it was wrong. Without experience in publishing, I stood up and spoke through a 319-page employment guide I researched and wrote all by myself. In only four months and at age 29 I was a published author. The prejudice moved my soul to write again. In the end the product of my heart and soul was a winning moment. The highest glory in addition to receiving several job offers following its publication was a strong message that Asians, just like any other immigrants and minorities, have a voice and place in this great country, the land of opportunity.

The 40 stories, reflections, poems and songs I wrote in 40 consecutive nights are a reminder on how prolific I was as a child. Colleen Wilson, my editor, reminded me I have exceeded the 60,000 words we initially expected in this book. It was now close to 90,000 words. Keeping too many things inside of us is a heavy load. We must unload them out of our system to truly be free.

Forty nights of reflections showed me how rich and blessed my life had been. The Barefooted Soul left me with special moments, powerful lessons, a realization of special gifts I have within me, and indelible footprints I would be proud to share to all and to leave behind on this earth!

This book, Barefooted Soul, is my soul-defining moment.

A Summary of Indelible Footprints in My Heart

Throughout my journey, my life has been sprinkled with the BAREFOOTED SOUL's inspirational quotes I gleaned from my own real stories. They are lessons that defined who I am today and what I continuously pursue to live a better life for myself and for those around me. You have come across these quotes in the beginning of each of the chapter of my life. They are what I call soul-defining attributes that are important to me – the acronym of the BAREFOOTED SOUL.

It is my strong belief that the BAREFOOTED SOUL defining attributes have a powerful place in our journey as we find our own place on this earth. I see them as footprints for a better world. I have also left the BAREFOOTED footprints after each chapter of my book with the hope that each chapter of my life leave an indelible footprint into your own soul.

As you read at the end of the chapter, My Soul-Defining Moment, I summarized the higher level of attributes and what SOUL means to me as I continue to seek a higher purpose in the things I do in life. It is a tall order, but with you and all others we can do it together.

Let the BAREFOOTED SOUL inspire you to unleash your inner gifts and leave behind your footprints for a better world!

Barefooted Soul

Footprints for a Better World

B
A
R
E
F
O
O
T
E
D
S
O
U
L

Belief — ***B***elieve in yourself and keep the faith within you. Believe that each of us have a special gift waiting to be discovered. It is up to us to unleash our innate calling.

Aspiration — ***A***spire to reach a cherished dream and a great ambition. You are the architect of what you want to become.

Resolution — ***R***esolve the issues of the heart and the mind as best as you can. The longer problems and pains linger in your life the more they pierce deeply into your heart. Claim your pain, and let your soul gain peace and strength from within.

Enthusiasm — ***E***nthusiastically perform whatever you choose to do in life including difficult life's tests; it fuels the heart to greatness.

Forgiveness — ***F***orgive even those who hurt you. It is in forgiving that the pain and agony within your heart finally finds peace.

Optimism

Optimism is an onward bound positive energy that lifts the spirit and where one sees and finds opportunity in the midst of difficulties. It is the light despite darkness, it is the smile within sadness, it is the laughter within our soul, and the wide wings that make us fly and soar against the wind.

Overcoming Adversity

Overcome adversity in life. Whether it is a tragedy, poverty of the heart, the mind, the spirit or poverty itself, nothing is greater than the beauty of life itself. The tenacity of human spirit cannot be underestimated. It is in difficult times when our spirit and courage rise and shine.

Tolerance & Trust

Tolerance is opening our hearts and minds to those who may be different from us, less fortunate than us, or who may believe differently from us. Tolerance of the heart means greater trust and understanding of the human being inside each one of us. Trust that there is innate goodness in people and that hope resides in each one of us.

Excellence

Excellence is symmetry of perfection as grand as the mountain, as wide as the ocean, and as sparkling as any gem. It is an ideal state and worth aspiring for.

Destiny

Destiny is your life's journey. Where you were may reflect upon your future, but you have the power to change the course of your journey and reach where you vividly envisioned to be.

BAREFOOTED SOUL

Seeking a higher ground through our SOUL...

Selflessness — **S**elflessness as you share the innate abilities you have in you to touch those around you, most especially the poor, the sick and the hungry.

Obedience — **O**bedience to the rule of law, the ethics of your profession, and to the Supreme Being that moves the human soul.

Unity — **U**nity for peace and for the sake of family, region, nation and the world.

Love — **L**ove for yourself, for your family, for your country and even for your enemy. The most powerful, free-living feeling that resides within us. Don't be afraid to love and be loved. Love is a great medicine for a bitter heart's adversity.

If we all do these, the storms of hatred, selfishness, greed, war, and all other evils that destroy our earth will vanish and once again our barefooted soul can fly away to a higher place, higher than any place we have ever been on earth.

We come to this world barefooted... we leave this earth barefooted – but our BAREFOOTED SOUL is a legacy we leave here on earth and will stay forever within the hearts of those we love.

I now leave behind BAREFOOTED SOUL – Footprints for a better world. I also leave you with two questions I've asked myself –

What would my future look like? What on earth would I leave behind?

I hope to see you in my next journey!

BAREFOOTED SOUL

My 40th night in completing the writing of this book was a perfect happy time. My night ended with what our future hold as I recall the last conversation my dear Jeff and I had with Matt Gilmore, an attorney and Jeff's son-in-law, about the 25-acre plot of land in New Market. It reminded me of the mountains, the blue sky, a vineyard, and something green that is soothing to the spirit I can gaze at while I write more stories to nourish my soul and share to the world. My favorite roses are blooming in spring and summer, the wind is breezy, the butterfly I've dreamt since I was a child is flying freely, and the morning is a fresh breath of air. Jeff will be on the veranda with his morning newspaper and a mug of hot coffee as he enjoys the beautiful vineyard he has been dreaming of. I envisioned both of us holding hand as we enjoy the pond and the grotto at our backyard that will be there to always remind us to say Thanksgiving to our Lord for the blessings, love and peace in our life.

The photo, Jeff took of me with blissful smile is a reminder of blessings, while the roses behind me speak of beauty and of thorns that surrounded my life. There is no perfect world I sigh, but I have to make the most out of the two worlds I live. My perfect paradise is my perfect state of mind – at peace with combining the very best of my two worlds. My life has been blessed with discovering my innate gifts and what this world means to me. I pass them on to you through this book, the Barefooted Soul and my heart songs!

No Perfect World, Only a Perfect State of Mind

Narration:
Dear Father,
We pray that in each and everyday
We count our blessings
And see this world as a better place to live in
Only in this way we could have a happy life.

I.
I've traveled long and far away
Now I see, there's no perfect world
Broken heart, broken dreams I hold
In my barefooted days, I found my way
In my soul, in my heart, my own perfect state of mind ...

II.
This is my soul-defining moment
The day I saw beyond my self
My soulful journey
where I can be truly free!

III.
Free to explore the world around
Free to live where dreams abound
Selflessly share to touch mankind
Freely reach your own perfect state of mind.

Refrain:
No perfect world, no perfect world
Only a perfect state of mind!
Can bring true peace, true joy for you and I

Repeat All
Let my Barefooted Soul
Inspire your own perfect state of mind!

###

See You in My Next Journey ...

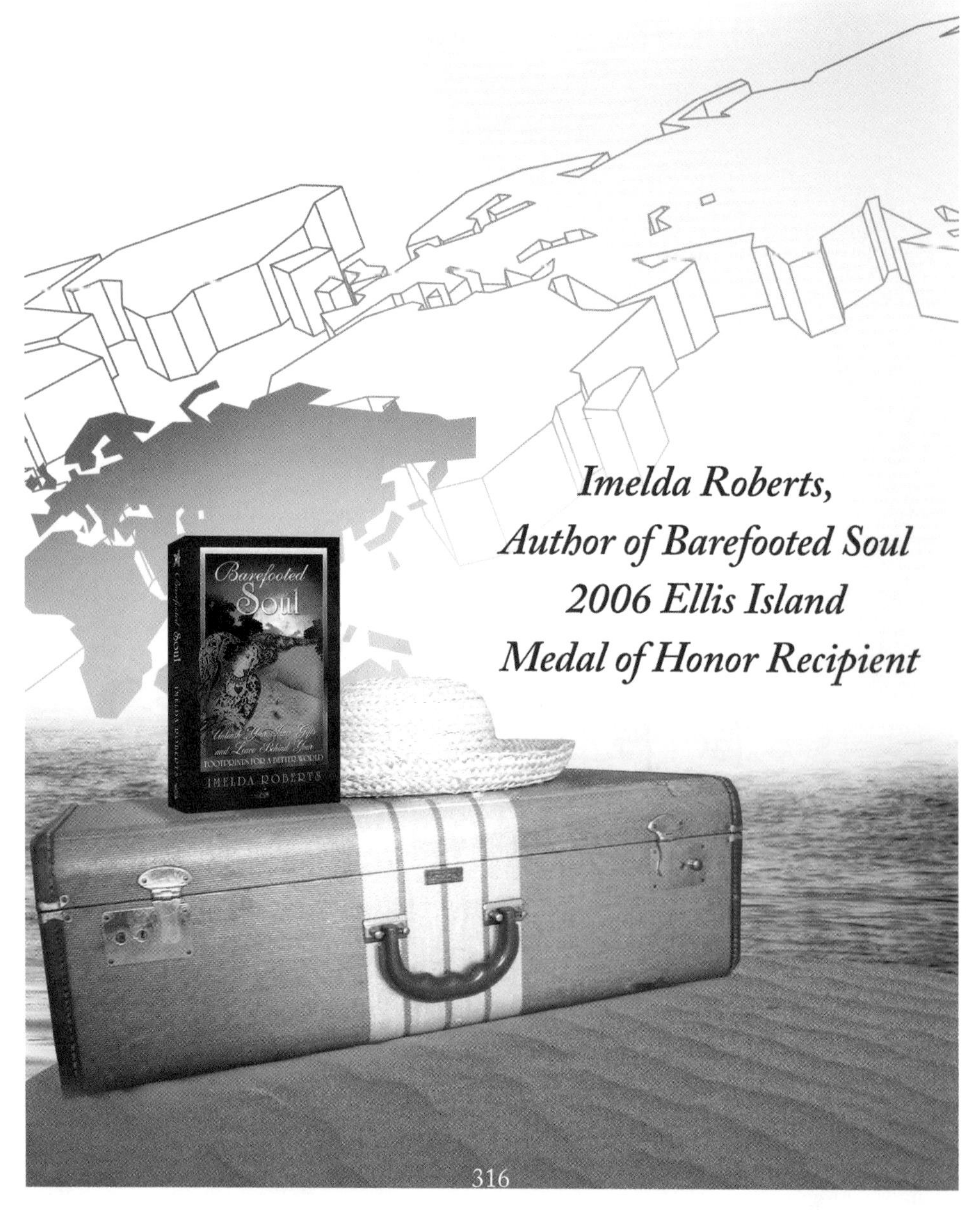

EPILOGUE

The Spirit of Ellis Island
From Barefooted Soul to the Bravest of Heart

March 29, 2006

"Congratulations on your selection as an Ellis Island Medal of Honor recipient for 2006. You will soon join the remarkable roster of distinguished American citizens who have received this singular honor."

- Rosemarie Taglione, Executive Director
National Ethnic Coalition of Organizations

Since sharing my Barefooted Soul journey with my family, friends, people important to me, as well as strangers, my life story resonated like a musical drumbeat with harmonious sound reaching as far as New York culminating in one of the highest honors I could ever dream of as an immigrant – an *Ellis Island Medal of Honor.*

In January 2006, over a month after I completed writing the Barefooted Soul, I received a nomination to the *Ellis Island Medals of Honor*. Considered as one of the most prestigious singular honors for Americans with recipients listed in the Congressional Record, the *Ellis Island Medals of Honor* was established "to pay tribute to the ancestry groups that comprise America's unique mosaic."

This remarkable recognition sponsored by the National Ethnic Coalition of Organizations representing 250 ethnic organizations, includes an impressive list of recipients such as at least six Presidents, Nobel Prize winners, well-known celebrities and other highly successful Americans. Being nominated was already an honor for my family and my native land, the Philippines. But being selected was totally overwhelming and humbling given where I came from.

On March 30, 2006, I received a special big envelope with a colorful imprint of an American flag. With excitement, I opened this beautiful package. Inside were impressive invitation and a letter from the National Ethnic Coalition of Organizations Foundation, Inc. (NECO), with one of the best news and the greatest honor of my life as a Filipino-American – a congratulation letter for being selected as a recipient of an ***Ellis Island Medal of Honor*** for 2006.

As a child it was my dream to see the Statue of Liberty. However, I never imagined that a day would come when I would stand side by side with many distinguished Americans to receive such a remarkable recognition. On May 13, 2006, in the very same place I saw in my childhood's dream, it is my greatest experience as an immigrant to receive the *Ellis Island Medal of Honor*. My heart was inspired by the tremendous thanksgiving for such an incredible gift.

Still relishing the joyful news about the awards ceremony and the gala night scheduled a few days after the launching of my book, I envisioned being in Ellis Island, New York. I saw the vision of distinguished Americans reaching the highest pinnacle of their lives being honored for their contributions to America. With sincere appreciation of another incredible journey and for being a part of this celebration, the lyrics of the "The Spirit of Ellis Island" was finished in less than an hour.

Another incredible door has been opened. I wonder what's waiting for me in my future?

The Spirit of Ellis Island

With burning hope in the American dream
You gave your heart like a new day in spring
Refreshing smile on each day you bring
Through sweat and tears touching your own skin.

From barefoot soul to the bravest of heart
You stood up high, with strength in your heart
Some lonely nights and faceless days
You kept your courage and found your way.

Chorus.
From barefooted soul to the bravest of heart
You stand for the spirit of Ellis Island
You are a child of this universe
You stand for the glory of your land
A pride and might of Ellis Island
Your footprints in our hearts and minds.

With burning hope for love, true liberty
You brave your fears through the Almighty
With passionate voice you stand high and tall
Dividing walls, your strength crushed them all.

Your day has come to rise and shine
Marching sound of America's freedom
Bursting fireworks in one great world
Ellis Island, we truly behold!
Repeat Chorus (2x)

From barefooted soul to the bravest of heart
You stand for the spirit of Ellis Island.

Paying Tribute to the Philippines

Now at 50, my life is at a crossroads, and I find myself looking back and then looking forward. Where will I be in the future? As a baby boomer in America, my life has been enriched in so many ways. I have experienced overwhelming life's graces and abundance so much so that even my family has been blessed. In a few years, my retirement will be on the horizon. My children, Alberto and

Alberto, Imelda and Andrea – November 2005.

Andrea, are now living their own life's journey and I am proud to have raised my two beautiful children.

My Filipino-American heart was nourished by my two beautiful worlds – America and the Philippines. The thought of sharing my story and incredible journey in America to my family, friends and others who may be touched by my book was heartwarming. I could not forget what happened one early morning a day after I finished writing the Barefooted Soul. I entered the shower room, and just as I always do when I am happy… I began to sing. But, instead of a familiar favorite American pop song, Filipino words started coming out of my belly, and just like that, a "Pinoy Boomer" was born. The melody and lyrics were completed in only half an hour, just in time for me to get out of the shower. It was an upbeat, almost "kenkoy"

(comedian) Filipino song about longing to visit my native land. It sounded just like me. The joyful, comedic personality my friends in SMC are familiar with. It was Imee! (Imee was a nickname my Filipino friends love to call me.)

I sprang onto the computer, bought the domain name ... and a future inscribed for a new Pinoy Boomer was reborn. There are lots of possibilities for what may be for this barefooted soul. One thing is sure: this baby boomer, or Pinoy Boomer, is up and about. It was a happy thought, for my barefooted soul is finally free!

"Pinoy Boomer" reflects a Filipino-American baby boomer dreaming of going back home relishing memories of the Philippines. I see myself enjoying summer to fall in America and traveling, and on winter time going home to the Philippines welcoming in my heart the tropical feeling of warmth and hospitality of my "kababayans" (fellow Filipinos). The time has also come to pay tribute to my beloved native land, the Philippines.

Pinoy Boomer

ni Imelda Roque Roberts

I
Ngayong ako'y tumatanda na
Pinoy Boomer sa Amerika
Ang puso kong naghahanap
Isang saglit ay nangarap.

II
Karitelang masarap sakyan
Maging jeepney ni Mang Julian
Hagikhikan at tawanan
Lahat ng iyan ay babalikan.

Refrain
Pinoy Boomer ako (2x)
Uuwi na sa bayan ko,
Pilipinas heto na ako
Pinoy Boomer ako (2x)
Tiya Dely ng puso ko
Humanda ka't heto na ako
Pinoy Boomer ako!

III
Tanda ko pa ang Divisoria
Intramuros at Tagaytay
May San Miguel Beer tuwing fiesta
Parang Pasko may lechon pa.

IV.
Tunay akong Pilipino
Hinahanap ang adobo
Halika na't umuwi na tayo
Pinoy Boomer, I'll see you
there!

V.
Kababayan may oras pa
Tumulong sa ating bayan
Ang Luneta'y naghihintay
Jose Rizal kumakaway.

Repeat Refrain

Adlib
Pinoy Boomer ako (2x)
Tiya Dely ng puso ko
Humanda ka't heto na ako
Pinoy Boomer ako (2x)
Uuwi na sa bayan ko
Pilipinas heto na ko
Pinoy Boomer ako (2x)
Tiya Dely ng puso ko
Humanda ka't heto na ako
Pinoy Boomer ako!

Barefooted Soul - Final Notes

My Love to All the Children in the World

It is my sincere hope that this book inspires you to think of the children of the world most especially the more than a billion children living in poverty today.

Through this book and my CD, it is my goal to reach out and share my love to all children all around the world. My song, ***We are the Children of the World***, has been translated into 17 languages. On the next pages are the Filipino version and the Spanish translation of this song. Both versions are included in my ***Barefooted Soul CD Album***.

Kami'y Anak ng Mundo

I

Kaming mga bata
Kami'y anak ng mundo
Umaawit upang
Ipadama'ng pag-asa
Kami'y anak ng mundo
Kami ang bukas
At lahat ng ito'y alay
Para sa inyo

(Chorus)
Habang iba ay lubos
And iba nama'y kapos
Habang iba'y sagana
Ang iba'y nagdurusa

Iba'y puno ng kaalaman
Iba nama'y kamangmangan
Kamangmangan nagdudulot ng
pagdurusa

II

Ang buhay ng tao
Ay aral sa mundo
Tingnan mo ang paligid mo
Ibukas ang palad mo
Ang buhay natin ay
Hubog ng tulad mo at tulad ko
Ating tanawin pag-asa ng
mundo

III

Kahit maging saan ka pa
Pilipinas o Amerika
Afghanistan o Africa
Tayo ay iisa

Habang iba'y sagana
Ang iba nama'y nagdurusa
Kamangmangan nagdudulot
ng pagdurusa

Repeat I
At lahat ng ito'y alay
Para sa inyo (3x)

CREDITS: Filipino Version of We are the Children of the World by Imelda R. Roberts (BMI) Filipino Lyrics by: Imelda Roberts, George "Butch" Albarracin, Aissa Corcoro, Paulo Masangkay, Christopher Cruz

Producers: George "Butch" Albarracin and Antonio Barcelo
Musical Arrangement: Michael DeLara
Studio: Venee Recording Studio, Manila, Philippines
Vocals: Roxanne Barcelo and Center for Pop Music Philippines' Angels: BG Albarracin, John Belarmino, Nino Non, Lenel Velasco, Jenaira Jalasco, Doreen Cardinal, Modelle Mae Ngking, Janet Terio

Somos Los Niños Del Mundo

Somos los niños
Somos los niños del mundo
Cantamos alfrente de sí
Compartir nuestro
amor y esperanza
Somos los niños del mundo
Somos su futuro
¡Pero hoy nuestro futuro
depende de sí!

Como jugamos otros niños
estan sufriendo
Como comemos otros
morirse de hambre
Aprendemos del mundo
La mente de otro
niño esta vacía
Y el vacío mata el
corazon y el alma

Los lecciones de vida que saben
No necesitamos proclamarlo
No decirlo todo
Pero vida es mordada
por lo que vemos

Asi miremos alrededor
vemos otros ninos del mundo
Si has nacido en America
Afghanistán o África
Nacidos puros y Sensibles
Moleados por el mundo

Enseñanos como vivir
Enseñar lo bello del mundo
Instalarse fe en Díos
permitimos sentir su amor

Somos los niños
Somos los niños del mundo
Suplicamos a ustedes
Para hacer un mundo mejor
Somos los niños del mundo
Somos su futuro
Piense en nosotros -
somos los niños del mundo
Piense en nosotros -
somos los niños del mundo

CREDITS: Original song by Imelda R. Roberts (BMI)
Spanish Version - Translated by Trowbridge & McClure
Producer/Engineer: Doug Benson, Thurmont, MD; Vocals: Jennifer Lori Soto
Musical Tracks: Doug Benson; Studio: Harvest Recording, Thurmont, MD

Acknowledgments

Writing these stories in 40 nights was a journey I took on with passion and commitment since my daughter, ***Andrea Grace Tabian***, gave me a copy of the book, ***The Purpose Driven® Life***. Thank you, Andrea, for your sweet, endearing heart and grace that inspired the very core of my being. You will always be my sunshine.

To my son, ***Alberto Tabian***, thank you for your insightful advice and contributions to my stories that have made me so proud of you. I love you and will always be proud of having taken the most difficult journey of my lifetime with you. Your presence in this journey saved our future. You were my child hero. I hope this experience will forever instill love in your heart.

Most of all, to my dearest love, ***Jeff Snively***, for always being there to give me moral support, encouragement, and assistance. I thank you for our patience during this time of self-reflection and perhaps even isolation as I crafted this book for the world to read the great things you and I have shared together as best friends and soul mates, forever, in our own way.

To ***Susan Romero-Vidal***, for inspiring me to write and for your untiring support and encouragement. I thank you for all the knowledge you passed on to me so that my book-writing journey would be a joyful and enriching experience. Your enthusiasm transfused life into my tired hand and mind. You gifted me with a friendship I will treasure.

To ***Johnny Pecayo***, for a beautiful write-up in the Manila-U.S. Times and for rekindling, once again, my long lost love for writing. You have been a great support and a generous ambassador of my projects. I am heartened to have your kindness and confidence. You became my public relations genius as you touched others to pay attention to what my book has to bring. You are a true ambassador of a Filipino's ingenuity and creativity. Your help went beyond and above. I thank you for your editorial assistance

and for your contributions in bringing the voices of prominent dignitaries into this journey. I am humbled by their presence.

To *Socorro E. Tiongson*, for providing editorial assistance and valuable input. I truly appreciate your words of encouragement, support and friendship. You inspired me to find true lessons and gems embedded in this book.

To *Colleen Wilson*, my editor, who made sure all my English words and grammar reflect excellent craftsmanship of my second language. I thank you for being with me in this journey and for all your kind words. Your small nuggets in between editing have enhanced my natural writing. It was a true blessing you were the only person I picked on the Internet to help me in this project. Though I have never even seen your face, your beautiful spirit is inscribed in my heart.

To *Jason Cangialosi*, thank you for your thorough and detailed assistance in researching statistics and information on social issues highlighted in this book. Your research and summaries on issues such as poverty, abused women, immigration, and other statistics I used in this book provided rich social perspectives that challenge our minds and hearts to look beyond our own life to help the less fortunate people of this world.

Thank you to *Jimmy Cabales* by providing his creative and skilled talents in illustrations and for giving life to some of my fond childhood memories through his artistic drawings.

Thank you also to *Patricia Cerrada* for helping us with some of the graphics used in this book. Her willingness to share her creative talents helped Johan Erik Cerrada, designer, finished the layout of the book.

To *Paul Emerson Marquez*, thank you for your technical assistance in some programming parts of the barefootedsoul.com website. I appreciate very much your prompt help that enabled us to share great news about this book.

Acknowledgments

To my relatives, ***Tony and Carmen Canda, Digo and Evelyn Asuncion, Cesar and Aurea Gironella, Vincent and Amy Asuncion, Danny and Ligaya Amante, Edgardo and Carmelita Gamallo, Willy and Liberty Chingcuangco, Sean and Christine Joi Canda, Ian and Princess Canda, David and Gemma Kerstetter, Jennifer and Art Besina, and the entire Asuncion, Buan, and Paterno family*** for being proud of me, for all your prayers and for your words of encouragement.

To my special friends and supporters like ***Stacie and Matt Gilmore, Brian Snively, Jill Tierney, Ashaun Jackson, Myrna Juat, Abot and Dan Mendoza, Josie Collins, Farimah DesRosiers, Pat Connelly, Mary Din, Tess and Duwain Dillon, Eleanor Alfonso, Arsenia Santos, Galo Elequin-Mungcal, Aisser Juat, Ray Vanneman, Jeanne Rockenbaugh, Joe Baldi, Jim Robinson, Sandra Robinson, Jack Lemons, Robbi Dreifuerst, Connie Pratt, Connie Harris, Marie Ricasa, Leny Mendoza-Strobel, Odette Jimenez, Ricky and Clair Bunuan, Steve Serra, Lita Foster, Siiji Abu, Eleanor Brown, Mildred Baynor, Pam and Ron Mata, Doug and Diane Auclair, Karen Cerrada and Daphne Hurd.***

Special thank you to ***Frank Ball*** and ***Angela Sanders, Georgetown University (GU), Center for Professional Development,*** for their support and assistance in sharing my project to others.

I am also heartened by the presence and support of His Excellency ***Ambassador Albert del Rosario***, and his staff at the Embassy of the Philippines, Washington, DC. Special thanks to ***Consul Patricia Paez*** and ***Consul Joy Quintana*** for their assistance and support in this project.

Thank you also to my colleagues and friends at the ***Metropolitan Washington Council of Governments***, especially ***David Robertson***, Executive Director, my staff - ***Larissa Williams*** and ***Janet Ernst***; members of the COG Board of Directors and the senior management team, and all friends from several organizations I am involved in.

My special appreciation to ***Michael Rogers*** for his friendship and support. To all others who helped in this journey, thank you!

A Special *Thank You* to the Great Talents Behind this Book and CD-Album

The Barefooted Soul comes to you in a stunning cover and layout because of one man whose creative talents are incredibly awesome. Thank you to ***Johan Erik Cerrada***, our brilliant graphics designer whose artistic abilities are heaven-sent. Johan, thank you very much for giving so much life into the cover and all other graphics I have used in this book. I thank you for making my book absolutely gorgeous with a world-class look. With ease, you interpreted my vision and crude drawings as if I were within you. I appreciate your dedication and patience as we worked together on every page and every detail of the graphics in this book.

I give special thanks to the ***team of artists from the Philippines and Nashville, Tennessee*** for their creative talents in bringing life to my new songs included in the companion CD-Album, *Barefooted Soul.*

To ***Antonio Barcelo***, for producing three of my new songs below, and for engaging great talents to give life to these songs.

To ***Roxanne Barcelo***, your soulful interpretation and angelic voice transformed the lyrics and melody of ***My Barefooted Soul*** and ***No Perfect World, Only A Perfect State of Mind*** into beautiful songs and music I am so very proud of.

To ***Pinky Amador***, I am heartened by your genuine heart to touch the Overseas Filipino Workers (OFWs) through your joyful voice. Thank you for bringing life and energy into my Filipino song, ***Pinoy Boomer.*** I am truly excited to share this special track to all our fellow Filipinos all over the world.

A Special Thank You to the Great Talents Behind this Book and CD-Album

Thank you to ***Gene Delfin***, Musical Arranger, ***Jane Januario***, Vocal Arranger and Coach, ***Media Exchange Network***, Recording Studio, and ***Donato Manalang***, Sound Engineer. Thank you also to the beautiful voices of the backup singers, the E-LAN group comprised of ***Jasper John Jimenez***, ***Jason Martinez***, ***Joyce Januario***, and ***Mariel Deocareza***. Thank you also to ***Rose Barcelo*** for helping in logistics and creative aspects of this production.

A very special appreciation also goes to ***Gerry Peters***, ***Midi Magic Studio***, Nashville, Tennessee for being the producer of my three new songs listed below and for mastering the entire Barefooted Soul CD-Album. Thank you Gerry for your exceptional work and for completing these three songs in such a short time!

To ***Cindy Shelton***, thank you for your beautiful rendition of my new songs, ***Secret Lies, Secret Stories*** and ***What On Earth Would I Leave Behind***. I also love your interpretation of ***With All My Heart and Soul*** with ***William Ray***.

Thank you very much for being a part of my Barefooted Soul journey!

Imelda Roberts and Jeff Snively, Executive Producers

First Magnitude International and Imena Azul – Blue Dreams USA

www.firstmagnitude.com

Barefooted Soul CD-Album

Original Songs by Imelda Roberts (BMI)

Barefooted
Soul
Original Songs by Imelda Roberts
Imena Azul

Barefooted Soul comes with a special CD-Album with 14 songs I personally wrote and composed plus a Spanish translation of my children song. Each song in this album anchors each chapter of my book and every song was inspired by my life's experiences. May these heart songs bring hope and love to you and may they touch you as much as they touched me!

		Lyrics Page
1. My Barefooted Soul	Roxanne Barcelo	1
2. We are the Children of the World	Jennifer Soto	18
3. Secret Lies, Secret Stories	Cindy Shelton	70
4. America, Land of Liberty, Land of Opportunity	Juli Hood and William Ray	88
5. You Are Our Hero	Jennifer Soto	114
6. Fly Away, Soar Like an Eagle	Cindy Shelton and William Ray	127
7. The Gift of Songs Story	Juli Hood	193
8. What on Earth Would I Leave Behind?	Cindy Shelton	208
9. With All My Heart and Soul	Cindy Shelton and William Ray	252
10. Forever (Song written with Jeff Snively)	William Ray	282
11. No Perfect World, Only a Perfect State of Mind	Roxanne Barcelo	315
12. The Spirit of Ellis Island	Cindy Shelton	319

SPECIAL TRACKS (14 and 15 are Filipino and Spanish versions of We are the Children of the World)

13. Pinoy Boomer *(Filipino Song)*	Pinky Amador	323
14. Kami'y Anak ng Mundo	Roxanne Barcelo	325
15. Somos Los Ninos Del Mundo	Jennifer Soto	326

Executive Producers: Imelda Roberts and Jeff Snively

www.firstmagnitude.com

Barefooted Soul

Footprints For A Better World

An Invitation from Imelda Roberts

Thank you for taking a journey with my family, loved ones, friends and me through the ***Barefooted Soul***. I invite you to visit our website, listen to the Barefooted Soul's CD-Album containing 14 songs I personally composed, and check out other information about my exciting journey.

I would love to hear from you. I would really appreciate if you could share your thoughts and experience in any of my creative projects, most especially how the ***Barefooted Soul*** has touched your life. Please send me your comments and thoughts by email, or through the address below.

May the ***Barefooted Soul*** inspire you to unleash your inner gifts, find your own perfect state of mind, and leave behind your own footprints for a better world.

May God Bless You!

Imelda Roberts
www.imeldaroberts.com

First Magnitude International
Imena Azul – Blue Dreams, USA

605 Hunting Ridge Drive Frederick,
MD 21703 301-695-1285
info@barefootedsoul.com
www.barefootedsoul.com